Mistress Blanche
Queen Elizabeth I's Confidante

Mistress Blanche
Queen Elizabeth I's Confidante

by

Ruth Elizabeth Richardson

Logaston Press

LOGASTON PRESS
Little Logaston Woonton Almeley
Herefordshire HR3 6QH
logastonpress.co.uk

First published by Logaston Press 2007, reprinted 2008

ISBN 978 1904396 86 4

Typeset by Logaston Press
and printed in Great Britain by
Bell & Bain Ltd., Glasgow

Cover illustration: Queen Elizabeth Receiving Dutch Emissaries (see also Plate 5). The lady standing on the left among the most powerful men of Elizabeth's Court may be Blanche Parry

I dedicate this book to my dearly loved family,
Terry, Paul, Hannah, David and Kathy,
to Maralyn, my own goddaughter,
and to Sue Hubbard, whose help has been invaluable

I hope that this book may encourage further research
into the life of Mistress Blanche, an elegant lady

I·PARRYEHYS·DOVGHTER·BLAENCHE·OF·NEWE·COVRTE·BORNE
THAT·TRAENYD·WAS·IN·PRYNCYS·COVRTS·WYTHE·GORGIOVS·WYGHTS
WHEARE·FLEETYNGE·HONOR·SOVNDS·WYTHE·BLASTE·OF·HORNE
EACHE·OF·ACCOVNTE·TOO·PLACE·OF·WORLDS·DELYGHTS
AM·LODGYD·HEERE·WYTHE·IN·THYS·STONYE·TOOMBE
MY·HARPYNGER·YS·PAEDE·I·OWGHTE·OF·DVE
MY·FRYNDS·OF·SPEECHE·HEERE·IN·DOO·FYNDE·MEE·DOOMBE
THE·WHICHE·IN·VAENE·THEY·DOO·SO·GREATLYE·RHVE
FOR·SO·MOOCHE·AS·HYT·YS·BVT·THENDE·OF·ALL
THYS·WORDLYE·ROWTE·OF·STATE·WHAT·SO·THEY·BE
THE·WHICHE·VNTOO·THE·RESTE·HEEREAFTER·SHALL
ASSEMBLE·THVS·EACHE·WYGHTE·IN·HYS·DEGREE
I LYVDE·ALLWEYS·AS·HANDMAEDE·TOO·A·QVENE
IN·CHAMBER·CHIFF·MY·TYME·DYD·TOOVERPASSE
VNCAREFVLL·OF·MY·WELLTHE·THER·WAS·I·SENE
WHYLLSTE·I·ABODE·THE·RONNYNGE·OF·MY·GLASSE
NOT·DOVBTYNGE·WANTE·WHYLLSTE·THAT·MY·MYSTRES·LYVDE
IN·WOMANS·STATE·WHOSE·CRADELL·SAWE·I·ROCKTE
HER·SERVANNTE·THEN·AS·WHEN·SHEE·HER·CROVNE·ATTCHEEVED
AND·SO·REMAEND·TYLL·DEATHE·MY·DOORE·HAD·KNOCKTE
PREFFERRYNGE·STYLL·THE·CAVSYS·OF·EACHE·WYGHTE
AS·FARRE·AS·I·DOORSTE·MOVE·HER·GRACE·HYS·EARE
FOR·TOO·REWARDE·DECERTS·BY·COVRSE·OF·RYGHTE
AS·NEEDS·RESYTTE·OF·SARVYS·DOONNE·EACHE·WHEARE
SO·THAT·MY·TYME·I·THVS·DYD·PASSE·AWAYE
A·MAEDE·IN·COVRTE·AND·NEVER·NO·MANS·WYFFE
SWORNE·OF·QVENE·ELLSBETHS·HEDD·CHAMBER·ALLWAYE
WYTHE·MAEDEN·QVENE·A·MAEDE·DYD·ENDE·MY·LYFFE

The inscription on Blanche Parry's memorial in St. Faith's Church, Bacton

Contents

	Acknowledgements	*viii*
	Preface	
	In Chamber Chieff ...	1
1	*Parry's Daughter Blanche*	
	Introducing Blanche's Family	7
2	*Of Newcourt Born*:	
	Blanche Parry's Early Life	25
3	*Trained.. in Princes' Courts*	
	Early Years in the Royal Household	37
4	*Where Fleeting Honour Sounds*	
	Blanche at Court	57
5	*Preferring Still the Causes of Each Wight*	
	Blanche's Influence	83
6	*Not Doubting Want*	
	Wardships, Lands and Wills	109
7	*A Maid Did End My Life*	
	Blanche's Death and Monuments	133
Appendix 1	What happened to Newcourt	149
Appendix 2	Blanche Parry's Wills	151
Sources and References		167
Index		179

Acknowledgements

I am most grateful to all the individuals and organisations who have helped with the research for this book. They include Sue Hubbard, Barbara Griffiths (who generously helped with pedigrees), Eurig Salisbury, Professor Gruffydd Aled Williams, Dr. A.C. Lake, Cynthia Comyn, Neil Barnes, Dr. Anna-Regula Beilstein, John Freeman, David Lovelace, Brian Smith, Mrs. B. Harron, Jenny Houston, Melvin Jenkins, Charles Hunter, the late John Kirkwood, Anthea Mackenzie, John Pilley, Terry Richardson, Dr. David Starkey, Pat Thornton, Dan Vickers, J.R. Webster, June Webster, Elizabeth Welsh, Robin Harcourt-Williams and Dewi Williams; Phil Thomas and Leonard Charlesworth of the Ellerton Church Preservation Trust, and John Holmes; Sue Andres (Ironmongers' Hall), David Beasley (Goldsmiths' Hall), Theresa Thom (Gray's Inn Trust Fund) and Pegasus Press (of North Carolina, U.S.A.). Hereford Sixth-Form College provided a small grant for initial photocopying, the Library staff being unfailingly helpful. Elizabeth Semper O'Keefe and the excellent staff of Herefordshire Record Office, the Staffs of the National Archives, the British Library, the National Library of Wales, Gwent Record Office, Cumbria Record Office, East Riding Archives (Beverley), the Borthwick Institute for Archives. Dr. Christiane Lukatis and archivists in Denmark, Norway, Sweden, Netherlands and Germany. My editor Karen Stout and publisher Andy Johnson provided both encouragement and expertise. (As my research has taken a number of years I may have omitted a name and, if so, I sincerely apologise.)

To everyone who has helped me — your contributions have been invaluable. Any mistakes or misinterpretations are mine alone.

I am also most grateful to the Marc Fitch Fund for their financial help in carrying out the research for this book.

Thank you.

Please Note

The spelling of the quotations has generally been modernised for clarity although names have often been retained in the original form.

For more information on Blanche Parry see the website:
www.blancheparry.co.uk

Preface
In Chamber Chieff ...

The soft scents of a fresh spring day permeated even the darkest corners of the Court of Queen Elizabeth I, unobtrusively relaxing the hundreds of men and women noisily bustling to retain, or acquire, any chance of preferment or restitution. As usual the Court was crowded, the strict order of preference causing people to vie for the permissions required to advance through the adjoining rooms. Only the highest in the land could hope to approach the Queen's own rooms. In the sumptuously decorated and gilded corridor outside her apartments the more favoured stood trying to attract the attention of the nobles who themselves passed through to gather in the Presence Chamber hoping to be noticed. Those nearest the inner doors tenaciously held the privileged positions which just might lead to favour. Conversations did not prevent everyone from keeping a close watch on all activity around those coveted doors. Heads turned as the door to the Privy Chamber opened and a lady emerged. As tall as the Queen, she stood erect, despite her 59 years, with an unlined, handsome and kindly face beneath her French hood. She was elegantly dressed in black satin, Queen Elizabeth's livery for her personal servants, but her dignified demeanour and the manner of her reception showed that she was far more important than a mere servant.

The lady stood by the door aware that her position was pre-eminent even in that distinguished gathering. She looked around, nodded pleasantly to several courtiers and beckoning a servant to her, sent him to the outer gallery to fetch John Dudley. Dudley was a distant relation of Robert Dudley, Earl of Leicester, whom he served as a man of business. The lady had been entrusted with a verbal message for him to pass on to Leicester — a personal message from the Queen marvelling that she had not heard from the Earl since the previous Monday. The lady had tried to make excuses for the Earl, she explained to John Dudley, telling the Queen that he would return quickly but, she stressed, the Queen expected to hear from the Earl before his return to Court. John Dudley bowed respectfully. As he was moving away, the lady was warmly greeted by the Earl of Ormond. They stood chatting and were soon joined by Edward Fiennes de Clinton, the Lord Admiral who six years later would be created Earl of Lincoln. John Dudley was still near enough to be able to hear Ormond ask the Lord Admiral if he would give him a command in Ireland. The Lord Admiral rejoined by asking when Ormond would return to Ireland, to which he replied that he was due to depart the following week without fail, especially as the Earl of Desmond had already left.

We know that this scene happened exactly as described because, having returned to his quarters, John Dudley immediately wrote a lengthy letter, dated 29 March 1566, to the Earl of Leicester, which included details of all that he had heard:[1]

> .... Mrs. Dorothy ... being absent, our best friend in the Privy Chamber is Mrs. Blanche (Parry), who told me to-day that Her Majesty much marvelled she had not heard from you since last Monday and willed me to advise you to send to her before you come. She excused it by your hasty return but the Queen said she expected to hear from you before your return. Standing at the Privy Chamber door, talking with Mrs. Blanche, the Earl of Ormond, meeting my Lord Admiral there, asked him if he would command him any service into Ireland; to which the Lord Admiral asked him when he would go; he said next week without fail, as the Earl of Desmond was already gone and he must follow after ...

These few sentences reveal much about the Elizabethan Court. The conversation between Ormond and the Lord Admiral related to the very latest political situation that was causing concern to the government, for the families of Butler (Earls of Ormond) and Fitzgerald (Earls of Desmond) were old enemies in Ireland. Despite this there had been a period of peace between them when Joan, Ormond's mother, married as her third husband the Earl of Desmond — a love-match, the two having been close during her second marriage. This meant that Desmond was briefly the step-father of Ormond, who was two years his senior. Ormond was a well-known figure about the Court, which he had frequented since Henry VIII's reign. Although he had helped to suppress Sir Thomas Wyatt's rebellion in the reign of Queen Mary, he nevertheless had connections, through her maternal great-grandmother, with Queen Elizabeth, whom he had met when they were both children. Indeed, Elizabeth knew him well and trusted his opinion and his loyalty. His adversary, Desmond, was a very different personality and his insolence before the Privy

Council in May 1562 had brought him imprisonment in the Tower of London. Desmond was allowed to return to Ireland in 1564, only months before Joan's death on 2 January 1565 (modern dating is used here — at the time this was considered 1564).[2] This ended the ceasefire and open war resulted between the Earls of Ormond and Desmond. Ormond defeated and captured Desmond in battle in Ireland in 1565. In London both were ordered to keep the peace and they only returned to Ireland early in 1566 to give evidence to a commission appointed to adjudicate in their disputes. The encounter at the door of the Privy Chamber shows that Desmond left just before 29 March while Ormond intended to travel the following week, evidently to keep a close eye on him.

The other topic currently of interest to the Court was the position of the Earl of Leicester, the man Queen Elizabeth came closest to marrying. Leicester, too, had known the Queen from childhood and was one of her oldest friends. The two had both endured the dreadful experience of being imprisoned in the Tower of London, with the ever-present fear of execution, and they remained close friends, despite his marriages, until Leicester's death in 1588. However, the 1560s were a difficult period in their relationship. Leicester's wife of ten years, Amy, was found dead in 1560. Her death is now thought to have been due to cancer but then it was widely rumoured to have been murder. With the Queen's support, Leicester was able to weather the situation. He was appointed a member of the Privy Council in 1562 and Earl of Leicester in 1564 to further a plan devised by the Queen that he should marry the widowed Queen Mary, Queen of Scots (though Mary eventually preferred Lord Darnley). This convoluted situation was compounded by the fact that Elizabeth herself had a suitor, the Archduke Charles of Austria, which led to frantic counter-proposals from France. Leicester was also jealous that the Queen welcomed attentions from one of the gentlemen of her Privy Chamber. Perhaps in some pique he began an affair with Lettice Knollys, the widowed Viscountess Hereford, and this led to quarrels with the Queen and to factionalism among the different sections of the Court, where many heartily disliked Leicester. The Earl renewed his marriage offer to the Queen at Christmas 1565, only for the Earl of Norfolk to tell him forcibly to desist in favour of the Archduke. Startled, Leicester agreed, but then the Queen, in March 1566, markedly began to favour the Earl of Ormond. Leicester was so incensed that he left the Court, hence his need for reports from John Dudley.

Leicester was now worried about his post of Master of the Horse, which carried with it the right to apartments in the overcrowded palaces and proximity to the Queen's person (for the Master of the Horse's role involved riding immediately behind her in any procession). John Dudley reported a conversation, overheard by Lord Hunsdon's man, between the Queen and Hunsdon, her cousin, in which it emerged that Hunsdon was likely to be made Master of the Horse, suggesting Leicester's demotion. Two days later John Dudley was writing that he had heard very different opinions about whether the Earl should return to Court: 'some say tarry, others, come with speed'. John Dudley advised that he should return 'hastily' as Her Majesty disliked his absence so much that she would not hear anything good of him. He said that he had discussed the situation with Mistress Dorothy (Bradbelt), one of the three or four Chamberers, or chambermaids, socially the lowest group attached to the Privy Chamber. Mistress Dorothy seems to have been John Dudley's best source but in her absence on the Queen's orders to attend a sickbed, he approached a far more important lady whom he described as 'our best friend in the Privy Chamber'. He named her as 'Mistress Blanche'.

Mistress Blanche was the usual designation of Blanche Parry, or Apparry. She was the lady with ready access to the Privy Chamber and the Queen's inner apartments. She was the lady who was able to pass on personal messages from the Queen, with her own appended comments, to the one man Elizabeth loved. She was the lady with whom the latest favourite at Court, the Earl of Ormond, chatted amicably by the doorway of the Privy Chamber. She was there when the Lord Admiral spoke delicate politics to Ormond and neither baulked at discussing Desmond in front of her. Her position at Court and in the Queen's life was evidently known and universally recognised. She was there at the apex of the power structure of the Elizabethan Court. Moreover, Sir William Cecil, Lord Burghley, the Queen's most powerful minister, would call Blanche his 'cousin' and would help her whenever she asked him.

So who was Mistress Blanche? Where did she come from? Who were her family? How did she come to be in such an important position at Court? Why has she been ignored or forgotten when the men at the centre — Burghley, Leicester, Sir Christopher Hatton, Francis Walsingham — have all had their lives, and those of their families, described and their actions analysed? Even in biographies of Queen Elizabeth herself Blanche is rarely given a line or even a footnote and when some mention is made of her the facts are usually wrong. This lady who was at the very centre of the Elizabethan Court, in daily attendance on the Queen, has virtually disappeared from the histories of the time.

This biography aims to rectify this situation and to place Blanche in her rightful place and prominence. Relevant published material has hitherto been sparse. The Oxford antiquary, George Ballard, who saw her tomb, included Blanche in his *Memoirs of several ladies of Great Britain…*, published in 1752. In 1935, Charles Angell Bradford, F.S.A., published a pamphlet entitled *Blanche Parry, Queen Elizabeth's Gentlewoman*. This gave an outline of Blanche's life but mentioned few details concerning her family history or the influences on her childhood. Bradford was also engaged in countermanding false information. Any biographer of Blanche will always be grateful to Bradford for his research, which provides a very useful starting point, especially as nothing significant has been published since. Untapped material does exist and is used here, having first been checked to ensure accuracy.

It can now be confidently stated that Blanche's family were connected with Dore Abbey, a Cistercian monastery in the Golden Valley of Herefordshire which held estates in mid-Wales and Gloucestershire. Her family played an important part in the Wars of the Roses in the area, being adherents of the Duke of York and King Edward IV. Several official documents have survived about the family's activities and even about Blanche herself. In addition, there is a group of nine Welsh bardic poems (six of which have never before been transcribed into modern Welsh nor translated into English) which concern members of her family and which give a wonderful immediacy to the events described.[3] They also show beyond doubt the importance of Blanche, Lady Troy (Blanche Parry's aunt), who had a key role at the Royal Court where she was in charge of King Henry VIII's children, Princess Elizabeth, Prince Edward and, for a time, Princess Mary.

Blanche Parry herself composed a brief biography in the form of the epitaph which she had inscribed on her monument in Bacton Church, her family's parish church and mausoleum in Herefordshire. In it she records that she was 'trained … in princes' courts with gorgeous wights' (with richly dressed, fashionable people), that she was the servant of Princess Elizabeth 'whose cradle saw I rocked' and continued to serve her 'when she her crown achieved'. She remained with the Queen 'till death my door had knocked' and thus 'with maiden Queen a maid did end my life'. In her epitaph Blanche describes herself as 'preferring still the causes of each wight as far as I durst move her Grace's ear', an influence that has been wholly unexplored and discounted, for it has been assumed that women had little influence at Court even during the reign of a Queen.

The reorganisation that resulted in the Privy Chamber had been made by Henry VII. In his reign and in those of his son Henry VIII and of his grandson Edward VI, the personnel were male. Their daily proximity to the sovereign meant that the personnel of the Privy Chamber also held the great offices of the government and were often members of the Privy Council as well. Under the Queens, Mary and Elizabeth, however, there had to be a separation of functions as the Queen's body servants were necessarily female.[4] Then the Privy Council was separated from the Privy Chamber and, according to Sir

James Croft, Comptroller of the Household 1570-1590, 'The Court is divided into two governments, the Chamber and the Household.'[5]

Although members of Queen Elizabeth's Privy Chamber could not be members of the government as their male predecessors had been in the reigns of the Tudor Kings, the value of their access to the Queen should not be underestimated. Blanche Parry herself became the Chief Gentlewoman of the Privy Chamber, which she called the Queen's Head Chamber, and she was the longest serving Lady of the Bedchamber. Her right of admittance to every room of the Queen's most private suite was accepted by all. She saw the Queen each morning and each evening, at night and at intervals during the day, so she was always available. Queen Elizabeth could discuss recent events with her, vent her feelings about recalcitrant courtiers, be consoled and share happiness. Blanche was discreet, trustworthy, fair in her expressed views and always there when wanted. When Elizabeth retired to her Privy Chamber, it was Blanche who saw that her private life ran smoothly. For 56 years, from the day Elizabeth was born until the day Blanche died in January 1590, scarcely a year after the defeat of the Spanish Armada, the Queen had never known a time when Blanche was not nearby.

Blanche's importance can be gauged by her official duties, the nearness of her accommodation to Elizabeth, the arrangements made for her servants and the evidence for her influence on the Queen. Blanche's views, however gently offered, must have helped the Queen to form her own opinions and Blanche's understated influence to some degree shaped Elizabeth's approach to personal relationships and religious observance. To understand Queen Elizabeth it is therefore important to examine the views of Blanche Parry (and those of her aunt, Lady Troy). So who was Blanche Parry, who were her family, and how did she come to be in such an influential position at Court?

1 *Parry's Daughter Blanche* Introducing Blanche's Family

As Blanche Parry was born between March 1507 and March 1508 she was of the same generation as Anne Boleyn, the mother of Queen Elizabeth I. Blanche, who would pass the greater part of her life in devoted service to Elizabeth, grew up in Herefordshire's Golden Valley, close to the present Welsh-English border and in the vicinity of Dore Abbey, a Cistercian monastery with which her family had had strong connections for generations. Although the area was a Welsh speaking part of the Welsh March (using a Herefordshire dialect), Blanche's father also spoke the English necessary for his official duties as Sheriff and Steward of Dore Abbey and he married an English lady. So Blanche's early years were passed in a bilingual, cultured Welsh household where education and music were valued.

Her family adhered to the Welsh system of nomenclature whereby children were named after their father, a son using 'ap' (or 'ab' before a vowel) meaning 'son of', while a daughter would be designated as 'ferch', meaning 'daughter of' (enunciated as 'verch', f being pronounced as v in Welsh). The use of 'ap' for a girl in Blanche's case may suggest a transitional phase prior to replacement by the English surname system. This did lead to confusion and as late as the 1589 Cox Indenture (see chapter 6) Blanche is named as Blanche Parrye and Blanche Apharrie within the same document. At the time Welsh people needed to know their family trees up to the ninth degree for legal purposes, Blanche's going back to Moreiddig,[1] whose land can still be traced in the farm name of Tremorithic.[2] It is often very difficult to be certain a family tree is accurate but in Blanche's case there is a remarkable surviving text that provides incontrovertible information about her pedigree.

Blanche's family were circuit patrons for several bards who entertained at great houses including Raglan Castle (of William Herbert 1st Earl of Pembroke, first creation), the home of the Stradling family (of Joan, Blanche's grandmother) and Newcourt (built by Harri Ddu, Blanche's great-grandfather, in 1452). These bards were honoured guests, with a place beside the master at high table in the hall. The poems, sung to a harp accompaniment, incorporating salient facts about the host and the surroundings, are primary evidence but have been little used as many are still in manuscript form. Fortunately, there is a corpus of nine poems extant that relate to Blanche's family, the bards concerned being Guto'r Glyn, Gwilym Tew, Howel Dafi, Huw Cae Llwyd and Lewys Morgannwg. Guto'r Glyn, the highly regarded bard working between the 1430s and 1493, was noted for praising his patrons, his descriptions, his satire and his humorous asides.[3] He followed the precepts laid down by the great Taliesin, the 6th century founding father of the praise tradition, in praising his patron's ability in warfare and largesse at home. He dedicated five of his 124 known poems to Harri Ddu, describing him as a 'soldier' and the 'Lord of Bacton' and he eventually performed in front of Harri's son and grandson, Blanche's father. In one song[4] Guto'r Glyn gives the family's definitive pedigree: Siôn (John) – Harri – Gruffudd – Harri Ddu – Miles ap Harri – Henry Myles.

Working backwards, Blanche's father was Henry Myles, her grandfather was Miles ap Harry / Harri, her great-grandfather was Harri Ddu / Henry ap Griffith and her great-great-grandfather was Gruffudd ap Henry. The list is complicated by varying spellings but the various permutations show that in this family it was during Blanche's generation and the succeeding one that there was a general change to English-style surnames, Parry rather than ap Harry. (Surnames were finalised over several generations in different families. It is only an accident of time that the Tudor / Tudur family was known by this name and not Meredith / Maredudd. The adoption of surnames by siblings could result in different surnames in the same family as, for example, in the family of the 1st Earl of Pembroke. In time, a person named ap Howell would anglicise it to Powell, ab Ithel would become Bethell, while Vaughan was a nickname from fychan meaning small, or the younger.)

Gruffudd ap Henry, Blanche's great-great-grandfather

As far as we know, Gruffudd (approximately pronounced Griffith)[5] was the first in Blanche's family to have a connection with Dore Abbey. His father was Harri ap Siôn (Henry the son of John) of Oldcourt, which has been variously identified as Poston, Oldcourt Farm by Tremorithic, or 'Old Hall' field west of the future Newcourt. Gruffudd, described by Guto'r Glyn as a 'brave … a noble man', married Mawd, the daughter and heir of Gwilym / William Llwyd of Tregunter / Trefgwnter (anglicised to Gunterston / Gonterston). Guto'r Glyn called her the 'generous Mawd … the faultless girl' and she is mentioned several times, suggesting a charming lady who made a considerable impression on all who knew her. Mawd's father was also a patron of the bards. It was through Mawd that the family acquired the manor of Trostrey in the lordship of Usk and it is through Gunterston and Trostrey that links can be made between Gruffudd and other family members.

Mawd's mother was the daughter of William de Barri (son of Gerald de Barri) or Barr, which gave her great-great-grand-daughter, Blanche, an armorial connection with the Sidney family (and through them with the Earl of Leicester) and with Sir James Croft, Comptroller of the Household of Queen Elizabeth. (Sir Thomas Parry, Elizabeth's Cofferer, who died in 1560, was the son of Henry Vaughan and so was only distantly related to Blanche.) Blanche's family were interconnected with all the local gentry families of the March and these included the Cecil / Sitsylt family of Sir William Cecil, Lord Burghley. Both families were also closely involved with Dore Abbey. Gerald Sitsilt was buried there in the 13th century[6] and his son, Owen, was a monk in the abbey. Baldwin Sitsylt was a benefactor, giving lands and liberties to Dore, while Thomas Sitsylt (Burghley's great-great-great-grandfather) cancelled a considerable debt owed to him by the monks.[7] Lord Burghley would describe himself as Blanche's 'cousin' and later Olive (grand-daughter of Blanche's great-uncle) would marry Walter Sisilt, who continued to live in the Cecil family home of Alt-yr-Ynys in Elizabeth's reign. The close family relationship of Blanche and Burghley would be a focal point of Elizabeth's Court.

Gruffudd's career demonstrates the utter lawlessness of the March in the 14th and 15th centuries, throughout which disturbances, raids and bloodshed were common. Described as 'the King's esquire' in 1403,[8] it is likely that his dispute with the Abbot of Dore was a part of the dynastic struggle that brought Henry IV to the throne in 1399. Abbot Jordan Bykelswade accused Gruffudd, his two brothers and two friends (including Sir John Oldcastle) of damaging abbey buildings and lands, killing cattle (enough to feed a small army), stealing mature oak trees and, most serious of all, seizing, imprisoning and ill-using three monks, probably abbey officials.[9] It is probable that this accusatory petition actually concerns disputes over ownership of assets, especially as one of Gruffudd's brothers was Deputy Steward of Breconshire 1396-1409 and Sheriff of Herefordshire in 1399.

Gruffudd evidently became involved in the uprising of Owain Glyndŵr for, at the height of the revolt, he received a royal pardon due to the intercession of Joan Beauchamp, Lady of Bergavenny (Abergavenny).[10] Her championing of him strongly suggests that, although originally a supporter of Glyndŵr, he had provided military aid against Welsh incursions, preventing the destruction of Abergavenny Castle. His pardon also demonstrates his status for he was locally very important indeed and the bards, who admiringly described his prowess as a man-at-arms, 'with horses and weapons', considered him a member of the nobility. His extensive lands, forfeit due to rebellion, were returned to him on a tenancy basis and he served as the King's official, his brothers fighting at the Battle of Agincourt in 1415. From this point too Gruffudd maintained good relations with Dore Abbey.

However, there are strong indications that Gruffudd was a Lollard, the name given to followers of John Wycliffe, who was concerned with the fundamental primacy of the Bible as the Word of God.[11] He rejected the doctrine of transubstantiation and all authority not derived from the scriptures, including the church hierarchy and monasticism, and contrasted the wealth of the church with the spiritually true Church available to God's chosen people. Wycliffe's most enduring legacy was the first complete English translation of the Bible from the Latin Vulgate version and he inspired itinerant preachers. Gruffudd was certainly closely associated with Sir John Oldcastle (said to be the inspiration for Shakespeare's Sir John Falstaff). Sir John's family were Lords of the Manor of Almeley in west Herefordshire, his estates reaching the River Wye at Letton on the opposite bank to Bredwardine. He had carried out a number of commissions in the Welsh March for Henry IV, represented Herefordshire in the Parliament of 1404 and was Sheriff of Herefordshire in 1406-7. When he married for the third time he became Lord Cobham in right of his wife and he was then summoned to Parliament as a baron. In 1411 he successfully fought abroad under orders from Prince 'Hal', the eldest son of Henry IV and the future Henry V, to whose household he was apparently attached.

Despite his government involvement it is clear that Sir John had long tolerated Lollardy on his manors, particularly around Almeley, where two cases are known from 1391 and 1393, this last indicative of a popular following. The case cited by Abbot Jordan of the abduction of the three monks by Gruffudd, his brothers, a friend and Sir John Oldcastle is suggestive of a Lollard denunciation of monastic authority. The monks were bound to trees using cords and iron chains as if crucified and then two were tied upside down by their feet. Either of these two methods of restraint used on their own could simply have been coincidence but together they suggest something far more radical. One was a parody of a crucifixion reminiscent of the familiar image of Christ in churches, while the act of tying the monks upside down was reminiscent of Saint Peter's execution. These acts, coupled with the presence of Sir John Oldcastle, all suggest Lollardy. In 1417 Gruffudd's brother was required by law to refrain from 'unlawful assemblies' and from adhering 'to John Oldcastle knight late lord of Cobham …'.[12] Sir John Oldcastle was executed the same year. Gruffudd's involvement may well have been more circumspect as there is no indication that either he or any member of his family was further adversely affected. There remains the possibility that the Lollard influence persisted and that the family maintained a tradition of reading the Bible in English.

Harri Ddu ap Gruffudd, Blanche's great-grandfather

Harri Ddu, the builder of Newcourt (Blanche's family home), was quite the most fascinating of her forebears. The English called him Harry Griffith and he used this anglicised form when dealing with Dore Abbey[13] but his Welsh compatriots called him Harri Ddu (pronounced 'thee'), meaning 'black', showing that he had dark colouring. His first mention in documents was in 1435 and the last mention in 1477.

He married a Welsh girl from the March and, although her identity is not certain, it seems that she was Alson the daughter of Eustace Whitney of Whitney, on the north bank of the River Wye.[14] Alson's mother was apparently the daughter of Sir Thomas Oldcastle, a reputed relative of Sir John Oldcastle and maybe it was this Lollard connection that made the marriage desirable. If Harri married twice his second wife was probably Joan de la Hay, despite Guto'r Glyn's description of Harri's ardent pursuit of the beautiful, generous Gwladus. Harri had at least two sons, Miles and John, who was known as John Parrie.

We know a great deal about Harri Ddu from the poems of Guto'r Glyn, who was Harri's herald and chief-bard in his earlier years, and an additional poem by Gwilym Tew. As a boy, Harri had fair hair, which darkened as he grew to maturity, hence his name, and he was very, very handsome, a 'black angel'. No wonder the ladies liked him! He was tall and graceful and liked to wear black clothes so that Guto'r Glyn describes him as a 'black prince'. He favoured black velvet and sable, with silk, complemented by jewels of coral. (His great-grand-daughter, Blanche would also favour sable.) To Guto'r Glyn, Harri compared with Hector, Ovid, Troilus, a lion (several times) and even the dark-haired Christ shown in the picture of *Veronica and her Veil* owned by Harri, which hung in the chapel at Newcourt, or perhaps over a family chantry altar in Bacton Church. Harri was brave, a good lord (the highest praise at the time), a 'pearl of faithfulness', discerning, diligent, open-handed and generous especially in his hospitality at Newcourt, where the mead and claret flowed freely. Once, when he was pursuing a girl, he briefly sulked because Guto'r Glyn had refused to sing for him but the poet stressed that Harri's anger was short-lived and could be pacified. Indeed he was 'a true son' of his noble father, both 'earls' according to the bard, and was a superb man-at-arms 'with horses and weapons'.

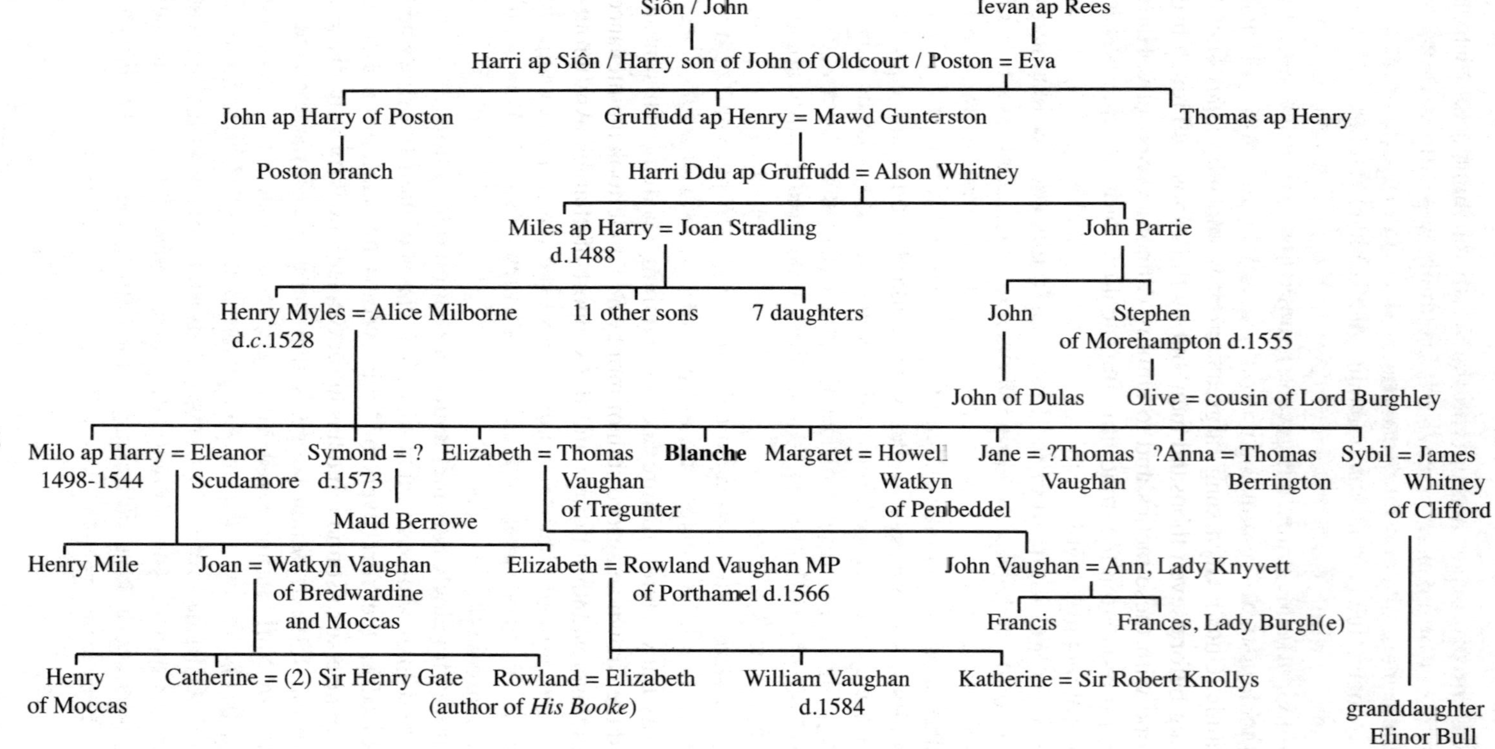

Simplified Parry Family Tree

Notes: Most names have several different spellings and sibling order is not necessarily as given here.

Henry Miles, Blanche's father, also had a bastard son, John ap Harry.

Alice Milborne, Blanche's mother, and her sister Blanche (Whitney / Herbert, Lady Troy) were daughters of Simon Milborne

Harri was also an expert archer with the Welsh longbow, a skill which resulted from years of constant practice. As this regime usually started at a young age the archers' skeletal bones adapted, showing enlarged upper arms and, indeed, Guto'r Glyn says he had 'the body of a soldier'. Archers inflicted enormous damage, firing ten to twelve arrows in the time it took a cross-bowman to reload. Longbowmen had given Henry V his victory at Agincourt and there was a long tradition of using a very long bow in the Usk area where Harri held lands. Guto'r Glyn sang 'a great arrow would my eagle [Harri] shoot, shooting before seven thousand men' but by the 1450s the French had learned to cope with these tactics and to employ cannon successfully. Harri also 'had a great reputation for stone-throwing', called *bwrw maen* in Welsh, a most competitive game involving distance throwing and accuracy in positioning. The popularity of stone-throwing in the 14th century meant that it was forbidden by European governments in favour of archery, an essential skill in warfare.

Harri, described as the Lord of Bacton (and so patron of Bacton Church), held two granges of Dore Abbey, where he was the Steward, a paid appointment, from about 1455.[15] He managed the monastic business affairs, representing the abbot in the manorial courts. Politically, he was also the Steward of Usk and Caerleon, his immediate overlord being Sir William Herbert (created Earl of Pembroke in 1468). Harri cemented this relationship by marrying his son, Miles, to Herbert's niece, Joan Stradling. His connections meant that he was also in a position to join his cousin in farming all the Warwick inheritance lands in Ewyas Lacy, Herefordshire and the adjoining March.[16] This meant that they paid the Crown an agreed sum of money and undertook maintenance of houses, enclosures and buildings and the support of charges. Any profits over and above this would belong to them. This inheritance was eventually conferred on the Neville family and resulted in a strong Neville-York influence in the Welsh March.

It was through Harri's personal recommendation that Guto'r Glyn was indentured as a soldier with Richard Duke of York and Gwilym Tew described Harri as 'dressed in' the York livery of 'gold colour and scarlet'. Further he noted that 'no one else of sound mind has burnt France as wisely as he [Harri] without suffering losses', which suggests that he was an efficient officer with the Duke of York's army when York served as the King's Lieutenant in France, 1441-1445. Howel Dafi enigmatically describes Harri as fighting in the area of the River Rhone. The duke's relative success in France was disturbing for the government of Henry VI, who replaced him with the Duke of Somerset. York was ordered to Ireland as the Lord-Lieutenant and Gwilym Tew makes it clear that Harri Ddu was on the duke's staff, where 'he impales an Irishman on spears'. York was successful in Ireland but returned without official authorisation in order to confront Somerset. After a year of political manoeuvrings York finally marched on London, where, disbanding his army, he was arrested. It is likely that Harri was involved in the rumoured attempt by York's son, Edward, to rescue his father, which resulted in York's release. In 1452 Harri not only forfeited the valuable farm of the Marcher Warwick estates to John Skydmore (Scudamore), of the local family from Kentchurch Court, but also agreed to be bound over for his good behaviour, the sum with which he was charged being a colossal £1,000 (over £455,000 in today's money).[17] This sum provides an indication of Harri's status, even among the estimated 1200 esquires in the realm. However, the following year, 1453, Harri not only received a pardon from the Lancastrian government but they also accepted his standing surety for Walter Devereux, another adherent of the Duke of York, both acts demonstrating Harri's official rehabilitation by the government.

In 1453 a son was born to the Queen but the King's first period of insanity allowed York to be appointed Protector in 1454. However, the King recovered, York was dismissed, and he finally turned to war in 1455. That Harri followed Herbert, his overlord, in being involved on the Yorkist side in the first skirmishes of the Wars of the Roses, was shown by Guto'r Glyn and it resulted in Harri and his son Miles being among the Welsh esquires again pardoned by the Lancastrian Queen Margaret in 1457, part of her ploy to attempt to gain the allegiance of Sir William Herbert, who was also pardoned. Herbert managed to retain all his lands and even added to them and in 1460 a grant was made 'for life to Henry ap Griffith of the office of Steward of the lordship of Ewyas Lacy in Wales, forfeit by the rebellion of Richard, duke of York and Richard earl of Warwick, with the usual fees and profits.'[18]

Although Guto'r Glyn described Harri as 'a sword in battle for Wales …', saying 'he was the best with his hand as far as Leicester', he also called him 'a courtier', suggesting that his attendance on the Duke of York included the several Parliaments held in Leicester. Howel Dafi would call him 'beloved one of the Crown'.[19] In 1460 Harri served on a commission with six other esquires, including Simon Milbo(u)rne (who would become his grandson's father-in-law) with powers 'to arrest certain persons of Herefordshire who wander about the country spoiling, beating, maiming and slaying'.[20] The area was still very lawless.

When Herbert returned his allegiance to the Yorkists so did those who owned him fealty, including Harri Ddu, now Steward of Usk, Caerleon and Ewyas Lacy (Longtown). Herbert was the most important Welshman to support Edward Earl of March, son of the Duke of York. In 1461 he fought for him at the decisive Battle of Mortimer's Cross[21] which led to the Earl becoming King Edward IV. Herbert was created Baron Herbert of Raglan (and in 1468 Earl of Pembroke). In 1462 he also bought the wardship of the young Henry Tudor (the future King Henry VII) from the King and Henry was to be brought up at Raglan Castle. Harri Ddu's mention in the 1464-65 Act of Resumption suggests that he had benefited by acquiring additional land during the war. He served on at least four further commissions, in 1463, 1465[22] and 1467 but Herbert's defeat and execution after the 1469 Battle of Edgecote affected the fortunes of all his followers. Lady Herbert and the young Henry Tudor fled from Raglan to her brother at Weobley Castle in Herefordshire.

Harri's tenure as Steward of Dore Abbey coincided with all the violence and mayhem resulting from the skirmishes, changes of allegiance and battles of this dynastic war. Dore, with land in the March and in mid-Wales, evidently experienced cash-flow problems and these were no doubt compounded by their steward's attention being engaged elsewhere. The result was a list of backdated, perhaps unfounded, complaints made against Harri by Abbot Philip Morgan in 1476-1477[23] and it is in these that the evidence is found that Harri built two houses, including Newcourt. This was named to reflect his considerable status as the Welsh *cwrt* meant a court or mansion where the lord of the manor would hold the manor court.

Harri seems to have died when he was in his late 50s or early 60s. Guto'r Glyn wrote this superb elegy for him and his fervent words are still powerfully moving. The mourning bell would have tolled for Harri as he was buried, according to custom, at night in the family vault under Bacton Church. He was so famous that stories of his life were handed down to his descendants. Certainly Blanche would have known all about him.

Marwnad Harri Ddu o Euas[24]	***The Death of Harri Ddu of Ewyas***[25]
Doe darfu'r Deau derfyn,	*Yesterday the South's frontier died,*
Dwrn Duw a roes dyrnod ynn.	*God's fist gave us a blow.*
Daearen Duw a oeres,	*God's earth turned cold,*
Dwyn gŵr oll a dynn ei gwres.	*taking a man completely drains away its warmth.*
Dyrnod hoedl drwy Went ydoedd,	*A mortal blow was it throughout Gwent,*
Dwyn Harri Ddu (dyn hardd oedd).	*taking Harri Ddu, he was a handsome man.*
Dyffryn Aur yn deffroi nos,	*The Golden Vale rouses night,*
Heb liw dydd, heb le diddos.	*without day's colour, without a shelter.*
Euas gynt wrth lais ei gorn	*Euas [Ewyas Lacy] once had the sound of his horn;*
Ac Erging heb gyweirgorn.	*and Erging [Archenfield] is without a tuning-key.*
Saethwyd yma'r saith dinas,	*The seven cities were shot down here,*
Swydd Henffordd, Cliffordd a'r Clas.	*Herefordshire, Clifford and Glasbury.*
Beth a dâl byth, o delir,	*Whatever holds a war-sloop, if it's held,*
Belinger heb longwr hir?	*without a tall shipman?*
Bro Wy oedd hon, briwodd hi,	*This was the Vale of the Wye, it wounded it,*

Byd perygl bod heb Harri.
Wylo mae llin Wiliam Llwyd,
Aml dolef am lew dulwyd.

a world of danger is it without Harri.
William Llwyd's line is weeping, [i]
a repeated cry for a dark lion.

Nid wyf syth na da fy sâl
Wedi ef, na diofal.
Fy nghariad, fy nghynghorwr,
Fy llyfr gynt, fy llaw fu'r gŵr.
Dug fi at y Dug of Iorc
Dan amod cael deunawmorc.
Fy ngwaith fu, eilwaith foliant,
Fwrw gwawd hwn i frig y tant.
Dengair o gellwair i gyd
Fu rhof a Harri hefyd.
O dywedais, da ydoedd,
Na rôi ei aur, anwir oedd;
Ni rôi gawn er a genynt
Glêr y dom, bwngleriaid ŷnt;
Ac i'r gwŷr gorau eu gwaith
Ar unrhodd y rhôi anrhaith.

I'm not erect nor well-paid
after him, nor carefree.
My love, my counsellor,
my book before, the man was my hand.
He brought me to the duke of York
on the condition of getting eighteen marks. [ii]
My work was (more praise)
to cast praise of him to the top of the string.
Ten words all joking [iii]
were also between me and Harri.
If I said (he was good)
that he didn't give his gold, it wasn't true.
He wouldn't give straw for what the minstrels of shit
would sing, they're bunglers.
But to men of the best work
by a single gift he gave wealth.

Rhydd fu'r Cwrtnewydd i ni,
A'r Drehir, dra fu Harri.
Gŵr oedd ef fal Gwrthefyr,
Gorau â'i law i Gaerlŷr.
Gwayw 'mrwydr i Gymru ydoedd,
Gard aur ysgwïeriaid oedd.
Cwrtiwr oedd y milwr main,
Cryfaf o Iorc i Rufain.
Ni thrwsiodd maen na throsol,
Ni bu neb na bai'n ei ôl.
Saeth fawr a saethai f'eryr,
Saethu 'mlaen seithmil o wŷr.
Nid âi i'w naid un dyn iach,
Nid oedd ieithydd du ddoethach.
Ni roes Iesu rasusoed
Un lliw ar ŵr well erioed.

Liberal was Newcourt for us,
and Longtown, while Harri lived.
He was a man like Gwrthefyr, [iv]
the best with his hand as far as Leicester.
He was a sword in battle for Wales,
he was the golden guard of the squires.
A courtier was the lean soldier,
the strongest from York to Rome.
No one ever trimmed stone or sceptre,
there was none who wouldn't be behind him.
A great arrow would my eagle shoot,
shooting before seven thousand men.
Not one healthy man would match his leap,
there wasn't a black linguist wiser.
Jesus of gracious life never put
a better colour on a man before.

Harri Gruffudd a guddiwyd,
Heno, Dduw, dwyn hwn ydd wyd.
Heddiw ydd aeth o'i haddef
Hydd y Cwrtnewydd i nef.
Dwyn o'r coed a wnâi ŵr call
Derwen a dodi arall.
Mae un o'i wŷdd yma i ni,
Mal yw pur, Mil ap Harri.
Impyn cadr a'm pen-ceidwad,
Impied ef gampau ei dad.
Gwŷdd ieuanc a weddïwn,
Gadu hil yn goed i hwn.

Harri Gruffudd was buried,
tonight, God, you're taking him.
Today the stag of Newcourt went from his home
to heaven.
A wise man would take an oak from the wood
and put another in place.
There is one from his wood here for us,
he too is pure, Miles ap Harri,
a bold scion and my chief keeper.
Let him engraft his father's deeds.
O young wood for whom I'd pray,
Leave progeny as his wood!

[i] A reference to Mawd, Harri's mother, daughter of Gwilym / William Llwyd of Tregunter / Trefgwnter.
[ii] Guto was brought into the service of Richard Duke of York, the 18 marks being the price of his indenture as a soldier.
[iii] Guto'r Glyn disowned this complaint in another song.
[iv] Gwrthefyr was one of the sons of Gwrtheyrn / Vortigern, the 5th century British ruler who gave land to the Saxons in return for military support against the Picts. Gwrthefyr was said to have bravely resisted these Saxons when they turned on their British hosts.

Miles ap Harry, Blanche's grandfather

Miles[26] heard himself described as 'pure ... a bold scion' ready to follow his father and as Guto'r Glyn's 'chief-keeper' or patron. His wife, Joan, was the daughter of Sir Harri Stradling of St. Donat's Castle, Glamorgan and Elizabeth Herbert, the sister of Sir William Herbert (the 1468 1st Earl of Pembroke). The Earl's mother, and Joan's maternal grandmother, was the daughter of Sir Dafydd Gam, the Davy Gam mentioned by William Shakespeare in *Henry V,* and this descent was proudly proclaimed by the bards. This marriage thus linked Miles with the family of his father's overlord, including the Devereux family of Sir William's wife, and with his father's friend, Harri Stradling. Indeed, the apex of his career, built on the achievements of his father and grandfather, was this very prestigious marriage to a knight's daughter and they started married life at Newcourt. Miles, associated with his father in the general pardon of 1457, was acclaimed as the chief, or the culmination, of eight generations by Howel Dafi in a poem about his son, Henry Myles, Blanche's father.

Like his grandfather and father before him, Miles ap Harry held the rank of esquire and he was entitled to a coat-of-arms. In the 1560s Sir Thomas Smith wrote *The Commonwealth of England*[27] in which he described the power structure of the four classes of society, namely gentlemen, citizens and burgesses, yeomen and the common people. He then divided 'gentlemen' into two, namely the *nobilitas major* / peers, who had the right to help rule the country and the *nobilitas minor* / lesser gentry who ruled locally. The *nobilitas minor* were further subdivided into knights, esquires and gentlemen. Blanche's grandfather had therefore attained the middle tier of the English lesser gentry and his coat-of-arms placed him in the upper echelons of his category. Such divisions were not just semantic, they really were important in the tremendously hierarchical society of the period. Miles had achieved this status by his and his father's support of Herbert in the Wars of the Roses.[28] His marriage cemented the connection.

On 5 November 1470 Miles became escheator for Herefordshire and the Welsh March, a position he may have held for two years.[29] Escheators, appointed by the Treasurer, were next in importance to sheriffs and both could act for two counties — in Miles' case, those in which his own estates were situated. The escheator acted on the death of a tenant-in-chief to determine the value of the deceased's estates, to identify the heir(s) and to decide if he/she was old enough to succeed. If so, the heir paid a year's income to the King but if there was no heir, the estate reverted to the sovereign. The heir would usually be the eldest son but if there were no surviving sons, the daughters would inherit equally. If the heir was under-age the estate reverted to the sovereign, who drew the annual profit, less the heir's and widow's maintenance and also had the right to arrange the heir's marriage. This wardship continued until the heir was old enough to inherit, or an heiress married. The sovereign could farm out the wardship of an heir or heiress, the Crown being paid a fixed agreed sum of money, and the 'farmer' retaining additional profit from the estate's annual income plus the sale of the marriage(s). Wardships were lucrative, as Blanche would later find.

Miles' appointment as escheator coincided with a Lancastrian resurgence. The Earls of Warwick and Clarence landed in September 1470 to oppose Edward IV, who fled abroad and Henry VI was restored as King in October. Miles was appointed a month later, in November 1470. Edward IV returned in March 1471, reclaiming the throne after the victory at the Battle of Barnet in April. General pardons were usually given at a change of government to facilitate good order and Miles certainly needed one as he had been appointed under the Lancastrian Henry VI and continued under the Yorkist Edward IV. Edward IV, concerned to pacify the March, sent influential commissioners to remedy the situation. On 6 June 1473, 'on the Thursday before the Feast of All Hallows' in Ross, the commissioner issued a 'general pardon to Miles ap Herry of the county of Hereford, gentleman, of all offences committed by him before 3rd June, 12 Edward IV' and he was the most important of those acquitted.[30] Miles was granted a second pardon relating to local disorders which suggests that he was being extremely cautious in his dealings with the newly restored King, while actively trying to consolidate his estates. He could obviously make use of the fact that he was Harri Ddu's son, given that Harri's support for Edward IV and his family was well known. Miles ap Harry was evidently widely respected. In 1484, four years before his death, he was twice named among those appointed to commissions of array for the county of Hereford led by William Herbert, Earl of Huntingdon, the son and heir of the 1st Earl of Pembroke. They were prestigious in their composition, for of the 18 commissioners, 10 were knights, including Simon Milborne who had finally been knighted,[31] an honour that Miles never received.

There is little mention of Miles in surviving Dore Abbey documents, though he did join with two others in lending the abbey £8 (£4,000 in today's money). His involvement in a legal matter concerning the chantry in Saint Katherine's Chapel, adjacent to Hereford Cathedral, only serves to demonstrate a conventional minimal religiosity, a view supported by the terse religious instructions in his 1488 Will written in Latin.[32] He was probably in his 50s when he died and according to his specific instructions was buried in the family vault in Bacton Church. His Will, which provides details concerning his family and lands, shows that he requested no masses and endowed no chantry chapels (as shown later in the 1524 Will of Sir William Herbert of Troy — see page 27). It is entirely possible that Lollard / Protestant views were still quietly held by the family. Perhaps an attempt by the formidable Joan to temper these resulted in the commemorative stained-glass windows erected behind the altar in Bacton Church, where Blanche would have seen them every time she attended a service (see Plate 7).

These windows are the earliest depiction of the family available to us. Miles and Joan are shown with their 19 children, all kneeling, in the lower portion of three windows, the upper two-thirds (now replaced) having depicted religious figures. Perhaps Joan felt the need for some tangible, Catholic, visual display but if so, it was a muted statement. When viewed from the front, Miles and Joan in the centre are flanked, left, by their 12 sons and, right, their 7 daughters. The Parry coat-of-arms of *argent a fess* between three *lozenges azure* has the central place above Miles and Joan and the altar tomb on which Miles has an open book turned towards him. He and his sons are bareheaded and wear long gowns, except for one son who is in armour. The foremost son is Henry Myles, Blanche's father. Joan wears a tight-fitting cap, while her daughters each have a more fashionable head-dress, the hair being drawn from the face into a hood at the back of the head which was then covered by a thin veil. Such clothes were perfectly suitable for their station in life, important considerations when clothes marked status. There are no names but the attribution appears secure and Miles' Will helps identification. In 1811 the windows were removed to Atcham Church in Shropshire, which had no connection with Blanche's family.[33] A further 19th-century window there commemorates Blanche herself.

Blanche never knew her grandfather but she did know her grandmother, Joan, who lived into Blanche's childhood. Theirs was a family with a strongly Welsh culture and care would have been taken that Blanche and her brothers and sisters would have known all about their ancestors. It was a family that prized its heritage.

Henry Myles, Blanche's father

According to Howel Dafi Blanche's father was 'revered in Christendom, grandson to two Harris' (Harri Ddu and Sir Harri Stradling), descendant of Dafydd Gam, a confident player at 'ball' and 'backgammon' and a skilled harpist, playing 'the harp with both his hands', for dancing.[34] He predicted that Harri Mil (Henry Myles), like his father and grandfathers, would receive 'his share in the world'. Although warlike when necessary, Henry Myles was a cultured and popular man who maintained the family's secure economic base. Over generations Blanche's family had attempted to build such a base under the auspices of the great families to whom they were bound. Family relationships helped to consolidate land holdings and families inter-married frequently within their own circles. Family connections really did matter. The Herberts, the Nevilles and similar families all expected to control local affairs and even the law courts to their advantage and their tenants were expected to follow the policies of their lord. At Henry Myles' level of society, family connections gave local influence and it was important to have a patron, a good lord, to provide a supporting network. Advantageous marriages were the most important means of acquiring new lands, connections and income.

Blanche's mother was Alice Milborne,[35] a daughter and heiress of Simon Milborne who, as an armiger, was then of the same status in society as Henry's father. It was a marriage with prospects for Alice as Henry inherited the manor of Newcourt and was Steward of Ewyas Lacy and Steward of Dore Abbey. However, while the wedding negotiations for the young Henry and Alice were underway, Howel Dafi provided an after-dinner entertainment at Newcourt. In public, he declaimed:

ytt Harri Mil gwr trwm wyf	*To (you) Harri Mil, I am a heavy (hearted) man,*
pa les o daw Saesnes hir	*What good (would come from the arrival) of a tall English woman*
y baradwys yn brodir	*To the paradise of our country?...*

He described Alice as a 'fair ageing girl', blonde, tall and older than was usual for marriage, and he begged Henry to take instead 'a Welsh knight's daughter', a 'slender twenty-year old' Welsh girl and not to 'seek the daughter of an Englishman from the Shire', who he inferred would be the first truly English woman to marry into the family, as previously wives had come from the March of Wales. Howel Dafi's intervention is even more dramatic when compared to his usual output. The many surviving examples of his work, 1450-1480, include the standard topics of religion and love but the majority are praises dedicated to his patrons among the gentlemen of South Wales. It is unlikely that he would have made such pointed remarks without the tacit agreement of his host, Henry's father, and yet both fathers had served together on at least one government commission. The families knew each other well but, nevertheless, this poem shows a degree of caution concerning marriage outside the gentry circles of the Welsh March. One hopes that Alice was not present to hear such views, however politely uttered, but she must have known for it would have been the talk of the family, servants and tenants — and yet the wedding went ahead. Henry seems to have been a quietly forceful person who was generally admired and usually achieved what he wanted. Marriage was normally a business arrangement but the evidence suggests Henry and Alice married for love, probably in 1497, as their eldest child, their son Milo ap Harry, was born in 1498. Alice must have worked hard to be accepted, especially perhaps by her mother-in-law, Joan (Stradling) and she would have spoken Welsh in order to deal with her new family, servants and tenants.

Henry's mother, Joan, had been a knight's daughter, related to the *nobilitas major*. Henry could not aspire quite so high in his own wife and he married into his own class in society, even though the lady was English. Alice Milborne's mother was Jane Baskerville, who had brought the manor of Icomb in Gloucestershire as dowry to her own marriage to Simon Milborne. The effigies of Simon's parents, Sir John Milborne and Elizabeth (Devereux), can still be seen in Burghill Church. Elizabeth's grandfather had fought at the 1402 Battle of Pilleth against Owain Glyndŵr. Sir William Herbert 1st Earl of Pembroke had married Elizabeth's niece, Anne Devereux and Anne's brother was to be the ancestor of Queen Elizabeth's last favourite, Robert, Earl of Essex. Simon Milborne was sufficiently important locally that negotiating the marriages of his 11 surviving daughters presented no problems for him. One of Alice's sisters was Blanche, who would become Lady Troy. Simon Milborne was Sheriff of Herefordshire in 1463-1464 and 1479-1480 and by 1484 he had been knighted.

Henry Myles continued the close links with the Herbert family first begun by his grandfather Harri Ddu ap Gruffudd. After the 1st Earl of Pembroke's execution his eldest son eventually became Earl of Huntingdon but he died in 1491, leaving a daughter Elizabeth who married Sir Charles Somerset. These were years rife with rumours of invasion which resulted in Perkin Warbeck's 1495 rebellion and a 1497 rising in Cornwall. In this atmosphere Henry VII, to neutralise any incipient trouble, offered 'the King's grace and pardon to all persons guilty or suspected of treason'[36] in Wales and the March in 1491. It may have been in connection with this policy that Henry Myles was summoned to London: 'Be it remembered that on October 18, 6 Henry VII [1491] Henry Miles gent was ordered by the Very Rev John, Archbishop of Canterbury [John Morton 1486-1500], Chancellor of England, under pain of £100 to appear personally before the Lord King in his Council on the Morrow of All Souls next and to have and bring there William ap Watkyn or his sureties. And further that the said Henry under pain of £200 shall not do any hurt to John Kyller.'[37] This suggests that Henry Myles was acting in a legal capacity, perhaps as a Justice of the Peace, on behalf of the King. Henry VII's policy was successful as the March remained quiet, partly because many Welsh men and women saw Henry Tudor as a British sovereign reclaiming the throne of England. He also had connections to the Mortimer family and his victory at the 1485 Battle of Bosworth brought him the enormous estates of the Earldom of March, which included three of Henry Myles' manors. Henceforth Henry VII was himself the most powerful border magnate, sentiments sufficiently persuasive to contribute to Wales and the March being largely sympathetic to the Crown even when parts of England were in rebellion.

In 1505 Henry joined William Herbert of Troy and his half-brother Sir Walter Herbert (both were illegitimate sons of the 1st Earl of Pembroke) in a recognisance to the King of 500 marks, a procedure similar to standing bail.[38] As the named persons were their tenants or dependants, they were acting for the King in a policing capacity, administering the areas concerned. For several years Sir Walter Herbert was left in charge of Raglan Castle and the lands around it. Although he had been a prominent Yorkist, he quickly supported Henry Tudor, whom he would have known when Henry briefly lived at Raglan. Sir Walter even entertained Queen Elizabeth, Henry VII's wife, at Raglan and, after his death in 1507, the castle and lordship reverted to Elizabeth Somerset. By 1508 this William Herbert of Troy was an annuitant of Edward Stafford, 3rd Duke of Buckingham (beheaded by Henry VIII in 1521) and William was regularly in attendance, with his family, at Thornbury Castle. William Herbert was Sheriff of Herefordshire 1515-1516, the year he was knighted. He retained connections with the family of Sir Charles Somerset, Baron Herbert who became the 1st Earl of Worcester in 1513 and William's son, Charles Herbert, became deputy to the 2nd Earl of Worcester as Steward for Monmouth in 1533.

Henry Myles was Sheriff of Herefordshire from 11 November 1499 to November 1500, from 15 December 1508 to December 1509 (when his little daughter Blanche was two years old) and finally, recorded as Henry Mile, from 7 November 1512 to the winter of 1513. This was certainly a higher office than his father attained as sheriffs were the most prestigious local appointments made by the King. They were local knights and esquires who were expected to deal promptly with any rebel rising or disturbance and about half of all sheriffs were also returned as Members of Parliament at some point in their careers. Being sheriff was thus a very sought-after position because of the influence attached to it. It may be that Henry Myles' initial appointment was due to his connection with Simon Milborne. In 1515 Henry Myles was appointed a Commissioner to collect the subsidy voted to Henry VIII.

Henry Myles was also the Steward of Dore Abbey, with a fee of 66s 8d and, as he said himself, there was a charter to prove it.[39] If he succeeded his grandfather, Harri Ddu, Henry Myles was Steward in the abbacies of the later years of Philip Morgan, Richard Dorston(e) (1495-1500), John Longdon (1500-1516) and Thomas Cleubery (1516-1523) until his own death in 1522. While Henry carried out his duties efficiently and with the apparent good will of the tenants there were periods of acrimony, from 1507, arising from the abbot's attempts to regain, or acquire, land and tithes to solve cash-flow problems. The abbot also seems to have misunderstood the parameters of Henry Myles' two roles as Sheriff and Abbey Steward.[40] In addition, the abbot was trying to replace him as Steward with George Neville, Lord Abergavenny, whom the monks considered a more influential patron. The documents show that matters escalated until in 1520 the abbot instigated court proceedings against Henry in the Council in the March of Wales. Although conclusive information has not survived, it is likely that Henry Myles won his case, for the Council's Lord President, Bishop Blythe, required the abbot to sign a bond (for a massive £100) to accept the Council's ruling. Henry was very ill in the last years of his life and indeed his son-in-law, Thomas Vaughan of Tregunter (married to Blanche's eldest sister Elizabeth), deputised for him at the manor court due to his being ill with 'diverse infirmities'. It is certainly possible that Henry's death was hastened by this long-running dispute with the abbot. That his family felt aggrieved by the abbey's treatment of their father is shown by his son Milo's view that 'the said monastery of Dore stands in a wild quarter where there resided divers and many persons of light demeanour and some of the monks of the house being of that condition ...'. The young Blanche may have been left with the impression that monasteries were rapacious landlords who treated loyal servants abominably. This is not anticlericalism, for her family had worked with the abbey for generations, but in future years it may have allowed her to acquire former monastic land without a qualm.

Henry Myles died on 27 September 1522 and was probably buried in Bacton Church. Although his Will has not survived, his Inquisition Post Mortem is extant and details the lands that he held.[41] His estate covered 260 acres, including 30 acres of woods and 8 messuages, which were dwellings with outbuildings and lands. His income was £44 13s 4d, less the rent of 3s 4d for Newcourt (designated a manor from 1488 to the 1520s), giving a net total of £44 10s, twice the income of the average esquire and the same as the lower ranks of knights. So Blanche's immediate family lived very comfortably, despite the harassment from the abbot.

Blanche's Inheritance

Blanche grew up in a Welsh culture, where care was taken to ensure that she and her brothers and sisters knew their ancestral pedigree. She had a happy, devoted family who prized their heritage and had accumulated the means for a prosperous life. Family influences also hint at qualities that would prepare Blanche for the life she was to lead: a sense of responsibility and stewardship for property and dependants; a sense of the consequences of disharmony between people and the importance of being able to find common ground; an ability to move with the times; perhaps a mistrust of dogmatism; and a strong sense of loyalty to those in power whom one was bound to serve.

2 *Of Newcourt Born*
Blanche's Early Life

Even though no specific information has been found for Blanche's early years, accounts of the time provide a good idea of the kind of childhood she would have enjoyed. The interesting question is how this young woman from the Welsh March came to be, as she said herself, 'handmaid to a Queen' and the answer lies in the circumstances of Blanche's adolescent years and her family connections.

The preparations in the house for the new baby included ensuring that the midwife was on hand, the birthing chair for Alice was ready and a vessel prepared for a possible emergency baptism. However, all we know about Blanche suggests that she was a healthy child and so she would have been taken, if possible on the day of her birth, or the day following, to the parish Church of Saint Faith at Bacton to be christened. The church would have been decorated for the occasion, red and black painted cloths being popular,[1] and a special candle would have been lit during the ceremony. The officiating priest was very probably Sir John ap Harry, her father's chaplain, who was perhaps also the vicar of Bacton. The service began in the church porch to allow as many people as possible to be witnesses. Her mother, though, would not have attended as she would have remained indoors until her churching about a month later. Although designed as a service of thanksgiving for a safe delivery from the hazards of childbirth, churching also served to provide all women, except the very poor, with a short period of welcome rest after the strain of giving birth. As baptism was thought to encourage the devil to redouble his attacks on the child's soul, confirmation speedily followed and was certainly carried out before the age of 3 years. As was usual in her sphere of society, Blanche would have been confirmed by Bishop Richard Mayew of Hereford in Bacton Church, her parents taking her chrism cloth (a linen band used at her christening) to cover the anointed area of her head. The chrism was then cherished as a memento.[2]

The baby girl would have had two godmothers and one godfather and at her christening all of them entered into a recognised relationship with her. Godparents were expected to help their godson or goddaughter in any way they could throughout life, not just until confirmation, and this commitment was taken extremely seriously. Often, to reinforce the connection, the baby would be named after the socially most important godparent, who could then be relied upon to further the baby's career and marriage prospects. It is therefore reasonable to deduce that it was her Aunt Blanche (later Lady Troy) who was the baby's godmother and who carried her on the embroidered cushion to the font that christening day.

Blanche Milborne

In 1494 Blanche (in Welsh Blaens) Milborne married James Whitney of Whitney and Pen-cwm. Her dowry was the manor of Icomb in Gloucestershire, which was later inherited by her elder son. However, James Whitney died on 30 June 1500, leaving Blanche with three small children: Robert, who at 6 years old was the eldest,[3] and the younger James and Elizabeth. Anne Morgan (of Arkstone, Herefordshire), one of Elizabeth's daughters, would marry Princess Elizabeth's cousin, or possible half-brother, Henry Carey, later Lord Hunsdon,[4] by licence on 21 May 1545.[5] Anne's grandmother, Blanche, who had seen her two elder sons die, was still at Court on the occasion of her granddaughter's marriage.

Blanche Whitney was not a widow for very long as she soon married, as his second wife, William Herbert of Troy Parva,[6] an illegitimate son of the 1st Earl of Pembroke by one of his mistresses, Frond verch Hoesgyn. Illegitimacy did not carry the stigma in Wales that it later did in England so this was a very important match for Blanche, who seems to have been some years younger than William. She was attractive and, from a practical point of view, she was likely to produce an heir for William as she already had small children. As Lewys Morgannwg asserts that she joined her husband in welcoming Henry VII, his queen and earls at the 'palace of Troy', Troy(e) House, south-east of Monmouth in August 1502, Blanche's remarriage must date between July 1500 and August 1502. In 1516, when her husband was knighted,[7] Blanche became Lady Troy. Their connections were with Elizabeth Somerset, whose husband had become Earl of Worcester in 1513, and with Sir William's nephew who would become the second 1st Earl of Pembroke in 1551 (and whose first language, despite a glittering Court career, remained Welsh for he apparently could not write easily in English). Although English, Blanche Herbert was bilingual for she lived in a Welsh cultural environment, with Welsh spoken not only to servants but also within the family, and close contact was maintained with Henry Myles and her sister's family. The Herberts had two sons, Charles and Thomas, both of whom were eventually knighted and became Sheriffs of Monmouthshire.

Sir William Herbert, described by Lewys Morgannwg as 'an outstanding knight', died in 1524 and his Will,[8] which he had drawn up a year before, was proved on 13 April 1524. After a conventional preamble he asked to be buried 'in the south side of the new chapel' which he had lately built in the parish church of Monmouth, and he directed his executors to build a marble tomb with an effigy of himself between those of his first wife Margery and his second wife Blanche, who outlived him, complete with an epitaph. Blanche was to be well provided with manors, lands and tenements for her lifetime and their son Charles needed Blanche's consent to make a jointure of other properties, indicating that William admired his wife's good sense. In addition, he added the pious hope that 'I trust that Blanche will keep herself sole'. Blanche's opinion of this is not recorded though, in fact, she did not marry again. Blanche and Charles were made executors and there was the stipulation that if both legitimate sons lacked issue then the next beneficiary would be 'Henry Somerset knight, Lord Herbert', then heir to the Earl of Worcester, 'trusting that he will be a good lord to my wife and children ...'. As Lewys Morgannwg said that Blanche Herbert had been a 'governess' when she was young, it is possible she first fulfilled this role for some of Henry Somerset's children. Sir William had made a very fair Will for his wife and all his children. The frequent references to Blanche certainly suggest that Blanche and William had been fortunate in having a loving marriage and it was during this period of her life that Blanche Herbert became godmother to her baby niece.

Blanche Parry's Childhood

Growing up in Herefordshire's Golden Valley, Blanche was still a long way from the life she would come to lead. Her brothers were Milo (Miles) and Symond (Simon), and her sisters were Elizabeth, Margaret, Jane, Sybil and possibly Anna, their spacing suggesting that Alice, their mother, breast-fed them herself. Although survival rates can be difficult to determine, it is apparent that Blanche's grandparents had raised most of their children and her mother and three of her aunts lived long enough to marry twice. Large families were the norm in those pre-contraceptive days but it is paradoxical that both mother and baby stood a greater chance of survival in Henry Myles' sphere of society than in the Court of Henry VIII. Two queens, Jane Seymour and Katherine Parr in her subsequent remarriage, both died in childbirth. Katherine died of puerperal fever while Jane was killed by a catastrophic haemorrhage 12 days after the birth, probably caused by the retention of the placenta, a condition which was apparently not noticed by Jane's male doctors but would have been recognised, and perhaps prevented, by an experienced midwife.[9]

Nutrition was another factor, for high-class ladies rarely ate as much meat as their menfolk, reducing their iron intake. This, compounded by monthly menstruation, could lead to a progressive anaemia. The use of wet nurses also removed the contraceptive effect gained by breast-feeding and led to debilitating annual pregnancies. The result was that her first pregnancy was the best chance a lady had to produce a live, healthy baby. Anne Boleyn's first baby was Elizabeth and she was followed by two miscarriages. Catherine of Aragon's first full-term pregnancy produced a son, who died at nearly two months from an infection. Thereafter miscarriages followed, exacerbated by her fasting, and she was extremely fortunate to have a live daughter, Mary. By contrast, Blanche's family would have had a more balanced, varied, nutritious diet of good fresh seasonal food: mutton, venison, game, rabbit, beef, pork, fish, sauces with spices including pepper, whole-wheat bread, with fresh vegetables (especially leeks), herbs and pulses for pottage, fruit and honey all washed down with claret, mead, ale and cider. Children were given fresh milk but not the red meat or fruit thought to induce the diarrhoea that killed through dehydration. In a year of bountiful harvests Newcourt, according to Guto'r Glyn, was 'a lively place' and he had delighted in the sugar candy.

Fieldnames and documentary evidence show that wheat and rye were available and Newcourt had a bakehouse (probably under the present-named Keeper's Cottage). Bread was the staple food, though the quality varied according to the grain, or mixture of grains, used, which depended on the soil (the Golden Valley's was good quality) and the climate during the growing season. When the harvest failed bread was made from anything available, and there were harvest failures in 1521, when Blanche was about 13 years old, in 1529, 1545, 1551, 1556 and 1587.[10] Blanche was still at home to see the catastrophic effects of the 1521 failure and although her father died in 1522, it is likely that she visited Newcourt in 1528 for the marriage of her sister Sybil. As she kept in contact with her family, Blanche would also have known about the later failures, and the one in 1587 was evidently the impetus for her bequeathing an annual dole of corn in her Final Will.

Young children learned all the familiar nursery rhymes followed by the running and skipping jingles of early childhood. For Blanche and her brothers and sisters the rhymes would have been in Welsh as for example *Ar y ffordd wrth fynd i Rhuthun*, which describes a man on the way to Ruthin to sell wool. Even respite / truce terms, used when wanting a rest in a game, were intensely regional and are so traditional that some used by the little Blanche would still be recognised by children today.[11] It is likely that Blanche had a painted, jointed, wooden doll as well as balls and hoops with which she could play with her sisters and with similarly aged children from among the upper servants. She would also have learned to handle animals and to ride a pony as her father was essentially a farmer. That she became a skilled horsewoman is indicated by her later career at Court. She would have learned her alphabet from her mother, following the admired example of Saint Anne teaching the Virgin, initially using a hornbook with letters and the Lord's Prayer written on paper under transparent horn and mounted on a board for durability. With initial instruction in Welsh, Blanche's English mother would soon have added the preliminaries of written English, probably reading from her Book of Hours. Frequent references to the past deeds of the family and their connections would have helped Blanche to become politically aware. Dancing, singing and playing the harp were usual family entertainments and were skills to be practised regularly.

As Blanche grew she would have also learned housekeeping from her mother as this was considered essential for girls who were intended to marry. Arithmetic was also useful for checking all the various accounts and paying tradesmen. Richard Mulcaster, a noted educationalist, headmaster of the Merchant Taylors' School from 1561 and later high master of St. Paul's, was particularly concerned with the education of girls as well as boys in Blanche's class of society.[12] He considered 'it to be a principal commendation in a woman: to be able to govern and direct her household, to look to her house and family, to provide and keep necessaries ... to know the force of her kitchen'. This entailed knowing how to manage the servants, the medicinal herbs needed for emergencies and how to feed the whole household. It was superb training for part of Blanche's later role at Court.

Newcourt, the Family Home

Blanche was born at Newcourt at the high point of its existence and she was so proud of it that she mentioned the house by name in her 1570s epitaph in Bacton Church. Built by Harri Ddu in 1452, and embellished with timber taken from the oak woods on the ridges (the sites preserved in names like Longwood), it was immediately adjacent to the long disused Norman motte-and-bailey which seems to have been utilised for service buildings. In Miles ap Harry's time Newcourt, as a focal point for the burgeoning family estates,[13] had a park added and for about 40 years it was considered a manor. In the tenure of Henry Myles (Blanche's father) the house reverted to being an estate house with a park, which is the way it was drawn on Christopher Saxton's 1577 map of Herefordshire, its earliest depiction. Blanche would have known

Newcourt as drawn c.*1814 (Pilley Collection, Hereford City Library)*

of this as it was engraved as one of the series of maps begun in 1574 under the patronage of her cousin, Sir William Cecil, Lord Burghley.[14]

In her Final Will Blanche would leave £10 to 'the Poor People of Newton near the Park Pale of Newcourt', these cottages probably housing the outdoor staff. However, she was remembering Newcourt as it had been 50 years before as it is unlikely that she had seen it since the 1520s. She mentioned the house in a property conveyance clause in her First Will, written for her by Lord Burghley.[15] William Vaughan, as the only son of the eldest son (he was the grandson of Blanche's brother Milo ap Harry) was to inherit 'New Court' so Blanche included the provision that he was to 'have £300 to be in the safe custody by the order of the Lord Treasurer's towards the repairing of the house of New Court until he shall come to full age'. Blanche also intended to leave William 'the bedding and hangings at Westminster and all the household stuff at Newcourt'.[16] This suggests that Blanche kept furnished rooms at Newcourt for her own use — her aunt, Blanche Lady Troy, had done something similar when she left the Court and retired to live at Troy House. Blanche was evidently making provision for herself if Queen Elizabeth died, and indeed, she did nearly die of smallpox in 1562. In the event, Elizabeth outlived Blanche, who never needed to retire to Newcourt, and so it is probable that the furniture, sold as the Jenkins' Collection (described later), really did belong to Blanche.

Blanche never owned Newcourt but she obviously had fond memories of it as she wished to see it maintained in good repair. To her great sorrow William died in 1584 and Newcourt passed to his sister, Elizabeth, who had married their cousin, Rowland Vaughan. In 1586 a survey was made which described the park boundary 'along a far green broad meare from oak to oak, where the pale did sometime stand, to be discerned by the burrs & knots of the said trees that have grown over the holes where the paling rails were let into the said trees: and at length it follows a great bank reared up on both sides to a little brook or gutter of water, which brook does bound it on the east to the corner…'.[17] Such a park was not only a food source and a venue for hunting, but also a very prestigious symbol. Henry Myles would have used Newcourt and its park when he needed to entertain both as Steward and Sheriff of Herefordshire. Local families, most interrelated, constantly visited each other, maintaining contacts and disseminating news, and the status of Henry Myles meant that he and his wife were an important part of this social round.

Blanche's Religious Background and Education

Until her father's illness and legal dispute with the abbey, Blanche's childhood could be considered idyllic. Her family's circumstances meant she was never hungry and she lived in a valley which her great-nephew Rowland Vaughan (in *His Booke*, published 1610) would describe as 'the pride' of Herefordshire and said was strewn with moss and apple-trees. 'Cow-slips, which was the chiefest flower' were used to decorate the maypole erected on the level ground by Bacton Church to celebrate May Day. The church was the focal point of the parish's activities and the bells from Bacton and Dore Abbey were used to regulate the day. On Sundays it was obligatory for everyone to attend services, usually early morning matins and then high mass, and on Easter Sunday everyone received Holy Communion. Depending on the ecclesiastical season the church would have been profusely lit by candles on the altars, before the many images and on the rood loft.[18] The gold and silver ornamentation would have sparkled and the rood screen with its paintings of saints would have gleamed in the softly pervading light.

Maintaining the nave, the church finances and the equipment used in services was the responsibility of the churchwardens, elected annually from the heads (including widows) of all households in the parish.[19] In addition each image had wardens responsible for their lights (candles).[20] The Maidens' Wardens, two girls old enough to take Easter Communion but unmarried, maintained lights before the statue of the Virgin and those of female saints. It encouraged the girls' social skills and gave them some financial awareness.

Blanche's Bacton epitaph emphasises that she as 'a maid did end my life'. She was comparing her state to the Queen's but it is also possible that she was making a reference to the Maidens at Bacton Church. At 12 years she would have joined this group and helped to raise funds for the lights before the Virgin and Saint Faith.

The funds were partly raised from the gatherings that took place in the church ale-house adjacent to the churchyard. This was the centre for the village's social activity and scene of boisterous fun when the ale and cider flowed freely. Additional funds came from the church stores. A typical example (known from Morebath in Devon) was a flock of about 20 or more sheep, called Our Lady's Flock, producing about 40lbs of wool each year, paying an income of over 30 shillings into 'Our Lady's Store'. Each image had a similar store to pay for maintenance and lights and Blanche suggests similar stores at Bacton. It was a parochial obligation to graze church animals with one's own. At the annual accounting the exact location of each animal was meticulously recorded and anyone refusing to take part was named, shamed and fined. It has been estimated that this system involved at least two-thirds of the parishioners. Other stores operated on profit-sharing whereby parishioners paid to keep animals and then kept the profit. This efficient system ended with the religious changes begun in 1538 but Blanche, remembering how they operated in her childhood, tried to reinstate a store of church cattle on the profit-sharing basis. In her First Will she directed 'And for further relief of the vicar I will there be bought 20 kine [cows] to be distributed to the poor parishioners of Bacton and they to give to the vicar 2s [shillings] by year for the use of every cow as long as may be by some composition agreed between the vicar and them that shall have the said kine'.[21] This practical measure would have both paid the vicar and provided help for the poor. It also demonstrates Blanche's awareness of, and involvement in, the parochial activities of her youth.

Sir John ap Harry, her father's chaplain,[22] probably instructed Blanche and her brothers and sisters in basic education and then the boys would have proceeded to further training, probably at Dore Abbey. Although girls usually remained at home, there was another possibility for Blanche and her sisters. This is shown in a letter[23] written during the dark days of the Dissolution of the Monasteries:

> To the right Honourable the Lord Cromwell Lord Privy Seal.
>
> Right honourable and my singular good Lord after my most hearty recommendations, it may please the same to be advertised that I am required by diverse of my loving friends in these parts to write to your lordship in favour of the poor house of Aconbury. Which house is of

> honest disposition and stands by the City of Hereford and is adjoining to the marches of Wales. In the which house the gentlemen of Wales as of Abergavenny, Ewyas Lacy, Talgarth with Brecknock with all other adjoining, and the aforesaid City and Shire have had commonly their women children brought up there in virtue and learning. It might therefore please your Lordship of your Charitable goodness to tender the same with your lawful favour, and to be a means to our Sovereign Lord the King's grace to take the same to Redemption and grace. Wherein trust you most surely my good Lord you shall acquire both laud and love of these parties as knows the Holy Trinity who long preserve your good Lordship in honour from Wygmore the xxvjth [26th] Day of December [1536].
>
> Your lordships most
>
> Bounden
>
> Roland Co. et Leh.

Rowland Lee, Bishop of Coventry and Lichfield, was Lord President of the Council in the Marches, 1534-1543. He was a powerful man with a wide jurisdiction and his letter was an attempt to save the Augustinian nunnery of Aconbury from being suppressed. This was a locally prestigious foundation, the Pope and the Abbot of Dore both having been involved in a dispute concerning its affiliation. Bishop Rowland Lee's letter had no lasting effect and Aconbury was not exempted, being dissolved in 1539 when the complement was six nuns and sixteen servants. By 1542 it was in the hands of Hugh ap Harry, one of Blanche's distant cousins.[24]

This letter gives an authentic glimpse of life at the time and may also provide an insight into Blanche's further education. The geographical area described was precisely the area of Henry Myles' lands and his family were of the social class indicated. The remit of Augustinian canons was the spiritual welfare of the laity and the equivalent cloistered nuns interpreted their calling as giving spiritual instruction to women and girls. Aconbury was an upper-class, genteel establishment and was, for a nunnery, wealthy. Bishop Rowland Lee confirms that girls from the families of local gentlemen were sent to Aconbury as, in fact, to a finishing school.

The names of ten Prioresses have been traced, from the earliest in 1280 to the last, Joanna Scudamore, at the Dissolution. The Prioress from 1489-91 to 1534 was Dame Isabella Gardiner, who was said to have been an excellent housewife as well as Prioress. She was credited with growing dwarf elder at Aconbury, where it still flourishes. This was used as a purgative, the berries as a blue dye, and the leaves in an embrocation or, due to their strong odour, scattered in granaries to drive out moles and mice. Among other medicinal herbs, she grew expensive saffron to colour sweetmeats and cakes for the nuns' table and to be distilled as a cordial. Dame Isabella Gardiner's nuns and pupils certainly lived well and she was the Prioress who would have been in charge when, as seems likely, Blanche and her sisters were educated at Aconbury. The 'learning' taught to them would have included enough Latin to understand Church services, writing in English and the arithmetic needed to supervise a large household. They would also have become more proficient in embroidery, sewing, singing, the making of possets and in all the social graces encompassing 'virtue'. That the Aconbury nuns provided instruction of the highest quality is evident for otherwise Bishop Rowland Lee, not an advocate of monasteries and Cromwell's political ally, would not have been prevailed upon to approach Thomas Cromwell on the priory's behalf. Such a superior education was precisely what was needed to fit Blanche for her later role at Court and the fact that she was chosen from her sisters to attend their aunt may have been due not only to her particular relationship to Lady Troy, but also to her aptitude in learning these skills.

Blanche as a Young Woman

Her father's death in 1522, when Blanche was about 15 years old, was the catalyst for change, though Alice waited at least six years until all the children were settled before her second marriage, this time to Thomas Baskerville, then the last Steward of Dore Abbey. Milo, the heir, was old enough to inherit in 1522 and his marriage to Eleanor Scudamore produced three known children, the two girls (aged 15 and 14 years) marrying the son and grandson respectively of Sir William Vaughan of Porthaml, near Talgarth, who had obtained their wardships.[25] Symond's family included two legitimate daughters, one of whom became Maud Berrowe on marriage. Elizabeth married Thomas Vaughan of Tregunter and their second son was John Vaughan, Blanche's adored nephew. Margaret married Howell Watkyn of Penbeddel and their sons were known by the surname of Powell. Jane also married a Vaughan and Anna (if she was one of the sisters) married Thomas Berrington. Sybil married James Whitney of Clifford[26] and one of their granddaughters was Elinor Bull, who married Richard Bull, sub-bailiff at Sayes Court, the manor-house at Deptford which provided meat for the Royal Court when in residence at Greenwich Palace. It would be at the widowed Elinor's comfortable house at Deptford Strand that the playwright, Christopher (Kit) Marlowe would be fatally stabbed in 1593.[27]

Blanche too was of marriageable age but she did not marry. Her later favouring of Hugh Bethell of Mansell might point to a suggested but aborted alliance with his family. Being unmarried was unusual at that time but it may be that her father's death allowed Blanche more choice if a contract had not already been agreed. She may have even decided to become a nun at Aconbury when her studies, if she studied there, were completed. The other possibility is that her talents were such that her aunt, Blanche, Lady Troy, who probably attended her father's funeral, took notice. Presumably there was a family discussion with Blanche insisting that she had no intention of marrying. Perhaps one can imagine her elders smiling tolerantly, thinking that time would solve that problem! It may be, however, that she made her point so well that her aunt was prompted to proffer the suggestion that Blanche go with her and serve her as her gentlewoman. This is all the more likely in that Lady Troy was Blanche's godmother. However it came about, when we next encounter Blanche she is in the company of Lady Troy.

No concrete information has so far been found for the 11 years of Blanche's life between 1522 and 1533, but all the indications are that she was serving her aunt Blanche Herbert, Lady Troy and that Lady Troy was herself in the household of Elizabeth Somerset, Countess of Worcester (Henry Somerset's second wife). It is likely that Lady Troy had obtained an appointment for John Vaughan (her great-nephew) as a page of the Chamber to Henry VIII by 1533, and he was a sewer by 1538. The long and continuing connections between Blanche Parry's family and the Somersets were also reinforced by mutual connections to the Vaughans of Porthaml, and Blanche's Final Will shows that by then she was godmother to one of the Countess' great-granddaughters. Countess Elizabeth had a personal role in the Coronation banquet of Queen Anne Boleyn, even though her father was a staunch supporter of Princess Mary. She was assigned, with the Dowager Countess of Oxford, to hold a cloth ready to conceal Queen Anne whenever she wished 'to spit or do otherwise'.[28] In 1536 Countess Elizabeth was said to have given information against Anne to whom she was certainly very close. She is unlikely to have done so, unless inadvertently or under pressure, as she was pregnant at the time and was very distressed by Anne's situation. Her sister-in-law, Henry Somerset's sister, was William Brereton's wife, and Brereton was one of the five accused who died at the same time as Anne, much lamented by his wife who kept his last token, a gold bracelet, bequeathing it to her son. (Another of the accused was Francis Weston, the first husband of John Vaughan's wife.) Members of the Earl of Worcester's family were personally extremely upset by the fate of Anne Boleyn, although the earl's position at Court was not affected.

The close relationship between Lady Troy and her independently-minded niece, Blanche, was a crucial one. Lady Troy was brought to the Royal Court partly at the behest of her late husband who requested the Somersets to remember her but it was her own personal qualities that brought advancement. She was a gracious, gentle, cultured lady who would provide the loving stability that so benefited Princess Elizabeth, Prince Edward and to some extent even Princess Mary.

3 *Trained in Princes' Courts*
Early Years in the Royal Household

Princess Elizabeth was born at Greenwich Palace on Sunday 7 September 1533. We know that Lady Troy was a member of the household because there is a record of her involvement in the choice of a wet nurse for the healthy baby: 'My mother was chosen and brought to the Court by my Lady Herbert of Troy, to have been her Majesty's nurse and had been chosen before all other had her gracious mother [Queen Anne Boleyn] had her own will therein.'[1] This suggests that Queen Anne was not allowed her own choice of nurse for her daughter, or possibly the woman was not suitable. Mrs. Pendred (a Welsh name pronounced and often spelled Pendryth) was actually chosen. She stayed with Elizabeth as she is recorded as having another baby at Hatfield in 1552 and, as detailed later, her husband was to approach Queen Elizabeth for help in 1582.

A royal christening[2] could not immediately follow the birth as additional preparations were needed and so three days elapsed before the magnificent spectacle of the Princess Elizabeth's christening took place in the adjacent Church of the Observant Friars. She was not the hoped for male heir but nevertheless she was the King's daughter and so her christening was a theatrical event designed not only to bring the baby into the orbit of the Church but also to declare the power of the King. The church and processional way were hung with rich tapestries. The font, lined with fine linen and raised on steps, was silver, the stage and surrounding rails were covered in red cloth and above all this was a crimson satin canopy fringed with gold. A brazier was provided in an enclosure where the baby was undressed and warm water was thoughtfully used in the font.

The procession of dignitaries was splendid. There were the mayor, aldermen and forty of the chief citizens of London, preceding lords, knights and gentlemen. The King's Council, barons, earls, marquises and dukes, with their wives and the clergy of the King's Chapel, all attended. Indeed a member of the Court had to have a very good reason not to attend; otherwise the King would suspect them of supporting the deposed Queen Catherine of Aragon. The Countess of Worcester would have been present (unless indisposed) and Lady Troy would have been among her ladies. Of the necessities for the Service, the Earl of Essex carried a gilt basin, the Marquis of Exeter a wax taper, the Marquis of Dorset the salt and Lady Mary of Norfolk the pearl and jewelled covered chrism. The Officers of Arms followed. The baby herself was carried by the Dowager Duchess of Norfolk, flanked by two dukes, while her long train was carried by the Countess of Kent with two earls holding it along its sides. A rich canopy was held over the baby by four lords, and many ladies and gentlemen followed, the key personnel being the Queen's relatives. The Service was conducted by the Bishop of London and the baby's godparents were Thomas Cranmer, the newly appointed Archbishop of Canterbury, and the dowagers Duchess of Norfolk and Marchioness of Dorset. The baby was named Elizabeth after her paternal grandmother, though it was also her maternal grandmother's name. Immediately after the christening, Archbishop Cranmer confirmed the little Princess. All the elements of every christening-confirmation were there, though on a far more magnificent scale and, as was usual, the baby's parents did not attend. The godparents gave the child gifts, refreshments were served and the procession reformed. The gifts were displayed, Archbishop Cranmer's being carried by Henry Somerset, Earl of Worcester. Thus, attended by this great throng and lit by several hundred torches, the baby was ceremonially brought to Queen Anne's chamber door.

Princess Elizabeth's nursery was headed by her Lady Mistress, Margaret, Lady Bryan, sister of Lord Bourchier, who had previously been Lady Mistress to Princess Mary, a position in which she was succeeded, when Mary was 3 years old, by Margaret, Countess of Salisbury. In December, before the crowds arrived at Court for the Christmas festivities, bringing with them a risk of infection, a separate household was arranged for little Princess Elizabeth at Hatfield, 20 miles north of London, a far more pleasant environment not affected by the turgid smells and ill-health of the capital. Her mother was able to visit her there the following spring. In March the baby was moved to Eltham, where her father had spent much of his childhood and which (being only five miles from Greenwich) was near enough for both parents to visit her. However, Elizabeth's childhood would largely be passed in Hertfordshire, where the household would move between Ashridge House, Hunsdon House, Hatfield House and Hertford Castle.

In May 1536 Elizabeth's mother was put on trial on a trumped-up charge of adultery, which in a Queen was high treason, and was executed. Anne's real fault lay in her two miscarriages, for King Henry was adamant in wanting a male heir to ensure the dynasty's succession. In the fraught atmosphere little Elizabeth was temporarily forgotten. A letter from Lady Bryan to Thomas Cromwell dating from this time shows that the little girl had outgrown the beautiful clothes previously supplied by her mother. Mention was also made of Sir John Shelton, who with his wife (Anne Boleyn's uncle and aunt) was in overall charge of the Household, now at Hunsdon, where the King's daughters, Mary and Elizabeth, were living together. According to Lady Bryan, Elizabeth was teething which made her more fractious than usual as 'she is toward a child and as gentle of conditions as ever I knew any in my life, Jesu preserve her Grace'.[3]

His wife dead, the King immediately remarried, his new wife being Jane Seymour. In October 1537, Prince Edward, the longed-for son, was born and Lady Bryan became the Lady Mistress in charge of the nursery for the new baby prince, with Sybil Penne as his wet nurse. Three days later he was christened, this time in the Chapel Royal at Hampton Court. This even more sumptuous occasion was again very well attended. Princess Mary, now known as the Lady Mary, was one of the godmothers, and her train was born by Lady Kingston. 'Then the chrism richly garnished borne by the Lady Elizabeth, the King's daughter; the same lady for her tender age was borne by the Viscount Beauchamp', with the assistance of Lord Morley. (That is, the 4-year-old Lady Elizabeth was carried when she became tired.) Both half-sisters took refreshments of spices, wafers and wine. When the procession re-formed after the Service 'Lady Elizabeth went with her sister Lady Mary and Lady Herbert of Troy to bear the train',[4] demonstrating that Lady Troy was now in charge of Lady Elizabeth and, while the sisters lived together, of Lady Mary as well.

Lady Troy's Position in the Royal Household

Information concerning Lady Troy has survived in the elegy composed for her by Lewys Morgannwg, an important Glamorgan bard writing between 1520 and 1565, a time of great changes in religion, language and law in Wales. A family bard of the Herberts, he was asked by Lady Troy's sons to celebrate her, probably a month after her funeral. The poem, accompanied by the harp, is in the form of a *cywydd*, the predominant Welsh strict-metre form of the period, with seven-syllable lines and alternately stressed and unstressed end-rhymes. Some poems of this period are very difficult to translate but Lewys Morgannwg's compositions are usually beautifully constructed and flow well. The content of the elegy is similar to a modern obituary, giving the highlights of her life, and it had to be accurate as the gathered relatives and friends would have known all the details anyway.

Marwnad yr Arglwyddes Blaens[5]	***Elegy to the Lady Blanche***
Rhos oer fyned sir Fynwy	*Monmouthshire has become a cold plain,*
Ail Elen Goel o lan Gwy.	*(Because of the loss of) a peer to Elen Goel from the banks of the Wye,*
Mae'r Farn ym am feirw'n nes,	*For me, because of the dead, the Day of Judgement is nigh,*
Marwgoel oedd am arglwyddes:	*It was the death-omen of a lady:*
Bwrw Arglwyddes, brig loywddoeth,	*Smiting Lady Blanche, (she of) bright, wise countenance,*
Blaens, un ddawn Sibli hen Ddoeth;	*(Whose) gift (was) akin to (that of) the old wise Sibyl.*
Arglwyddes, teÿrnes bwrdd tâl,	*The lady of the royal Herbert household,*
Bord Troe, tŷ Harbart rial,	*Queen of the high table, the table of Troy,*
Mal y wraig gynt, mawl rhag cam,	*Similar to the lady Marcia of yore, praise lest there be wrong,*
Marsia *ar* ôl marw Syr Wiliam.	*Following the death of Sir William.*
Bwrw iawn henwaed brenhinoedd	*Smiting the ancient Milborne bloodline was akin to*
Mal bwrw hen waed Mylbwrn oedd,	*Smiting the ancient true bloodline of Kings.*
Ei llin o Went i ieirll Nordd	*Her lineage, from Gwent to the northern Earls,*
O'r lle hanffont ieirll Henffordd	*Is that from which the Earls of Hereford trace their ancestry.*
Arglwyddes breninesau,	*(She was a) Lady (in charge) of Queens,*
Gofrner oedd ban oedd yn iau.	*A governess she was in her youth.*
Hi a wyddiad yn weddus	*She knew in a fitting manner*
Wybodau iarllesau'r llys,	*The accomplishments of the ladies of the court,*
Gorcheidwad cyn ymadaw	*(And she was the) guardian, before she passed away,*
Tŷ Harri Wyth a'i blant draw.	*Of Henry VIII's household and his children yonder.*
I Edwart Frenin ydoedd,	*To King Edward she was a true*
Uwch ei faeth, goruchaf oedd,	*(And) wise lady of dignity,*
Waetio yr oedd at ei Ras,	*In charge of his fosterage (she was pre-eminent),*
Gywirddoeth wraig o urddas.	*(And) she waited upon his Grace.*
Arglwyddys plas a gladden',	*(She, whom) they buried, the Lady of the palace of Troy,*
Troe, a'i llew lletyai'r ieirll hen.	*And her lion (i.e. William), gave hospitality to the old Earls.*
Bu i frenin, bu fawr unwaith,	*A welcome was given to the King, Henry VII,*
Roeso, a'i ieirll, Harri Saith.	*And his Earls; he was great once.*
Gwedd*u* y bu tra fu fyw	*She gave service all her life,*
Hon sydd frenhines heddiw.	*To the one who is Queen today [i.e. Mary I].*
I dlawd gwan didlawd gin*i*aw,	*(She gave) to the weak and poor a worthy meal,*
I'r dall hen rhôi fwyd â'i llaw.	*To the old (and) blind she would give food with her hand.*
Â'i llaw draw llywiai druain,	*With her hand yonder she would guide those who were forlorn,*
Lle da, rhoes dillad i'r rhain.	*A good place, (and) she clothed them.*
Diwarth y rhoes da *wrth* raid:	*She honourably gave generously in response to need,*
Dêl hyn yn dâl i'w henaid!	*Let this be a reward for her soul!*

Gwely Gonstans ag Elen	*Akin to Constantine and Elen*
Merch Coel, hi a'i marchog hen,	*Daughter of Coel, she [Blanche] and her old knight,*
O! Dduw gwyn, ni ddug annoeth,	*Woe (that) blessed God did not take away an unwise (one),*
Ysbeilioedd ddwyn Sibli Ddoeth.	*He caused devastation by taking away (the) Wise Sybil.*
Aeth wraig. Nid â fyth ar ôl	*The lady has gone. Never again will the ages witness the loss*
O'r oesoedd wraig mor rasol.	*Of a lady as full of grace as she.*
Mae *i* Blaens feibion fal Tonwen:	*Blanche has sons who are like Tonwen's:*
Beli o'i bron hi, Brân hen;	*Beli from her bosom, (and) old Brân,*
Dau frodyr, gwŷr difredych,	*Two brothers, men of honour,*
Dau f*eirch* cad o farchog gwych:	*Two battle-steeds issuing from an outstanding knight [i]:*
Syr Siarls o hil Syr Wiliam,	*Sir Charles of the line of Sir William,*
Mor wych cawr â'r Marchog Cam.	*A giant as great as he Marchog Cam [ii],*
Arhowch cloi aur Marchog Glas	*(And) delay the sealing of the Blue Knight's [iii] wealth*
Tros wart Hvmr, Meistr Tomas.	*On account of the Humber's defender, master Thomas.*
Dau filwr y'u dyfelynt	*Two soldiers whom they compare*
Wrth wŷr o gwrt Arthur gynt.	*With men of Arthur's court of yore.*
Oes hir, eleirch Syr Wiliam!	*Long live the swans of Sir William!*
Yn fyw maent. Mae nef i'w mam.	*They are alive - heaven awaits their mother.*

[i] The original has *freich*, a mutated form of *braich* / arm, which could be used metaphorically as 'defender', in which case this line would be 'Two defenders in battle …' instead of 'Two battle-steeds …'.
[ii] Sir Dafydd Gam (Davy Gam in Shakespeare's *Henry V*), great-great-grandfather to Sir Charles and Sir Thomas (and Blanche Parry's great-great-great-grandfather through her Stradling grandmother). *Marchog Cam* translates loosely as 'the crooked knight', apparently on account of a physical peculiarity (possibly acquired in battle).
[iii] Sir William ap Thomas Herbert, great-grandfather to Charles and Thomas, known as the 'Blue Knight of Gwent'.

Lewys Morgannwg's poem describes Lady Troy's position as 'in charge of Queens', and she was responsible for the proper accomplishments of the court ladies. This suggests that her position included the teaching of good manners, basic education, etiquette, protocol and perhaps the enjoyment of music and dancing. As the elegy was written before Sir Charles Herbert died in 1557 (before Queen Mary), the Queens mentioned are unlikely to include Elizabeth as her elevation was by no means certain before 1558. The phrase may refer to Lady Troy's having responsibility in the household of

Queen Anne Boleyn. It certainly refers to Queen Mary, who acceded in 1553 and who had lived with Elizabeth and Edward for a time, for it is supported unequivocally by the line that Lady Troy 'gave service all her life to the one who is Queen today'.

It may be that she was put in charge of Mary's household as early as 1531, when Mary's vindictive father separated her from her mother, Catherine of Aragon. Perhaps Mary's brief stay in Ludlow Castle in 1526 gave Mary and Lady Troy some common ground, though everything suggests Lady Troy was very easy to be with and perhaps even Mary found her so despite the difficult situation. Lewys Morgannwg's choice of words when he says that Lady Troy 'was the guardian … of Henry VIII's household and his children yonder' shows not only how careful one had to be in mentioning Elizabeth before her accession but also how tenuous Elizabeth's position was right up to the very moment that her sister died. The only one of Henry VIII's children named in the elegy is King Edward and here there is no equivocation: 'To King Edward she was a true and wise lady of dignity, in charge of his fosterage — she was pre-eminent — and she waited upon his Grace.'

Lewys Morgannwg states that Lady Troy, 'a wise lady of dignity', was a 'governess … in her youth' and the 'guardian' of the royal children. She was a governess, possibly of the Somerset children but also of Prince Edward and Lady Elizabeth, though not of the older Lady Mary. Prince Edward later wrote in his *Chronicle* (or journal) that until the age of six he had lived 'among the women' and this was the household presided over by Lady Troy. The evidence suggests that it was Lady Troy who taught both the little Elizabeth and then Edward, her half-brother, their letters. Kate Champernon / Ashley was appointed as Elizabeth's governess in 1536, so Lady Troy taught Elizabeth the rudiments of education for her first three years. Edward was born in 1537 and male tutors were appointed for him in 1540 so again Lady Troy taught him for his first three years. (Both children started their more prescribed education at the same age.)

A formal household was arranged for the prince in 1538 with Sir William Sidney as his chamberlain. Lewys Morgannwg states that Lady Troy was 'in charge' of Prince Edward's 'fosterage'; evidently she became his Lady Mistress when Lady Bryan relinquished the post and, as such, remained in charge of the domestic side of the household. Initially though, Lady Bryan was concerned with the prince and so Lady Troy first took over as Elizabeth's Lady Mistress, a post for which she was eminently suitable, being related to the Earls of Worcester and Pembroke and having raised five children of her own. All the surviving evidence suggests that Lady Troy was a pleasant, graceful and charming person whose own children loved her, making her quite capable of fulfilling the role of mother to the younger royal children.

Her training of Elizabeth can be credited with being at least partly responsible for the Princess' self-possession and ability to handle discerning visitors. In 1539 the courtier Thomas Wriothesley was most complimentary about the six-year-old Lady Elizabeth's upbringing and education. It is quite possible that Elizabeth and Edward did not later remember Lady Bryan's tenure at all and that their earliest memories were of Lady Troy as their Lady Mistress and the mother-figure who provided the security and love that is so important in the early years of childhood and could easily have been lacking in the lives of these particular children.

Lady Troy's position is confirmed by four lists of personnel in the Letters and Papers of Henry VIII, two for 'the Lady Mary' and two for 'the Lady Elizabeth'. Although filed under 1536, the documents are undated and internal evidence suggests three different dates. The first list for 'Personages appointed to attend on the Lady Mary' predates the appointments of Susan Clarencieux and Mary / Margery Baynton, who according to a letter of Princess Mary to Thomas Cromwell were both in her service in 1536. Their names appear in the second list of her household, which must therefore date from 1536 or later. This list in turn suggests a date after 1536 for the following list of Lady Elizabeth's household: 'Ladies and gentlewomen: Lady Troy, Mrs. Chambrum, Lady Garet, Elizabeth Candysche, Mary Norice.'

The same women appear on a separate list which Nichols wrongly dates 1558.[6] Both lists then continued with named Chamberers, Gentlemen, Chaplain, Grooms of the Chamber, Yeomen, a Laundress and a Woodbearer giving a total personnel of 32, ten less than the 42 staff for Lady Mary.[7] Mary's list includes Stables' personnel, which indicates that Elizabeth was then too young for such arrangements to have been necessary. However, neither of these lists was complete as the named persons do not match the totals and Princess Mary's letter mentions a maid, Mary Brown, who did not appear in either of her lists.

The Mrs. or Mistress Chambrun(/m) in the list is Katherine, or Kate, Champernon (Kat / Cat was Elizabeth's nickname for her), a knight's daughter, and she is second in the list of ladies after Lady Troy. The date can be established from a letter written on 10 October 1536 by Kate Champernon, from Hunsdon, to Thomas Cromwell.[8] In it she thanked Cromwell for speaking well of her to the King and 'preferring her to her present' position. She continued that she needed a yearly stipend and asked that this be brought to the King's attention. However, Kate's position was not that of Lady Mistress (as has been asserted) but that of governess. Lady Bryan was replaced by Lady Troy. Kate Champernon's letter does show that all the important personnel were appointed with the King's approval. Lady Troy's was, therefore, an official appointment.

As the guardian of the royal children Lady Troy was responsible for their early religious education. She would have encouraged Blanche, her niece, and Prince Edward and Lady Elizabeth, her royal charges, to pray regularly. While at Court she must have favoured a form of worship reflecting the Catholicism of the last years of Henry VIII's reign, as if she had shown any overt Protestantism it would have at least been noted. From about 1544 Elizabeth seems to have become aware of the theological discussions at Court, particularly in the household of her step-mother Queen Katherine Parr, an awareness further fostered by the Protestant leanings of Kate Ashley. That Elizabeth kept her religious interest within the bounds of her father's dictates may well have been due to the influence of Lady Troy and Blanche Parry.

In 1545 Roger Ascham (Elizabeth's tutor from 1548, who may have had a connection with Lady Troy through John Whitney, his page and favourite pupil[9]) wrote to Kate Ashley, as she then was following her marriage to John Ashley in the same year.[10] As Ascham asked that she commend him to 'my good Lady Troy and all that company of gentlewomen', it provides clear evidence that Lady Troy was still in post. However, she is not mentioned in the second household list for Lady Elizabeth, which dates from about 1546, by which time Elizabeth needed personnel for the Stable. This list gives the first known reference to Blanche Parry (with her correct Welsh name) as a gentlewoman in Lady Elizabeth's service: 'Personages appointed to attend on the Lady Elizabeth, the Kings daughter. Gentlewomen: Kateryne Chambernowne, Elizabeth Garret, Mary Hyll, Blanche ap Harrye.'

Exactly what had happened is described in a letter written a few years later, on 31 January 1549, by Sir Robert Tyrwhitt to the Duke of Somerset.[11] Kate 'Ashley [née Champernon] … was made her mistress by the King her father … For her [Elizabeth's] desire to see the King, she confesses that her [Ashley's] pallet was removed from her [Elizabeth's] bedchamber because it was so small at Chelsea. But four of her gentlewomen confess that Ashley first removed Lady Troy, who has lain there continually for about two years and then her successor (Blanche) Parry and could abide nobody there but herself …'. Sir Robert Tyrwhitt's letter suggests that Kate Ashley was not popular with the other ladies in the household. Her post as governess had been curtailed by William Grindal's appointment as Lady Elizabeth's tutor in 1544 and she then succeeded Lady Troy. Perhaps her marriage made her eligible, if this was the preferred status for a Lady Mistress. King Henry, who died in January 1547, had approved the change and Kate was in place before Elizabeth went to live with her step-mother Katherine Parr at Chelsea later in 1547.

Lady Troy was probably in her late 60s when she retired, having been Lady Elizabeth's governess and Lady Mistress for three years and then continuing as her Lady Mistress for a further ten years. Although Sir Robert's letter seems to suggest 'removal', there is no reason to suppose the change was other than amicable. It certainly appears that Kate Ashley and Blanche Parry subsequently managed to have a calm working relationship, which might not have been possible if Blanche Parry had felt her aunt had been badly treated. Lady Troy retired to Troy House, where she was still living in 1552 when her son, Charles Herbert, mentioned her in his Will. It is probable that Lady Troy had found retirement to the beautiful rural area she had known when younger an attractive proposition. Lewys Morgannwg provides a picture of a dignified, graceful and wise lady who personally gave food and clothes to the poor, blind and needy.

The Household Accounts of the Princess Elizabeth, which survive for 1551-1552 when she was at Hatfield,[12] include the item: 'Sent to my Lady Troy, as by warrant appears, with v shillings [5 shillings] given to the Knights Marshall's servant - lxx shillings [70 shillings, or £3 10s].'

This is the only item in these accounts where a sum was 'sent' and not just 'paid'. Lady Troy remained on the Princess' payroll and her pension was especially delivered by the Knights Marshall's servant, who was paid to do this. In the same accounts 'Katheryn Ashley' was paid £7 15 shillings and 'Blaunche Parrye for her half years annuity Cs [£5]'. The accounts make it clear that Blanche was paid twice a year, on the last day of June and in December. As other payments mentioned in the accounts were half-yearly as well, it seems certain that this was also true of Lady Troy's pension. The reference to 'by warrant' shows that it was a regular payment. Certainly Elizabeth remembered her former Lady Mistress and made sure that she received her pension, and comparison with Kate Ashley's shows that it was about half of the wage she was given when she was in post. These sums place Lady Troy's pension in a context and show her enduring importance to the Princess.

By the time she retired both her Whitney sons had already died and her granddaughter was married to Lord Hunsdon. Her son, Sir Charles Herbert, in his 1552 Will,[13] bequeathed her: 'Item I will that Dame Blanche Herbert widow, my mother, shall have that part of my said capital house of Troy wherein she now lies together with all the stuff and implements in the same to be freely used, occupied and enjoyed for term of her life and, after her decease, I will all the said stuff' to Joan Herbert, Sir Charles' daughter. This shows that Lady Troy had her own furnished apartment in Troy House where her son and daughter-in-law, Cicill, lived and where she received her pension. The phrasing meant that Sir Charles did not need to change his Will but it is also possible that he did not have time to change it, in which case Lady Troy died in 1557 just before her son. Certainly Queen Mary was on the throne,

Charles was still alive and Lady Troy was probably in her late 70s, a marvellous age for the time. She was presumably buried in Monmouth Parish Church next to Sir William, her second husband.

It is reasonable to ask why the contribution of Blanche Herbert, Lady Troy has never been acknowledged in the accounts of the childhoods of Queen Elizabeth and indeed King Edward. The answer is partly an accident of history and partly due to her own personality. Lady Troy apparently kept a harmonious household without the unpleasant undercurrents that caused trouble and necessitated correspondence during Kate Ashley's later tenure. Documents have either not survived for Lady Troy's period in office, or did not need to be written in the first place. Her elegy has only recently been translated and it demonstrates the ambiguity of Elizabeth's position at that time. However, it is clear that Lady Troy is to be appreciated for providing happy and secure childhoods for both Elizabeth and Edward.

Blanche Parry and the Young Elizabeth

Blanche makes clear in her Bacton epitaph that she was with Princess Elizabeth, 'whose cradle saw I rocked', from Elizabeth's birth. Blanche was then about 25 or 26 years old. Four rockers seems to have been the usual complement, judging from those hired by Catherine of Aragon, and they rocked the cradle in turn. There were two cradles, one for normal use and one a cradle-of-state, furnished with a canopy and the royal arms, which was used to impress visiting dignitaries. The rockers had the important job of keeping the baby quiet and amenable, essential if favourable reports of the royal infant were to be publicised. Blanche's statement suggests that she was in charge of Elizabeth's rockers. Such was the beginning of an association that would last for more than 56 years. Sir Robert Tyrwhitt's letter clearly shows that Lady Troy had groomed her niece as her successor. That this did not happen straightaway was possibly due not to her age, or even her perceived social position, but to her single status.

Academically, Blanche was not as qualified as Kate Ashley to be Elizabeth's governess. In about 1545 Roger Ascham wrote to Elizabeth[14] and he tried to discourage Kate from pushing Elizabeth too hard and too fast with her learning:

> And although I know for sure that your education, in which distinguished teaching is linked up with your own great worthiness, has its source in Plato's discipline, I do not hesitate to affirm that your own volition and fine judgement have sustained you most. Mistress Champernon's excellent counsel has advanced you much and the best instructions of my William Grindal have helped and assisted somewhat.

Kate's responsibility was for Elizabeth's primary teaching and she continued to assist when William Grindal, a noted Latin and Greek scholar, was appointed in 1544; when he died in 1548 Roger Ascham succeeded him. Princess Elizabeth became fluent in Latin, Italian, French and Spanish and fairly proficient in Greek. It is occasionally asked if she could speak Welsh. This seems very unlikely but as Elizabeth clearly had a gift and fascination for languages, she may well have understood how to pronounce Welsh words and to have enjoyed Welsh lullabies sung to her as a child by Lady Troy and Blanche Parry. Elizabeth was fond of music, making payments at Hatfield in 1551-1552 to a lute player and to a harpist, which could perhaps suggest a possible Welsh influence. (Blanche's father had played the harp well.) Elizabeth could play the lute and virginals herself and she paid the expenses for Lord Russell's minstrels and for visiting theatrical players. She loved dancing and would have needed to be taught basic steps and popular measures, especially those danced at Court. She also enjoyed literature and is recorded as purchasing a Bible, also deemed politically correct at that time. Reading the Bible was very probably a discipline that Blanche Parry had followed all her life and one that she and Lady Troy may well have passed on to their royal charge.

Blanche was fully trained by Lady Troy to be a competent, efficient, discreet and sympathetic Gentlewoman of the Household. The first reference to her among Elizabeth's personnel shows Blanche as the last, although probably the oldest, of the four Gentlewomen. She was the closest in age to Elizabeth's mother and was also about the same age that Prince Edward's mother would have been. Despite being ousted by Kate Ashley from her very close contact with Elizabeth, Blanche retained her position. Her influential Herbert / Somerset connections may have been useful. Katherine Parr had married Henry VIII in 1543 and Katherine's sister, Anne, had married William Herbert, the second 1st Earl of Pembroke, the son of Sir Richard Herbert of Ewyas, who was himself the half-brother of Lady Troy's husband. In addition Katherine's stepson, John Neville, 4th Baron Latimer, married Lucy Somerset, daughter of the Earl of Worcester, in 1545. Blanche's removal from her close proximity to Lady Elizabeth could have caused great unpleasantness within the household but everything shows that Blanche had an amenable and kind personality and was not one to hold a grudge. Also she really loved Elizabeth. For more than 13 years she had been in close, regular contact with the little girl and it is quite possible that she simply put her first, refusing to become embroiled in a domestic conflict. After all, she probably argued to herself, she was still in daily contact with the Princess.

That this contact continued to be very close is again shown by Sir Robert Tyrwhitt. His letter, written at the time of the Seymour affair and already quoted, concerned the suspicion that Kate Ashley had aided the suit of Sir Thomas Seymour to marry the Princess Elizabeth. His letter continued 'May it please your Grace to be advertised that after my Lady's grace [Elizabeth] had seen a letter, which I devised to Mistress Blanche from a friend of hers, ... she [Elizabeth] was marvellous abashed and did weep very tenderly a long time.' Tyrwhitt had evidently forged this letter and sent it to Blanche to show Elizabeth. The fact that he chose Blanche clearly demonstrates that her closeness to the Princess was well known in court circles.

In January 1549 Kate was sent to the Tower of London, while her husband was incarcerated in the Fleet Prison. Always solicitous for her personal servants, Elizabeth pleaded for Kate in a letter sent from Hatfield on 7 March 1549, to the Duke of Somerset and the Council:[15]

> .... I shall speak for ... Kateryn Ashley, that it would please your grace and the rest of the council to be good unto her ... First, because that she has been with me a long time and many years and has taken great labour and pain in bringing of me up in learning and honesty and therefore I ought of very duty speak for her. For Saint Gregory says that we are more bound to them that brings us up well than to our parents, for our parents do that which is natural for them, that is bring us into this world; but our bringers-up are a cause to make us live well in it ...

Elizabeth was — and would remain throughout her life — intensely loyal to her servants and here she was pleading, as she thought, for Kate's life. It confirms Kate's position and long service but it is noteworthy that Elizabeth writes in the plural of 'our bringers-up'. (That nothing similar has survived for Lady Troy, or even Blanche Parry, only shows that Elizabeth never had occasion to plead on their behalf.) During the weeks Kate was in prison it was Blanche Parry who fulfilled her duties. Kate was released by August 1549.

Evidence of Blanche's progress in Elizabeth's household is to be found in the Hatfield Household Accounts of 1551-1552, which place Blanche after Kate Ashley in the list of ladies, treating her as a special case. Princess Elizabeth was a careful overseer of her accounts and she signed each page. The majority of the payments shown were for food, drink, fuel and stabling. Most members of her large staff were male, with only 13 female domestics, five of whom were the Princess' paid gentlewomen, receiving regular wages. All the servants received board-and-lodging and their livery, the clothes worn on duty. When she was Queen, Elizabeth would also pass on her own worn clothes to her ladies for re-fashioning and these were often very welcome wardrobe additions due to the costly fabrics and decorations involved. Sumptuary laws which limited the cloth or decoration of clothes, certain fabrics being a mark of rank, were not applied to the important Ladies of the Household.

Kate Ashley headed the five Gentlewomen and she was reimbursed for material to make towels, linen cloth, damask and crimson satin, velvet, other necessities, apples, hay and diverse items 'bought by her for my Lady's grace', though Kate was not the only purchaser of such items. There was also a payment for her wages, 'as appears by warrant for £ vii and xv shillings [£7 15s]', which suggests that she was paid, while in post, £15 per year. Blanche Parry was now next in prominence. On 14 December she was paid £5 'for her half years annuity' and on the following 28 March she was again paid £5 'for one half years annuity ending the last of June, as by warrant appears'. So Blanche was paid £10 per year, a substantial sum of money. In addition, on 6 March she was paid £1 10s 'in reward toward her horsemeat, as by warrant appears', which shows that she kept a horse, presumably to accompany Elizabeth when she went hunting, a sport which Elizabeth considered healthy exercise. Evidently Henry Myles' early training of his daughter in riding was now a further useful accomplishment. Of the ladies, only Blanche was reimbursed for horsemeat so accompanying Elizabeth on horseback must have been a part of Blanche's job description. Blanche was officially now considered the second of Princes Elizabeth's Gentlewomen after Kate Ashley and, now in her 40s, she may well have served as a mother-figure to the little group of women.

Queen Mary's Reign

The tenor of life remained relatively uninterrupted for Elizabeth's household until the untimely death of her brother, King Edward VI, and the abortive attempt to place their cousin, Lady Jane Grey, on the throne in 1553. At Queen Mary's triumphant entry into London, Princess Elizabeth rode just behind her half-sister, ahead of the peeresses and gentlewomen who attended the Queen. Such a display of sisterly loyalty did not, could not, last, as there were too many memories from their father's divorce perhaps aggravated by perceived religious differences. After the new Queen's Coronation their relationship soured and Elizabeth found it prudent to leave the Court for Ashridge where she celebrated Christmas. In January 1554 the plans were discovered for what became known as Wyatt's Rebellion, though his was to have been only one of four co-ordinated rebellions, another being Sir James Croft's attempt to raise the Welsh March. In February Queen Mary had her finest hour in the speech she made to steady the resolve of Londoners in forestalling Sir Thomas Wyatt's capture of the capital. His failure led to a far more ruthless government policy and among the first executions was that of the 17-year-old, blameless, Lady Jane Grey. The 20-year-old Princess Elizabeth had also been named, although she claimed without her knowledge, as a possible figurehead for the rebellion, and there is no doubt that her life was also now in very real danger. She was most fortunate that the incredibly brave Sir Thomas Wyatt, despite torture and inducements, refused to incriminate her and indeed positively exonerated her.

Summoned to London, Elizabeth pleaded that she was unwell and delayed her journey as much as she dared. Initially she was taken to Whitehall, where, after investigations, she was charged with involvement in the conspiracies. Despite her vehement denials and her desperately measured letter to her sister, the Queen, she was sent to the Tower on Palm Sunday, 18 March 1554. She was accompanied by three Gentlewomen, two Grooms of the Privy Chamber and a Yeoman of the Robes,[16] and further kitchen personnel were lodged outside the Coldharbour Gate entrance to the Tower's inner ward. Their names have not been recorded but Blanche's specific statement that she had never left Elizabeth from the time she was a baby strongly supports the view that she was one of the three Gentlewomen. It is unlikely that Kate Ashley was among them, as the government continued to be wary of her influence and she may already have been separately imprisoned. As second in the precedence of Elizabeth's gentlewomen, Blanche must have been included, the other gentlewomen most probably being Blaunche Qwrtnaye (Courtenay) and Mistress Stafford, possibly the same Dorothy Stafford who became Lady Stafford.

In early May 1554 Princess Elizabeth was transferred to house arrest at Woodstock, with the same small group of servants in daily attendance, under the gaolership of Sir Henry Bedingfield. On 5 June 1554 one of the Princess' ladies, Elizabeth Sandes, was removed from her duties due to her Protestant opinions and Queen Mary refused to allow either of Elizabeth's preferred replacements. Elizabeth Sandes went abroad, joining a group that included the strongly Protestant Sir Francis Knollys / Knowles, who was married to Catherine Carey, daughter of Mary Boleyn and Elizabeth's cousin (or possibly half-sister if her father was Henry VIII). Elizabeth Sandes married and, as Lady Berkeley, returned to Elizabeth's service when she was Queen.

The Princess' gaoler, Sir Henry Bedingfield, found it extremely difficult to control the religious tendencies of the household for his removal of Elizabeth Sandes was only removing the most overtly Protestant of the Princess' women. As commanded by the Catholic Queen Mary the ladies were supposed to attend fully Catholic services but some refused. It is likely that Blanche was accommodating in this, especially if she had grown up, as seems probable, in a household imbued with Protestant doctrine but with Catholic ceremonial. Certainly she seems to have worked for the good of Princess Elizabeth within the constraints imposed.

The government also thought that Sir Thomas Parry, Elizabeth's Cofferer (household manager), was involved in incipient conspiracies. He was certainly most successful in keeping Elizabeth's land-holdings and finances intact and in helping to lay the foundations for her smooth transition to the throne. He is generally little known because he died in 1560, early in Elizabeth's reign. Sir Thomas Parry claimed to be Sir William Cecil's cousin but was only very distantly related to Blanche.

In July 1554 Queen Mary finally married Prince Philip of Spain, the reign henceforth being designated that of King Philip and Queen Mary. In April 1555 Elizabeth was summoned to Hampton Court, where she eventually had an interview with the Queen, probably at the behest of King Philip. On 20 May 1555, a warrant was issued directing Sir Roger Cholmley 'to set at liberty Katheryne Ashley who has long time remained in his custody', which suggests that she had been imprisoned for many months and that she may already have been in prison when the princess was herself imprisoned in the Tower in 1554. In the following October Princess Elizabeth was given permission to leave the Court for Hatfield. However, further conspiracies gathered around her and in June 1556 Kate Ashley, described by the Venetian ambassador as Princess Elizabeth's 'chief governess', was re-arrested, with Elizabeth's Italian teacher and three other women, and again taken to the Tower. She was said to have been found in possession of 'writings and scandalous books against the (Catholic) religion and against the King and Queen ...'. Kate Ashley was a most indiscreet servant for the Princess at such a time. Her overt Protestant beliefs and those of her husband were an immense liability for Elizabeth in such appallingly dangerous times; at least 300 Protestants were burned at the stake in Queen Mary's reign. Kate was extremely fortunate that she was again released in October 1556, although she was forbidden from returning to the Princess' Household and was only able to do so after Elizabeth's accession.

For the whole of this difficult time Elizabeth's acting Chief Gentlewoman was Blanche Parry. The danger was still all too real and Elizabeth owed her life at this point to the timely intervention of King Philip on her behalf. She remained circumspect, with nothing proved against her despite unrelenting pressure. Blanche must also have played her part in ensuring that no further religious nonconformity was apparent in the conduct of Elizabeth's Household and Blanche, evidently conforming as required, was perhaps tolerated by the government because she was older than Elizabeth's other women. There is no doubt that it was Blanche who provided a steadying environment for her beloved Elizabeth.

Queen at last

Then the danger was over. The desperately ill Queen Mary finally nominated Elizabeth as her heir, sending Jane Dormer to Hatfield to inform her sister and to plead, futilely, for Elizabeth to retain the religious changes Mary had revived. On 17 November 1558 Mary died. Elizabeth was now the new Queen and, even if the future was uncertain, she was in control of her own life for the very first time. In future years the Queen's Accession Day would be celebrated with church services and a tilt held at Whitehall. Now the priority was forming her household and her Council and planning the Coronation.

Loyal supporters were rewarded. Sir William Cecil (Blanche's cousin and closest friend at Court) and Sir Thomas Parry came to the fore, taking their places on the Council. Kate Ashley was now Chief Gentlewoman of the Privy Chamber, with Mistress 'Blaunche Apparey' as the second Gentlewoman, soon designated Ladies of the Bedchamber. Kate Ashley was also in charge of Elizabeth's very private close stools, the velvet upholstered commodes used as lavatories in the royal apartments.[17] This crucial appointment gave unrivalled opportunity for an exceptionally close relationship with the sovereign (previous male holders of the office under the Tudor Kings had enjoyed enormous power). After Kate's death Blanche would have been in charge.

Kate Ashley by an unknown artist

The propitious Coronation date was devised by Dr. John Dee, mathematician, Greek scholar and astrologer and set for 15 January 1559. Material for new livery was issued to the household, which now included 56 or more women, for the processions and festivities were meant to be the visible expression of the new reign. The Queen's entry into London, accompanied by a series of pageants, was a triumph of public relations. The watching

Londoners noted that the Queen was immediately followed by Robert Dudley as Master of the Horse. Blanche was issued with '7 yards of scarlet, 15 yards of crimson velvet, 1¼ yards of cloth of gold yellow with work and ¾ yard cloth of gold black with work',[18] which must have been made up into truly beautiful dresses for this very special occasion. Expensive 'Scarlet' (French escarlette) was a very finely woven worsted, which although usually bright red, could be blue, green, white or black. Of the four Ladies of the Bedchamber, Kate Ashley and Blanche (the only untitled ladies) were allocated 7 yards, the same yardage as Catherine Lady Knollys, while the fourth, Mrs. Elizabeth Norwich (on marriage Lady Carew), had 5 yards. (Mrs. is an abbreviation for Mistress and did not then signify a married woman.) The Bedchamber women were considered immediately after the Chamberlain and Vice-Chamberlain (who each received 16 yards of material) and it is clear that Blanche's position and allocation placed her at the forefront of the members of the Queen's Chamber.

The quality of Blanche's dresses can be gauged by comparison with a similar crimson velvet gown that was sufficiently sumptuous to be bequeathed by the dowager Duchess of Norfolk to her successor as duchess. Such elaborate dresses were worn on state occasions especially in the processions to open Parliament, the women being required to robe the Queen. Otherwise dresses were in the Queen's livery of black-and-white, though white was often preferred for attendance at church. Blanche is listed by name among the Gentlewomen attending Queen Elizabeth on the evening preceding the Coronation. On the day itself, she would have attended Elizabeth in the curtained, heated enclosure behind the altar in Saint Edward's Chapel designated for the Queen to change her dress as dictated by the ceremonial.

The Coronation roll categorises the personnel of the Queen's Majesty's Chamber. Headed by the Lord Chamberlain and his deputy, the Bedchamber had precedence, followed by three Chamberers, seven women of the Privy Chamber without wages, six maids of the Privy Chamber, the Master of the Jewel House (John Ashley) and a gentleman usher. The six Maids of Honour, the responsibility of the Mother of the Maids, were followed by 11 women who could be called on when required and then by at least 18 Ladies of the Household.

This is augmented by a 1587 Household list[19] which notes when members first received their warrants (that is were first employed). Only two of the original Ladies of the Bedchamber remained (Kate Ashley died in 1565, Catherine Lady Knollys died in 1569). 'Mrs Blanch a Parry' and Lady Carew (died in 1594) were still in post in 1587 and still being paid £33 6s 8d a year (a decline of 25% in real terms). They were joined by Frances Brooke (née

Newton) Lady Cobham (died in 1592) in the 1570s,[20], a familiar face to the Queen as she had been a Chamberer since 1558 (and continued to be paid the same £20 wage). She had married William Brooke, Lord Cobham on 25 February 1560 and was evidently Blanche's friend as she would be remembered in her Final Will.

Of these, Blanche served the Queen by far the longest — for at least 56 years — and it is evident that Elizabeth, whose girlhood had veered from one change to another, preferred continuity in the more senior personnel of her Privy Chamber. In fact it is extraordinary how little change there was in her 45-year reign, apart from the six Maids of Honour who were replaced when they married, several becoming Gentlewomen. Indeed Elizabeth preferred continuity among all her servants, appointing additional or replacement staff from among the families of the people she knew well whenever possible. This meant that many of the nobility and gentry had a succession of relatives with access, however fleeting, to the Queen.

Of the five 1587 Gentlewomen of the Privy Chamber, only Lady Haward and Lady Stafford, each paid £33 6s 8d, were noted as having been appointed in the first year of the Queen's reign, when Lady Haward was a woman of the Privy Chamber without wages. Bequeathed £10 and forgiven an £8 debt in Blanche's First Will, her omission from Blanche's Final Will suggests that by then she had died. It is likely, therefore, that Blanche was referring to Margaret Lady Howard (née Gamage), who died in 1581. The second wife of the 1st Lord Howard of Effingham, at least three of her daughters became Maids of Honour and her second son was the commander of the English ships which successfully fought the Spanish Armada in 1588. (In 1574 he had married Catherine Carey, daughter of Henry Carey, Lord Hunsdon and Anne Morgan of Arkstone; Catherine too served in the Queen's household and in 1598, then Countess of Nottingham, she was recorded as Groom of the Stool, only the second time this office was specifically mentioned for Queen Elizabeth, although other women must have been appointed after Blanche's death.)

Dorothy Lady Stafford, the second wife of Sir William Stafford of Grafton (whose first wife had been Mary Boleyn, Queen Elizabeth's aunt), had lived in Geneva, where she knew John Calvin, until Sir William's death in May 1556, and returned to serve Elizabeth in August 1559. Lady Stafford was Blanche's greatest friend among the women at Court (remembered in Blanche's Final Will) and her caring personality is demonstrated by her continued support for a mentally ill servant. However, Dorothy Stafford had to be circumspect due to her connections. The Queen clearly liked to keep any lady with a close relationship to the Crown within her own household, as with Lady Jane Grey's sisters, and Dorothy Stafford was the great-granddaughter of George Plantagenet, Duke of Clarence, brother of Edward IV and Richard III. Her maternal grandmother, Margaret Duchess of Salisbury, Princess Mary's Lady Mistress, had been gruesomely executed by Henry VIII when he was eliminating possible claimants to the throne. Dorothy's paternal grandfather, Edward Stafford, 3rd Duke of Buckingham, and one of her brothers were also executed. Those of her family who survived did so by being politically uninvolved, or by being too poor to count. Dorothy sensibly avoided intrigues and loyally served the Queen all her adult life, dying after Elizabeth in 1603. Her monument in Saint Margaret's Church, Westminster is a plainer mirror-image of Blanche's own[21] and her epitaph records that '... She served Q[ueen] Elizabeth 40 years lying in her bedchamber, esteemed of her, loved of all, doing good all she could to everybody, never hurt any, a continual remembrancer of the sues of the poor.' All her life Lady Stafford, managed to blend into the background but on her epitaph she proudly and finally proclaimed her pedigree. She was four years younger than the Queen but 21 years younger than Blanche. Perhaps this gap in age meant that Blanche viewed Dorothy as a daughter or a niece. Blanche's other close friend in the Household (as opposed to the Court in general) was Sir Christopher Hatton and he and Thomas Knyvett (John Vaughan's stepson), appointed Groom of the Privy Chamber in 1570, are also remembered by name in Blanche's Final Will.

The 1561-1562 list of New Year Gifts to the Queen (set out in the State Papers Domestic) include those of 21 named Gentlewomen, headed by 'Mistress Ashley, Chief Gentlewoman of the Privy Chamber' who gave the Queen 'twelve handkerchiefs edged with gold and silver'. Second in the list is 'Mrs. Blaunche Apparey', who gave 'one square piece unshorn velvet edged with silver lace', which was velvet with the looped pile uncut. The Queen reciprocated Kate Ashley's gift with two bowls, a salt with a cover, a spoon and a pepper box, all in gilt, with a total weight of 45.5 ounces, a handsome gift which showed the affection the Queen had for Kate. These entries also show that Kate Ashley was very conscious of her status as it was given in full for both entries. Clearly she did not want anyone to forget her position. Blanche was given a gilt 'stoup [or beaker] with a cover' of 16.75 ounces, one of the most expensive of the other gentlewomen's gifts. Thereafter, future New Year Gift Lists placed Blanche Parry as the first Gentlewoman of the Privy Chamber, a post which Blanche's Bacton epitaph designates as the Queen's 'Head Chamber'.

Blanche's subsequent position can be partly determined by examining the evidence for Kate Ashley's influence. Apart from her Council, Elizabeth (now an anointed Queen) could be approached directly by only a few people.

Kate Ashley controlled access to the Queen, facilitating a meeting for Richard Bertie, second husband of the Duchess of Suffolk and corresponding with supplicants, even recommending an appointment to the Earl of Rutland. Indeed, she went further still. With another gentlewoman and eventually with her husband she started to meddle in the important and delicate question of Queen Elizabeth's marriage, by corresponding with the King of Sweden. The Ashleys were said to have passed on comments that Queen Elizabeth had made. (John Ashley, designated a Groom of the Privy Chamber, was paid £33 6s 8d, more than the other seven grooms, presumably due to his additional post as Master of the Jewel House, a position which brought him into contact with Blanche.) These incidents demonstrate the power Kate Ashley wielded because of her proximity to the Queen, though it is possible that the Ashleys were colluding with Elizabeth to spread disinformation, as despite such indiscretions Kate Ashley remained in charge of the Privy Chamber until her death on 18 July 1565. The Spanish ambassador noted that 'Her Majesty went to see her the day before and I am told she is greatly grieved'. He also added an assessment of Kate, adding 'what a heretic she was'. The English agent at the French Court complained that he now had no 'friend' close to the Queen 'to make his moan to'[22] which, indicating the circle of Kate's contacts, also demonstrates Blanche's role in the Court.

Blanche was not as concerned with titles as Kate Ashley had been, for she placed her welfare firmly in Elizabeth's hands: 'not doubting want whilst that my mistress lived ...'. In the past such security had been rare for a single lady outside the confines of her family or the restrictions of a monastic life. It was unusual even in Tudor times, and the Court could be a difficult place to live. In a letter to Roger Ascham, Sir Anthony Denny wrote: 'The Court, Mr. Ascham, is a place so slippery, that never so well done, is not a staff stiff enough to stand by always very surely, where you shall many times reap most unkindness where you have sown greatest pleasures and those also ready to do you most hurt to whom you never intended to think any harm.'[23] Blanche placed her trust firmly in her mistress, Queen Elizabeth, and it was not misplaced. Elizabeth returned her loyalty and complete devotion, for Blanche would be well looked after throughout her long life.

Plate 1 Edward VI

Plate 2 Queen Mary (National Portrait Gallery, London)

Plate 3 Princess Elizabeth c.*1546 (The Royal Collection © 2007 Her Majesty Queen Elizabeth II)*

Plate 4 William Cecil, Lord Burghley

Plate 5 Queen Elizabeth Receiving Dutch Emissaries

(Gouache on paper. Staatliche Museen - Graphische Sammlung Kassel 10430)

The lady standing by the window among the most powerful men of Elizabeth's Court may be Blanche Parry (see page 82)

Plate 6 An Elizabethan Maundy Ceremony, c.*1560*
(Watercolour on vellum by Lievine Teerlink b.1510-20, d.1576; Beauchamp Collection, UK)
Could the lady carrying the Queen's train be Blanche Parry? (see page 65)

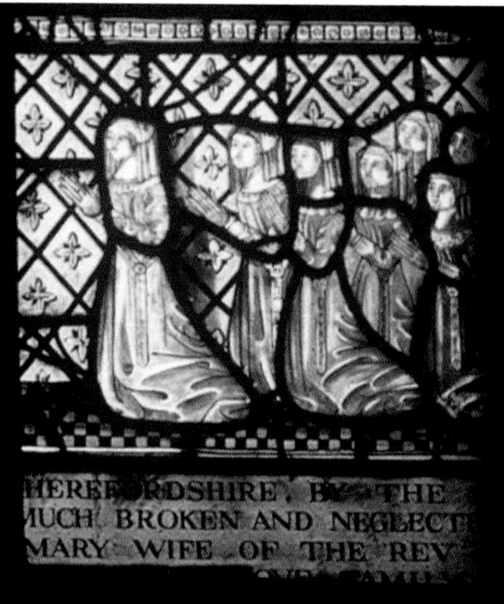

Plate 7 Miles ap Harry and his wife Joan Stradling, Blanche Parry's grandparents, with their 12 sons and 7 daughters. The foremost son is Henry Myles, Blanche's father. In 1811 the windows were removed from Bacton Church to that at Atcham in Shropshire (see page 19) (Ruth Richardson)

Plate 8 Dore Abbey (Terry Richardson)

Plate 9 Blanche Parry commissioned this map of Llangorse Lake in Breconshire in 1584, at which time she owned a fishery and lands there (see page 117) (NA SP/46/36/10)

Plate 10 Blanche Parry commissioned this memorial for Bacton Church before November 1578. Pevsner called it 'a very curious memorial' due to the relative heights of the statues of Blanche Parry and Queen Elizabeth (see page 143) (John Wilson)

Plate 12 An image of St Faith at Conques Abbey, the probable inspiration for the depiction of Queen Elizabeth on Blanche's memorial in Bacton Church (see page 147 and Plate 11 below)

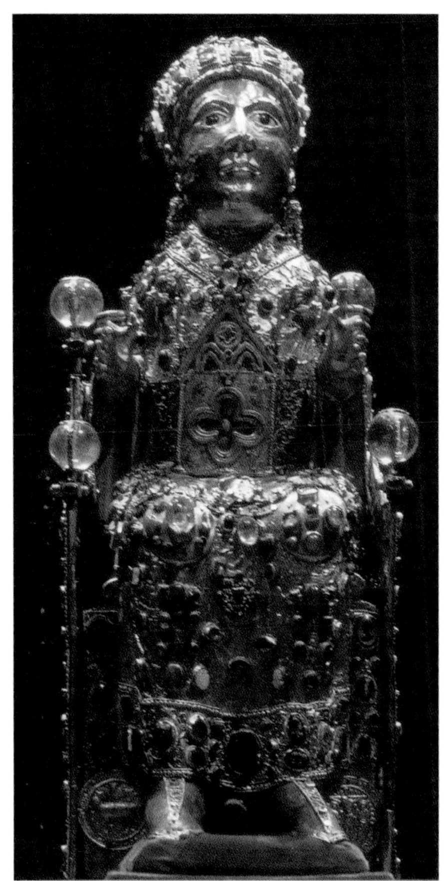

Plate 11 Bacton Memorial detail showing Blanche Parry and Queen Elizabeth

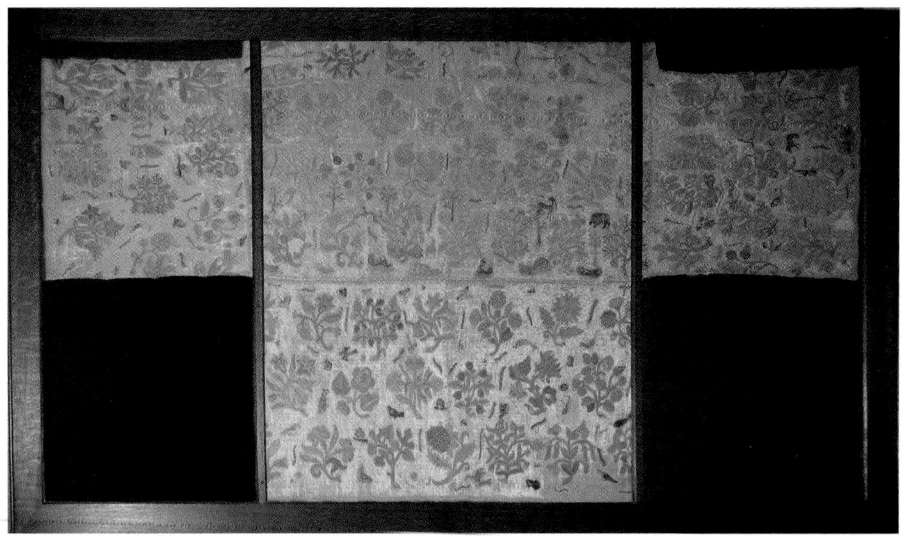

Plate 13 An altar cloth displayed in Bacton Church which tradition asserts was cut from an Elizabeth court dress embroidered by Blanche for herself (see page 62) (Karen Stout)

Plate 14 Depiction of Blanche Parry on the memorial in St Margaret's Church, Westminster (see page 140)

4 *Where Fleeting Honour Stands* Blanche at Court

Elizabeth was 25 years old when she became Queen and Blanche was 51. In a system of government where the sovereign was pre-eminent, those who controlled access to him or her held the key to power. Anne Boleyn and Katherine Howard had been destroyed by factions at Court, neither having been able to contact Henry VIII at the time of their arrests. Henry disliked unpleasantness to impinge upon him personally and so had taken good care to be unavailable. Katherine Parr was more fortunate, narrowly missing the same fate as her predecessors by managing to reach the King in time. In the wider Court circles, peers of the realm also had the right to approach the Sovereign directly but gentry only had the right to attend the Court and usually had to wait to be specifically invited to approach the higher officials.[1] Blanche's background placed her in the gentry category at the English Court and as a woman she would have been at an added disadvantage if the sovereign had been male. Blanche was a gentlewoman but, uniquely, she stood at the pinnacle of access solely because of her relationship with the Queen. A King's male servant in a comparable position to Blanche's would have wielded immense power. Blanche's influence was more subtle but she was undoubtedly Queen Elizabeth's confidante.

Discussion of the position of the ladies of the Privy Chamber has been adversely coloured by Rowland Vaughan, Blanche's great-nephew,[2] whose main purpose was to publicise his waterworks scheme for the Golden Valley in Herefordshire. He wrote that 'I remember in Queen Elizabeth's days, my Lady of Warwick, Mistress Blanche Parry and my Lady Scudamore, in little lay-matters would steal opportunity to serve some friends' turns ... because none of these (near and dear Ladies) durst intermeddle so far in matters of Commonwealth.' This has been taken to mean that such ladies were only concerned with the domestic and had no political influence.[3] What has been generally ignored was Rowland Vaughan's margin note describing them as 'a Trinity of Ladies able to work miracles'. Never sufficiently important at the Elizabethan Court to know exactly the political influence the women had, he nevertheless attempted to belittle and denigrate what he did know of them. In fact Blanche had employed him as her attendant as a letter of 30 April 1597 from William Cecil of Alt yr Ynys to his cousin, Sir Robert Cecil (second son of Sir William Cecil, Lord Burghley), makes clear: 'I forgot to crave your honour to prefer this bearer [Rowland Vaughan] to be one of Her Majesty's Guard, there being divers wanting and he being a sufficient man for that place. And Her Majesty, lately taking the air in Islington Fields, noted this bearer then, there being a shooting and of her goodness said he was a feat man to attend her service. He is strong and active and attended my good friend Mrs. Blanche Parry, his aunt, when he was a youth and if God had pleased, she would have preferred him to a better room, for that he is son to a good honest gentleman.'[4] It was Blanche's death and so the diminution of her influence, which had prevented Rowland's advancement at Court, his own merits apparently being insufficient.

Rowland himself wrote of this time in *His Booke*: 'After I had spent some years in Queen Elizabeth's Court and saw the greatness and glory thereof under the command of Mistress Blanche Parry (an honourable and Virtuous Gentlewoman, my Aunt and Mistress), my spirit being too tender to endure the bitterness of her humour; I was by her careful (though crabbed) austerity forced unto the Irish Wars, where I continued three or four years ...'. Blanche had tried to find Rowland suitable employment, a thankless task as his subsequent career shows him to have been unable, or unwilling, to work at anything for long. Not charmed by his sulkiness, she had refused him money and had made clear that his only practical option was to enlist in Ireland, where he claimed he fell ill and returned to Herefordshire for his health. Marrying his cousin Elizabeth, it was these two, 'my nephew Roland Vaughan and his wife', who granted away the house the vicar used in Bacton, which greatly upset Blanche. Nevertheless, her anger was short-lived. Preferring to avoid discord she left him £100 in the June 1589 codicil to her Final Will (calling him 'my cousin', meaning kinsman).

Rowland Vaughan makes it clear that Blanche had influence at Court and that she could and did arrange appointments. In this she was acting in the same way as most of the Queen's senior ladies whose access to patronage gave them undoubted power. However, Blanche's epitaph in Saint Margaret's, Westminster states she was pre-eminent as the 'Chief Gentlewoman of Queen Elizabeth's most honourable Privy Chamber and Keeper of Her Majesty's Jewels'. Rowland Vaughan is an unwitting witness to Blanche's true position for he categorically associates her with 'the greatness and glory' of Queen Elizabeth's Court. Blanche was at the centre of this Court and her position was known and fully recognised by everyone at the time.

The Privy Chamber

The design of the palace rooms reflected function. The further you could penetrate through the guarded doors, the more important you were deemed to be. Thomas Platter, a Swiss tourist, in 1599[5] described the more public Presence Chamber at Nonsuch Palace and the apartments leading into it, as 'hung with fine tapestries' on the walls and strewn with straw (or hay) on the floor. Carpets were laid as a path for the Queen to walk to her low red-damasked chair, furnished with gold-thread embroidered cushions and placed under a canopy of state ornately fixed to the ceiling. It was in the Presence Chamber (at Whitehall Palace) that Queen Mary's third Parliament had been convened in 1554 and it was in this room that tables were set up for the sovereign's official meals.

However, Queen Elizabeth rarely ate here as she preferred to use her more private rooms, where she retired with her very personal servants who, for most of her reign, were headed by Blanche Parry. Beyond the Presence Chamber was the Privy Chamber, a day-room for the sovereign which the Queen's accounts showed had curtains for greater comfort and privacy[6] with two further rooms opening from it. The first of these was the Privy Closet, a small room which was furnished as a private chapel but could also be used for interviews. The second was the sovereign's Bedchamber,[7] where the Ladies of the Bedchamber took it in turns to sleep either with the Queen or on truckle beds. Only a very few, very privileged, ladies were allowed into the Bedchamber, which was apparently searched every evening to prevent intruders and was cleaned by the Chamberers. Elizabeth's palaces each needed a well-stocked library for she prided herself on reading or writing each day, often, as Thomas Platter noted, annotating her books in Latin.

Although removals between palaces facilitated the cleaning and airing of rooms, to move over three hundred carts of baggage, tapestries and ornaments required meticulous organisation. In addition the Queen's Summer Progresses, reminiscent of the peripatetic journeys of mediaeval monarchs, allowed subjects a close view of the sovereign while the Court avoided London in the warm months when sickness could be rife. Although the Queen, accompanied by her Privy Chamber staff (leave was normally only permitted for sickness), usually visited courtiers' houses and towns in several counties each year, she never went to the north of England and, in the west, she barely crossed the River Severn. This Tudor Queen, unlike her sister, visited neither the former

Welsh March nor indeed Wales. So Blanche never saw her lands in Yorkshire and never returned to her home county. By the autumn the Court was usually in residence at Hampton Court, Richmond or Windsor while Whitehall in London was the venue for the Queen's Accession Day tilt held from 1581 until after Blanche's death in 1590. This was an eagerly awaited social occasion for otherwise tilts were only arranged for celebrations such as weddings.

At Richmond Palace, the Privy Lodgings, in a large three-storied stone building, consisted of 12 rooms[8] — the extra rooms being used by the members of the Queen's personal staff, their nearness to the Queen's bedchamber being dictated by the position in the household that each held. Blanche's importance can be gauged from the indications for the sleeping arrangements. When the Queen was on progress suitable lodgings had to be found which housed the staff in approximately the same nearness to their mistress as in her own palaces. On Wednesday 19 May 1574 arrangements were made by Simon Bowyer, whose job this was, for the Queen's visit to the Archbishop of Canterbury at his palace in Croydon. Rooms were allotted to the various Lords, to Ladies such as Lady Warwick, Lady Howard and Lady Stafford, to the 'Ladies and Gentlewomen of the Privy Chamber' and to grooms, physicians, department heads and kitchen staff. The harassed man added that 'I cannot then tell where to place Mr. Hatton' (then Captain of the Queen's Bodyguard). 'For my Lady Carew here is no place with a chimney for her but that must lie abroad by Mrs Aparry and the rest of the Privy Chambers ... Here is as much as I have any ways able to do in this house[9].' Evidently Blanche Parry had her own room and it was one of the first to be agreed.

The Queen visited Sir William Cecil, later created Lord Burghley, at his house, Theobalds, on 12 occasions, the first in 1564. He found it an expensive privilege, each visit costing £2,000 to £3,000, as the Queen stayed between three and six weeks. The arrangements needed care and tact. For the visit which commenced on 27 May 1583 Burghley himself recorded the allocation of the rooms. Blanche was the only untitled lady mentioned by name. She was allotted two rooms, namely 'a chamber in the uppermost part of the south-east turret and another over the Queen's bedchamber'[10], on the same floor as Sir Christopher Hatton, the Vice-Chamberlain. Blanche was then 76 years old and so was not given rooms adjacent to the Queen to fulfil any mundane tasks but simply due to her special position in the Queen's life. Of the other ladies, Lady Stafford's single room was immediately below the Queen's bedchamber, while the Gentlewomen of the Bedchamber had to share two rooms between all of them, one of which had a chimney and so could easily be heated if necessary. The remaining Gentlewomen of the Privy Chamber had to share a further two rooms together with their servants. Blanche's allocation was a privileged one.

Blanche's importance can also be gauged by the number of her personal servants as only a very few of the Household were allowed to keep servants at Court. The 1576 account of the Daily Expenses of the Queen's Table[11] provides 'a diet for two services' allotted to the servants of all the five or six Maids-of-Honour, 'one service' (£54 15s) to Mrs. Blanche's servants, the same for Lady Dorothy Stafford's servants and a total of 'two services' to the servants of all the Gentlewomen of the Privy Chamber. Both Blanche and Dorothy Stafford were noted as having their own chambers and they were the only named women. In her First Will Blanche mentioned that she had her own waiting woman and three men servants, while in her Final Will she detailed two gentlewomen, a male servant, a male chamber-keeper and a boy. It certainly appears that the women lived at Court even if the males were housed nearby. The care taken to provide rooms for Blanche and the number of her living-in servants places her in an almost unique position.

Daily Routine

Day staff came on duty at about 9am and probably had to exercise considerable tact in dressing the Queen as she was not at her best in the mornings. Queen Elizabeth had breakfast, then often sat at her window for a while, or worked on a translation, all before dressing for the day. The process of dressing, brushing her hair and selecting and fastening jewellery could take more than two hours. Washing required pewter bowls, although baths were available and close-stools of leather with pewter pans were used as toilets. All this required the attentions of several women and a Lady of the Bedchamber would have been in charge. This is where Blanche was pre-eminent and, as a result, she had private conversations with the Queen for hours during most days — unrivalled access at a time when Elizabeth, once she had shaken off her early morning mood, was relaxed and amenable.

The women were also responsible for receiving and caring for a variety of small animals given to the Queen as presents and kept in her rooms. They included a pet dog, a steel-chained monkey (eventually the concern of Lady Knollys) and a parrot in a specially made cage.[12] Blanche took delivery of the Queen's New Year gift of larks in a cage. There is also a warrant showing that Blanche took charge of 'our musk cat'.[13] Exactly what this was is debateable, for contemporary natural history books[14] describe a musk cat as a zibeline-ferret, a deer, or a Bengal bondar similar to a genet. It is most likely to have been a ferret with soft dark brown or black fur and sharp teeth, useful for catching the mice endemic in such open rooms. Perhaps Blanche's country childhood helped her to cope with the animal, though the little ferret did require 'a chain with a collar'. It must have been strong as within months it needed first a new collar, this time specified to be 'of iron with joints made full 'of holes with a hasp' and then a longer replacement chain with three swivels — or perhaps it had just grown.

All the ladies were expected to entertain the Queen with dancing, music (the Queen herself played the virginals), cards and theatricals. (Blanche's goddaughter, Lady Blanche Somerset, one of the daughters of the 4th Earl of Worcester, would be recorded as one of the eight masked dancers at Lord Cobham's house in 1600.) Music was performed by Court musicians and the singers of the Chapel Royal and intelligent disputation was fashionable. Gambling was popular and Blanche mentions debts owed to her which included the considerable amount of £20 from Blanche's great-niece Frances Vaughan, then a Maid of Honour. It would seem that Blanche was a successful gambler (though she did conventionally request that 'my debts may be paid' in her First Will). The Queen went hunting and riding (in which Blanche had accompanied her since before her accession) and enjoyed bear-baiting. Sewing and embroidery were considered suitable pastimes. The Courts of Catherine of Aragon and Anne Boleyn had been particularly noted for this but Queen Elizabeth does not seem to have really enjoyed producing such work herself. Among her ladies Blanche's friend Lady Cobham was particularly noted for her needlework skills.

There is a lovely fragile altar cloth displayed in Bacton Church which tradition asserts was cut from an Elizabethan court dress embroidered by Blanche for herself (Plate 13). This could be true and as the Queen handed down dresses to be altered for her women to wear, it is possible that it originally belonged to Elizabeth herself. Such gifts were considered to cement a relationship and were viewed as significant in the power politics of the time. The Bacton embroidery is a large panel of white ribbed silk with an additional weft of silver threads, then called silver chamblet and embroidered with polychrome silks. The original motifs by an expert embroiderer are flowers, with sprigs of columbine and vine, and it would have looked similar to that worn in a painting of *c*.1600,[15] of Elizabeth Vernon, Countess of Southampton, a Maid of Honour and indeed to the Rainbow Portrait of the Queen herself (painted by Isaac Oliver, and now in Hatfield House). The Bacton embroidery has tiny additional motifs of lesser quality: birds, butterflies, caterpillars, fish, dogs, stags, frogs, squirrels, dragonflies and tiny rowing boats with their minuscule occupants, the work of a gifted amateur and perhaps Blanche's own work.

Privy Chamber staff also made the Queen's underclothes, smaller day-clothes, night-clothes and edged sheets. The Queen's several thousand dresses and outer garments were the preserve of the Wardrobe of Robes. All clothes and jewellery were supposed to be recorded and signed for and many of these records have survived. In addition staff had to be able to make drinks and possets and cook small delicacies to tempt Elizabeth's appetite, especially as she ate sparingly though with a marked taste for sweetmeats. Blanche was recorded as having comfits delivered to her for the Queen in the New Year gifts.

Those ladies and gentlewomen who were paid received the same wages throughout the reign, although those who had served Elizabeth as Princess were given a pay rise on her accession. The highest annual payments were £33 6s 8d for most of the Ladies of the Bedchamber and several of the Gentlewomen of the Privy Chamber. However, it was evidently far more difficult for women to augment their wages, except by marriage, than it was for men and Blanche tacitly accepted this restriction when she noted that she had personally been 'uncareful of my wealth'. It helped that the household members also received livery for daily wear, the clothes being normally russet (that is undyed, natural colour) velvet or satin edged with black velvet, although Queen Elizabeth favoured black-and-white for her staff. In 1563 Kate Ashley took delivery of two dresses: a round black velvet kirtle (an under-dress) lined with taffeta and with a removable train and a French (that is with a square neckline, fitted bodice and full skirt) russet velvet kirtle lined with russet taffeta,[16] and similar dresses were issued to other ladies of the household. Black was also used for mourning, while white seems to have been used for attendance at Sunday Church Services, which were public occasions involving well ordered, stately processions. The beautifully decorated dresses were Court dresses for important events.

The Household also received accommodation and food, lights and fuel, known as bouge of court. Their food was allocated as a number of messes, each mess feeding four people, allocated according to rank. The Queen's women were fed by her messes or by the Privy Kitchen. Usually about 20 of the women ate from pewter dishes in the Great Chamber, which was probably either the waiting chamber or near to it, while the more important were served off plain silver dishes in the adjacent Presence Chamber. A 1576 record[17] has survived indicating that Elizabeth normally ate in the Privy Chamber with a chosen few (here four) of her ladies. Usually she ate dinner at about 11am and supper at 6pm. She ate fish (white meat) but avoided it on 'fish days' to indicate that she did not adhere to Catholic religious affiliations.

As advancement was contingent on the Queen's notice, important families strove to place a wife or daughter in proximity to her. The lack of this close contact was noticeable in the families involved in the Northern Rebellion and may have been a contributory cause. Even the Earl of Leicester ensured that his sister Mary (who became Lady Sidney) was an attendant. An official summons was required before arrival at Court and permission to attend from the male head of a woman's own family was also needed. None of the ladies in constant attendance on the Queen was a major landowner in her own right for, although Blanche did acquire small estates, aristocratic ladies such as Lady Warwick only attended the Queen intermittently. While status depended on that of a lady's husband or father, once appointed the Queen's women also had this acquired status. As a result, though most married, not all felt impelled to do so, becoming in effect career women, prominent examples being Blanche and also her successor Mary Radcliffe / Radclyffe. Mary, though, was the granddaughter and sister of successive Earls of Sussex and so had an inherited status of some note. She became a Maid of Honour in 1567, was noted as handling small jewels in 1577, succeeded Blanche as being in full charge of the Queen's sables, furs and jewels in July 1587, and finally took charge of her books, remaining in post until the Queen died.

Blanche's great-niece Frances Vaughan was one of the Queen's Maids of Honour from 1578/79, when her name first appeared in the New Year gifts, and it is extremely likely that Blanche was instrumental in her appointment. Through Blanche the Queen knew Frances' father, John Vaughan, whose career had culminated in his being appointed a member of the Council of the North, while her mother had been Lady Anne Knyvett / Knevet, a Lady of the Queen's Household. These Court connections meant that Frances was in a position to marry well and in about 1580 she married Thomas Burgh(e), who would become 5th Baron Borough/Burgh of Gainsborough in Lincolnshire, Knight of the Garter and the Lord Deputy of Ireland. Frances' half-brother, Thomas Knyvett, was a Groom of the Privy Chamber[18] and her half-sister, Katherine Knyvett, had been a Maid of Honour to the Queen. Blanche's cousin, John Parry of the Parrys of Poston, was one of the four Clerks of the Green Cloth, in charge of the Queen's Household finances, while his brother James was a Huntsman to the Queen. Other relatives were at Court because they served Blanche herself, the most notable of these being her niece Katherine Vaughan, who married Robert Knollys, fourth son of Sir Francis Knollys, Treasurer of the Queen's Chamber, and Catherine Carey, Lord Hunsdon's sister (Lady of the Bedchamber 1558 to 1569). Further relatives obtained posts through their connection with Blanche and it is likely that her influence continued after her death as one of the Queen's chaplains at the end of her life was Dr. Henry Parry. Descended from the Parrys of Wormbridge, he was Blanche's distant cousin.[19]

Glimpses of Blanche

On 8 September, 1560 Blanche was a guest at a dinner given by Sir Thomas Hoby at his house at Bisham Abbey. The guests, several of whom were related, were the Marquess of Northampton, the Earl of Arundel, Lord Cobham, Sir Roger North, the Earl of Hertford, his brother Lord Henry Seymour and sister Lady Jane, who was a Maid of Honour. Two other Maids present were Mary Mansfield and Lady Katherine Grey, the Queen's cousin, who would two months later, helped by Lady Jane, contract a secret marriage with Lord Hertford which incurred the Queen's extreme displeasure. The other guests were Lady Mildred Cecil, married to Sir William (a Lady of the Household and Sir Thomas Hoby's sister-in-law) and Blanche Parry. Blanche, the oldest lady present, did have a connection with Sir Thomas, who was born in Leominster, Herefordshire, through his mother who was a Vaughan. Nevertheless, the guest list clearly demonstrates the company in which Blanche moved.

Lady Katherine Grey's sister Lady Mary (both the younger sisters of the ill-fated Lady Jane) remembered Blanche in her 1578 Will: 'I give to my very friend Mrs Blanche a Parre a little gilt bowl with a cover to it.'[20] Blanche also received a bequest from Lucy (Lucie) Somerset Lady Latimer in her 1582 Will, proved 1583.[21] Lady Latimer was connected to the Herberts and her daughter had married Lord Burghley's son. She bequeathed 'Mrs. Blaunche Apparie a piece of gold called a portague', from Portugal, of the value of £3 10 shillings (about £550 today). Lady Latimer had three of these gold coins and they were used as token keepsakes.

In the Queen's accounts a payment of £20 was recorded to 'Mrs. Blaunche Apparie, 28th of January 1565 [1566] for the Funeral of Mr. Vaughan',[22] showing that the Queen actually paid these funeral expenses (of about £3,400 today). This was unusual and strongly implies a royal favour for Blanche. The deceased was Rowland Vaughan of Porthaml (Blanche's nephew-by-marriage), who died in 1566 and Blanche may have been required to make the arrangements as he died in London where he was serving as a Member of Parliament for Brecon. He was also one of the six Grooms of the Queen's Chamber but this appointment would not explain the Queen's generosity, whereas a personal favour to Blanche would. Married to a daughter of Milo ap Harry (Blanche's brother) Rowland Vaughan was buried at St. Margaret's, Westminster on 19 January 1566. Subsequently Blanche favoured his son, William, arranging for him to inherit under her First Will, though he sadly pre-deceased her in 1584.

It is possible that Blanche has been depicted in two pictures of the Court. The first is *An Elizabethan Maundy* c.1565 by Levina Teerlinc (Plate 6). Although crowded with people, this miniature shows the Queen clearly, with her train carried by an apparently older gentlewoman wearing the Queen's livery colours. It is this which makes it unlikely that she is an aristocratic lady. If the miniature was one of Levina Teerlinc's New Year gifts to the Queen and if the date is correct, then the gentlewoman could be Kate Ashley, who died some three months after the Maundy Thursday Service, on 18 July 1565. However, as the gentlewoman appears older than the other ladies, it is possible that Blanche is shown, perhaps because Kate was already ill. However, there can be no certainty about such a tiny picture.[23] Bradford suggests that Blanche is possibly also numbered among those shown in the illustrations for the *Noble Arte of Venerie* by George Turberville but this must remain conjectural.

In September 1575 the Queen stayed at the Palace of Woodstock, where the delightful entertainment included a banquet in an arbour, a 'woodland house', the masque being written by the poet George Gascoigne, at the time considered pre-eminent, and perhaps instigated by Robert Dudley, Earl of Leicester.[24] In it the Queen of the Fairies offered Queen Elizabeth an embroidered gown of 'great price' with accompanying poetry in Italian. She then offered nosegays, each with an English posy of a rhymed couplet, to every one of the Queen's 17 ladies. To Blanche Parry she said:

> For long and faithful service sake which hath abidden tuche,
> Good Parry is a paragon, show me another such.

The evening concluded with music. Gascoigne subsequently translated his work into Latin, French and Italian to present it to the Queen. The pun on Blanche's name obviously demonstrates the esteem in which Blanche was generally held and she presumably enjoyed such festive occasions.

New Year Gifts

It was traditional for gifts to be presented to the sovereign, as a statement of loyalty, on New Year's Day, 1 January (as Christmas Day, usually kept at Hampton Court, was considered a religious festival). There was a defined pattern to this giving as recorded by Henry 5th Earl of Huntingdon in 1605 for the Court of King James I:

> The manner of presenting a New-year's gift to his Majesty from the Earl of Huntingdon: You must buy a new purse of about v s [5 shillings] price and put therinto xx [20] pieces of new gold of xx s apiece and go to the Presence-Chamber, where the Court is, upon New-year's day, in the morning about 8 a clock and deliver the purse and the gold unto my Lord Chamberlain. Then you must go down to the Jewel House for a ticket to receive xviii s vi d [18s 6d] as a gift to your pains and give vi d (6 pence) there to the box for your ticket; then go to Sir William Veall's office and show your ticket and receive your xviii s vi d. Then go to the Jewel House again and make choice of a piece of plate of xxx [30] ounces weight and mark it and then in the afternoon you may go and

> fetch it away and then give the gentleman that delivers it you xl s [40 shillings] in gold and give to the box ii s and to the porter vi d.[25]

The procedure was not quite so stereotyped at the beginning of Queen Elizabeth's reign but a pattern did quickly form. Lists of New Year gifts were recorded for every year of Elizabeth's reign but have only survived in full for 1562, 1578, 1579 and 1589, in all of which Blanche is mentioned. These can be augmented by partial lists including gifts delivered to the Jewel House. All gifts were handed to the person who would be responsible for looking after them on behalf of the Queen. The format for recording them remained the same throughout the Queen's reign, noting what the gifts were, their whereabouts (which usually meant to whom the gifts had been delivered) and usually the names of the givers (men first) categorised according to social status. The Queen's reciprocal gifts were invariably an assortment of gilt plate, cups, bowls, stoups, tankards, sometimes with a cover and occasionally a salt,[26] weighted to reflect the value of the gift made to her.

Only occasionally does it seem that the Queen chose a specific gift for a particular person. She is recorded as giving Blanche sables (which Blanche bequeathed back to the Queen). Blanche also mentions two girdles in her Final Will. The first, left to 'my cousin Anne Vaughan, wife of Francis Vaughan, esquire', was 'a chain of gold and a girdle which the Queen's majesty gave me'. The other, left 'to my cousin, Katherine Knowles', was a 'girdle of friar's knots of gold with a jewel of masonry work set with stones'. This could be the same as the valuable girdle with friar's knots which Mary Southwell exchanged with the Queen for another girdle in February 1557.[27] If the Queen had passed this on to Blanche she had clearly had it a long time and it was evidently a favourite piece, especially as Blanche bequeathed it to Katherine, who had been Blanche's gentlewoman before her marriage.

The type of gift to the Queen was determined by rank, status and gender. Most noblemen usually gave her money, while their wives evidently had more imagination, often preferring to give commodities. Bishops invariably favoured a purse of money and a sliding scale operated from Archbishop of Canterbury's £40 to seven bishops including Hereford at £10.[28] In 1562 Elizabeth acquired the huge sum of £1,262 11s 8d (over £215,000 in today's values). It is clear, however, that members of the Queen's Household were also more likely to choose commodity gifts for her. The considerable thought given to these is evidenced by Sir William Cecil's choice of a beautiful writing set in 1562, although in subsequent years he often gave money while his wife chose a gift, perhaps reflecting how busy Cecil was administering the country.

In 1562 the Queen's incoming gifts were delivered to 14 different people according to the type of commodity. Many of the gifts were items of clothing or handkerchiefs, though there was also a crossbow and food, the Servant of the Pastry giving a delicious 'pie of quinces'. Most (20) were delivered to Lady Cobham. Blanche received the second largest group of six gifts, which included a purple velvet desk embroidered with gold, a painted and gilded wood coffer containing 'combs, glasses and balls', a piece of 'cambric in a box', an inkstand covered with crimson satin embroidered with Venice Gold and silk, an embroidered and jewelled bag of 'taffeta' and a second 'piece of fine cambric'. She also seems to have received the book (beautifully covered in tinsel, that is, silk woven with silver-gilt metal threads) showing the arms of the Knights of the Garter from Sir William Dethicke / Dethyk, Garter King of Arms. This was about the time she took delivery of a hasp for a newly mended coffer for the Queen's books.[29] In 1578 Blanche received Sir Gilbert Dethick's gift of a book of the states in William the Conqueror's time. A similar book, perhaps a third book in this series, was in her care in 1584[30] when it was noted as 'containing the arms of the noble men of England in the time of King Richard the second'. Further books handed to Blanche in 1584 were one entitled *Explicatio Orationis Domini*, bound in gold-embroidered white velvet, two books of Latin verse and a fourth book bound in vellum. Interestingly, Blanche, who was depicted with two books on her tomb in Saint Margaret's Church, Westminster, did not mention any books of her own in either of her Wills. Clearly she had the use of the Queen's library and it may be that she had already given away her own books when she went blind.

Queen Elizabeth was noted as thriftily recycling gifts and in 1562 John Ashley's gift of a gilt bowl with cover was speedily passed to the Earl of Pembroke. The consolation for the giver was that she usually did this only with gifts from those closest to her. In the list of jewels presented to the Queen in 1572 Blanche gave her 'one fair flower of gold, being a rose enamelled white and red in the top and other flowers also, all set with 3 diamonds, 3 rubies and one little pearl in the middle; half an ounce and a farthing gold weight'. This very pretty gift was promptly recycled and given 'by her Majesty to Mrs. Elizabeth Howard'. Lady Cheake's gift was also recycled and the following year, in 1573, this happened to gifts from the Countess of Derby, Lady Mary Sidney, Lady Woodhouse and Lord Howard. In the same year Blanche gave 'one jewel, being a scrippe [a small wallet] of mother-of-pearl, garnished with gold, hanging at three little chains of gold and a small agate pendant' and this Queen Elizabeth kept. Blanche could now clearly afford to buy jewellery, even if the jewels were small, for the Queen.

In 1574 Blanche gave 'a jewel, being a crystal garnished with gold; Adam and Eve enamelled white and a crystal pendant, garnished with gold and four small pearls pendant'. Often the key to successfully giving to Queen

Elizabeth was the size and/or number of pearls, as large or as many as one could afford and Blanche's gift of this jewel must have been frequently worn as it was later noted to be broken. Blanche's 1575 gift was also noted as having a broken gold chain, again suggesting heavy and immediate use, on which hung a green enamelled gold flower with three white roses 'in either of them a spark of rubies and the midst thereof a fly', a design clearly based on the Tudor rose. In heraldry white roses represented love, faith and purity, yellow showed achievement, while a fly was a symbol to ward off evil and pestilence. In 1576 Blanche returned to pearls with a gift of a crystal jewel set in gold 'with two storeys' appearing on both sides, with a small pearl pendant. In 1577 her gift was another jewel of gold set with a white agate and four small 'sparks' of rubies and a small pearl pendant. The following year, 1578, Blanche gave the Queen a charming 'little box of gold to put in comfits and a little spoon of gold, weighing all 3 oz. 1 qr.', receiving the usual gilt plate in return. Indeed, over the years Queen Elizabeth was given a number of comfit-boxes for sweetmeats as New Year gifts, which stayed in the Privy Chamber being classed as jewellery not plate.[31] Queen Elizabeth's fondness for sweets resulted in agonising toothache later in life.

In 1578 three boxes of ginger candy, green ginger and orange candy were given by Mr. Morgan, the apothecary who was the Queen's and Blanche's medical attendant (and remembered in Blanche's Final Will).[32] In all, some dozen people were involved in receiving this particular multitude of New Year gifts, Blanche only receiving four gifts including three pieces of lawn given by Mrs. Margaret Dane, a seamstress (Leicester's account books show that she was paid to hem napkins).[33] She probably served the Queen in the same capacity, being mentioned in several lists of New Year Gifts. The widow of William Dane (a liveryman of the Company of Ironmongers, master of the company, Sheriff 1569-1570 and Alderman in the City of London), her portrait hangs in the banqueting hall of the Ironmongers' Company in London. Blanche kept her money and chests of plate at Margaret Dane's house, using her secure premises as one would a safety deposit box in a bank vault today. Margaret bequeathed Blanche, 'my friend', a black gown in her Will dated 16 May 1579,[34] Blanche heading a lengthy list of recipients which included the Queen, Leicester, John Dudley and his brother. Katherine Vaughan, then Blanche's waiting woman, was to have a cup worth £20 on the day of her marriage to Robert Knollys. Margaret made numerous bequests to help the sick, the poor and the imprisoned. Her bequests to help scholars included loans to 20 young men of the Company, those retailing linen cloth to be preferred. Although an ironmonger, William Dane was also a merchant who dealt in cloth, for he is recorded as supplying canvas and holland to the Great

Wardrobe in the 1560s.[35] After his death in 1573, Margaret ran his business[36] and it is probably from her that Blanche obtained the 'two pairs of Holland sheets' mentioned in her own Final Will.

These New Year gift lists show that Blanche usually took charge of any material, rather than finished parts of garments, which could be used to make the Queen's underclothes or could be made up into additional parts of outer dresses. Cambric was a plain woven fine white linen, while lawn was an even finer linen, both eminently suitable for these purposes. The decorated linen creppins or coifs were worn under headdresses to keep the hair clean. It is clear, therefore, that Blanche had charge of the Queen's very personal linen. In 1579, only weeks after her serious illness, Blanche only received three gifts, the two mentioned and 18 larks in a cage given by Morrys Watkins. Her gift to the Queen that year was 'a pair of bracelets of carnelian heads, two small pearls between every head, garnished with gold'. It must have been a success as she repeated this twice.

Blanche's other gifts to the Queen were nearly all jewels. The following year, 1580, she gave 'a pair of bracelets of gold, 12 pieces of goldsmith's work and the rest agate'. In 1581 she gave 'a jewel of gold, being a crane, with mean [meaning good quality] pearl pendant'. A crane was a symbol of vigilance, justice, longevity, duty and gratitude, all very suitable as a gift from the 73-year-old lady who adored the Queen. Her 1583 gifts of 'a double porringer and four boxes, with covers of silver and gilt' were still in the Jewel House collection in 1597 when the Inventory recorded that one cover, weighing 1oz, was missing. A porringer was basin-shaped and was used for pottage, soup or perhaps broth. Blanche reverted to 'a pair of bracelets of gold', 1oz qa in 1584, though she seems to have made a special effort in 1587 when she gave 'a jewel, being a serpent's tongue set in gold, enamelled, garnished with three sparks of rubies, two sparks of emeralds and three very little pearls pendant'. A serpent's tongue represented wisdom and knowledge, again most suitable from such an elderly lady. It is evident that Blanche continued to give thought to the presents she chose for the Queen and that they were very personal and well-chosen. After she had resigned her responsibilities for the Queen's jewels, her 1589 New Year gift for the Queen was 'one long cushion of tawny cloth of gold, backed with taffeta'. It must have been beautiful, made by using a warp of tan coloured silk thread and a weft of fine gold wire with a taffeta backing. Blanche had good taste right to the end of her life.

'Keeper of all jewels and other things belonging to her majesty'

Blanche's pre-eminent position in the Queen's Household meant that she was in charge of items personal to the Queen, some of which were intimate and many of which had high intrinsic value. Blanche is probably one of the first women known to hold such a position of trust.

Blanche had charge of the Queen's jewels. This was a considerable responsibility, as the person designated to be in charge of any item had to account for it and remedy its loss if it proved untraceable. If the explanation for loss was accepted a letter of discharge resulted. Jane Dormer had had to account for the deficiencies in Queen Mary's jewels, which, to her great relief, she was eventually able to do in 1559. The enquiry was conducted by Catherine Lady Knollys (née Carey), Margery Lady Norris and Blanche Parry. One interesting item was a little ring set with a small ruby which 'Mrs. Pary confesses the Queen's Majesty to have this jewel sent from the late Queen [Mary I] for a token'.[37] The fact that Blanche knew this clearly shows that she was in charge of Elizabeth's jewellery, even of such a politically significant ring, before Queen Elizabeth's accession.

Blanche remained in charge of all moveable jewels for most of the reign (though Lady Howard first received some New Year gifts). These were kept, locked, in the Bedchamber or Privy Chamber or were placed in the Jewel House in the Tower of London for maintenance, repair or re-fashioning. The foot-long jewel boxes (or coffers) were segmented and lined with protective cotton, with rings on special sticks and loose buttons and beads on laces. Particular items had individual boxes some of which were of gold. The Queen's personal jewellery was kept in the Bedchamber, in coffers such as the 'little jewel coffer covered with purple velvet embroidered with gold' that was delivered to Blanche by warrant in 1562.[38] This was well-used as only a few months later its lock required a new hasp. Blanche was also issued with a new key for another small jewel coffer lined with crimson velvet and later with another key for an ebony jewel coffer whose lock had been mended.

From about 1579, when she was over 70 years old, Blanche's responsibility for the Queen's linen was increasingly taken over by Mary Scudamore, who was known for her beautiful sewing. Mary (née Shelton) was the Queen's second cousin who, in January 1574, married without permission John Scudamore of Holme Lacy in Herefordshire, a cousin of the senior branch of the Scudamores of Kentchurch Court. Mary, initially a Chamberer, was promoted to become a Gentlewoman only after the Queen's reconciliation to her marriage. The Queen's embroidered and bejewelled dresses, often with detachable sleeves, were issued by the Wardrobe of Robes (part of the Great Wardrobe in the Palace of Westminster), while each palace had a wardrobe chamber for the current clothes and accessories. Such a system required organisation and forethought so that the designated outfit would be ready for a particular occasion. The Keeper was in charge of maintenance, repair and renewal and a required item had to be signed for, the person concerned undertaking to be responsible for its safe return. The documentation accumulated over a long reign, especially as duplicate books were required for the main office and for the Privy Chamber. Such a daybook arrived at Holme Lacy House through Mary Scudamore for she frequently signed the entries. It concerns over 381 items dating from 1561 to 1585 and as a redundant daybook was evidently returned to the Gentlewomen of the Privy Chamber; Mary took it home, perhaps to use the spare leaves or perhaps simply as a souvenir of her time at Court.

Two entries record gifts to Blanche Parry, 12 entries record Blanche taking delivery of items and one entry shows her authorising delivery of an item. The first item, dated 29 December 1569, records the Queen's gift of two valuable sable skins each to Lord Hunsdon, his wife Anne, Lady Elizabeth Clinton, Lady Margaret Howard, Lady Frances Cobham and Mrs. Blanche Parry, and was signed by all the ladies concerned. The significance of this is considerable, as the sumptuary laws specifically reserved sables for the nobility, placing them in the same categories as cloth-of-gold, cloth-of-silver, tinselled satin and silk. (Although the Queen could be flexible on the application of these laws to her favourites, Blanche would, nevertheless, bequeath her sables back to the Queen.) All the ladies mentioned were at this time baronesses and Lord Hunsdon was a baron. Queen Elizabeth never granted any woman a title in her own right and certainly did not create any titles but it is abundantly clear that Blanche was treated by the Queen as a baroness. Blanche knew this and everyone evidently accepted this as her status.

These were the sables that Blanche mentioned in her First Will of 1578 when she bequeathed them to the Queen: 'I will that there be delivered to her Majesty a pair of sables garnished with 8 claws of gold.' She had evidently added the gold claws herself. The Queen's own sables also had gold heads and were garnished with jewels. It seems probable that it was Blanche's recovery from serious illness that led the Queen to make her a further, very personal, gift for on 9 April 1579, 'two pieces of old sables taken out of a cloak and two pieces of like sables being taken out of a night gown of chequered velvet were given to Blanche by her Majesty's commandment'. So Blanche now had three pairs of sables. The fine soft fur was likely to have been a beautiful very dark brown or black and to have come from the *mustela zibellina*, an animal related to the weasel family that looks a little like a marten. The skins were at that time brought into England from Russia by the Muscovy Company whose ships sailed from Deptford (where Blanche's great-niece, Elinor Bull, was now living after her marriage in 1571).

The 12 items delivered to Blanche and which became her responsibility included (on 30 July 1565) two yards of yellow sarsenet, a light-weight silk used for linings. She also took charge of the Queen's tippets (a narrow stole worn above the elbows), signing for one around New Year 1578 made of three sable skins lined with black wrought, or embroidered, velvet. The same, or a similar, tippet of three sable skins was delivered to Blanche on 26 January 1580 'by her to be kept to the Queen's Majesty's use'. Evidently the Queen found these comfortable wear for winter.

In this age of recycling, small, special and valuable items were personal and could be of particular importance to the user. It is in this context that Blanche's charge of the jewelled ornamentations mostly for French hoods needs to be viewed. These were known as *habilliaments* or bilaments, often now termed buttons (or studs). One delivery, on 23 November, makes it clear that these gold and bejewelled buttons were sent to her by Mrs. Twist (Anne Twist, the Queen's laundress, a position of trust) after she had removed the ornamentation prior to cleaning the garments. That this happened regularly is shown by a note dated 17 April 1581 attached to a group of 14 pieces comprising roses of diamonds, 23 pieces of another sort of diamonds and 13 spinel rubies in a delicate rose red variety, 'being all of her [i.e. Blanche's] own charge before'. Two deliveries in 1581 place Blanche at Whitehall Palace.[39] The wealth involved was so considerable, and the items were so easily lost, that only someone close to the Queen could be entrusted with such a meticulous responsibility.

As Blanche was in charge of the Privy Chamber, she was involved in giving clothes away. In 1583, Mary Scudamore, Bridget Chaworth and Jane Brussels signed for discarded garments to be given to an Irish gentlewoman, noting that this was done 'by all the gentlewomen's consent of the Privy Chamber'; 'Mrs. Blanche' is expressly named as giving the required consent. Blanche's position and influence in the Household are further exemplified by the phrasing of an authorisation: 'Item delivered by the commandment of Mrs. Blanche and Mrs. Skidmore to Mr. Jones' (William Jones, the Queen's tailor) on 1 May 1585 one round kirtle of white tuft taffeta (taffeta woven with tufts of silk) with two pair of bodices decorated with a narrow lace (strings as fasteners) of gold and silver to make a gown for Mr. Harvey's (possibly Leicester's steward) daughter. Mary Scudamore was involved because she signed for the dress. This authorisation is quite extraordinary as normally only the Queen is noted as 'commanding' but here the term is specifically used of Blanche.

The system of signing for items and then being responsible for them meant that letters of discharge were essential so that the heirs of those involved were not encumbered with demands for the return of untraceable items. When Blanche was seriously ill in November 1578 she was concerned to ensure her heirs were protected, especially as the value of the commodities she had cared for was enormous. She requested her cousin, Sir William Cecil Lord

Burghley to intercede with 'the Queen's Majesty, my dear sovereign lady and mistress, that a favourable account may be made of all jewels and other things belonging to her majesty within my charge that my heirs may thereof have a discharge'. This covered the jewels, furs and books that had been her especial charge. It was particularly important when it is realised that of 111 jewels and precious trimmings lost between the 1560s and the 1580s only one was traced. The statistics may be deceptive, however, as such items were re-used, records have not always survived and some items were given away. However, Blanche recovered her health and she continued in her duties for several more years, until 1587, the same year as this entry in an Inventory of the Jewel House in the Tower of London:[40] 'Received of Mrs. Blanch Apparry. One Great Seal of silver, 108 ounces.'

According to the Close Rolls, this Great Seal was brought into use on 26 January 1559 and was wearing out as it 'by much use, waxes unserviceable'. It had been used by the Queen's first two Lord Chancellors and Keepers of the Great Seal, namely Sir Nicholas Bacon and then, in 1579, Sir Thomas Bromley. (In 1587 Sir Christopher Hatton succeeded to the position.) A second, more artistic Great Seal, designed by Nicholas Hilliard, was ordered to be engraved in silver on 8 July 1584, coming into use before 20 November 1585. However, the Queen kept her first Great Seal in her Privy Chamber before sending it to the Jewel House and so for at least two years Blanche had had charge of the first Great Seal of England of Elizabeth I. It contained enough silver for it to be re-fashioned into two silver jugs, for jewels, gold and silver were regularly dismantled, a practice even extended to the Imperial Crown of England in Henry VIII's reign. At the same time as Blanche delivered the first Great Seal to the Jewel House she also handed in 'two collars of gold, 66 ounces 3 quarters', which were official chains of authority used by the judiciary and therefore by the Lord Chancellor, the principal legal officer of the realm.[41]

It was also in July 1587 that Blanche handed over responsibility for the Queen's jewels to Mary Radcliffe. An inventory[42] of more than 628 listed jewels was compiled to provide Blanche with a letter of discharge. When Mary Radcliffe in her turn needed her discharge letter a note was appended recording that her list was a 'part of such jewels as were in charge of Mrs. Blanche Parrye', clearly indicating that Blanche had had charge of even more jewellery,[43] additional pieces including the Great Seal, the collars and other jewels depicted in Queen Elizabeth's portraits. Of the 68 gold chains, one was 'enamelled black with pearls in gold links' measuring 6¾ yards.[44] Books were only counted if their covers were of gold, silver or gilt and there were nine of these. Among the 104 rings was a seal ring with the arms of England engraved on it and there was a 'standishe of silver gilt with an ink pot and a sand box with a ring of gold having a black engraved stone in it', presumably another seal ring.

While there was an abundance of the pearls of which Queen Elizabeth was especially fond, the collection shows she also loved diamonds, often enhanced by rubies, emeralds and other jewels, one gold tablet, or pendant, having 'an agate engraved with the Queen's picture'. The listed collection charts the history of the Queen's suitors for the four little frogs, three of enamelled gold and one of mother-of-pearl, were probably gifts from the Duke of Anjou, who she nicknamed her 'frog'; one is 'a little flower of gold with a frog thereon and therein Monsieur his picture'. One pendant may originally have belonged to Queen Mary as it contained a picture of King Philip. Such were the items Blanche had cared for and they were meticulously counted. For instance, a tablet of gold 'being a whistle' depicting Cleopatra was noted as having one diamond missing. Mary Radcliffe's list has an appended Latin note was that 'it agrees with the original', showing that a master list was employed against which individual jewels were minutely compared.

This summary demonstrates the enormous value of the items that were Blanche's responsibility and the trust placed in her integrity by the Queen. This aspect of her responsibilities was so important that it was recorded by Blanche's executors on her Saint Margaret's, Westminster Epitaph, which described her as 'Keeper of Her Majesties Jewels'. Blanche relinquished her charge of the jewels when she was 80 years old, an incredible age for the time. The evidence suggests that she had been coping efficiently with the responsibility and it is likely that she only resigned this function due to her failing eyesight. As she became blind she would not have known when jewels fell from their settings and such a failure of diligence would have been upsetting for the careful old lady. Perhaps with help, she remained in charge of the Queen's books, which could account for the two books shown on her tomb. However, even when she had handed on her responsibilities, Blanche's status did not diminish as she remained the most important Gentlewoman at Court, with Mary Radcliffe in second place.

Blanche's Further Responsibilities

As Blanche was the Chief Gentlewoman of the Privy Chamber she was in charge of the Queen's personal papers, while the Officers of State and secretaries kept the state documents. She was also in charge of considerable sums of money. Gifts were given and received throughout the year, notably by ambassadors and at christenings. On 2 January 1569 Blanche took receipt of £500 (nearly £87,000 at today's values) 'as given to the Queen's Majesty at the late Lord North's house at the Charterhouse, by the Merchant Adventurers'.[45]

Blanche served the Queen in an administrative capacity, as what today would be termed a personal assistant. Blanche used secretaries but enough of her letters survive to suggest that she would dictate, or at least indicate and subsequently check, the contents.

Mr. Pendred / Pendryth was the husband of Queen Elizabeth's wet-nurse and in 1582 he approached the Queen for help. A close reading of the subsequent letter[46] signed by Blanche confirms her true position at Court:

> Right honourable and my very good Lord, these are to desire your Lordship's lawful favour on the behalf of Mr Pendryth whose wife nursed the Queen's Majesty and also is one of her Majesty's tenants of the manor of Norbourne [Northbourne] in the county of Kent.
>
> The cause, as I am informed, is that the Bishop of Canterbury hath ~~appoyy~~ appointed certain persons, viz Mr Bostock, Conyers and others, to carry away the said Mr Pendryth's tithe corn which he ever quietly enjoyed till now and further they seek to pluck from the Q[ueen] tenements within the manor which they withhold from her Majesty without suit commenced in law for the same. Wherefore seeing there as a Commission of Survey sued forth by Mr Pendreth directed to the Surveyor and others for severing [surveying] and better knowledge of her Majesty's lands, therefore I beseech your Lordship to consider of the old man and of his quietness, for so at as her Majesty's pleasure the which I am bold so to signify unto your honour.
>
> Thus with my most humble duty and prayer I commit and commend myself unto your good Lordship from the court at Nonsuch this xvith of August 1582.
>
> Your Good Lord to Command
>
> Blaunshe Pary

Blanche Parry's signature on the above letter (Cecil Papers 12/59 Hatfield House)

Although written in compassionate terms, emphasising Mr. Pendred's 'quietness', or inoffensiveness, it is clear that this is a business letter written at the command of the Queen: 'for so at as her Majesty's pleasure the which I am bold so to signify unto your honour'. Mr. Pendred had contacted the Queen about his dispute with the agents of Archbishop Edmund Grindal of Canterbury (1576-1583). Elizabeth wished the matter to be examined but instructed that the resolution must be within the law, and Blanche wrote this letter on her behalf.

Once this aspect of Blanche's real position has been recognised it can be further confirmed by other references and shows her being aware of even difficult politics. Ireland was always a fraught situation and at the time was administered by appointees from London with the help of local gentry who often came from families in the English Pale around Dublin. One such administrator was Sir Nicholas White, Master of the Rolls in Ireland, who would be knighted by Blanche's friend Sir John Perrot (remembered in her Final Will) when he was Lord Deputy of Ireland. In 1579 the Earl of Desmond (the same as mentioned in the Preface) rebelled against the Crown, Desmond being much influenced by Nicholas Sander, the papal envoy who seems to have been trying to incite a Catholic rising.

On 22 July 1580 Nicholas White wrote to Lord Burghley mentioning that among the various items he had appropriated from Desmond and Sander, was a 'toy after the manner of a cross supporting a book which I have sent to your lordship with the remainder of them, when you have done, to Mistress Blanche'.[47] There is no point to this unless the implication was that Blanche would show the items to the Queen. In another letter to Lord Burghley, dated 31 May 1586, Sir Nicholas White wrote: 'My singular good lord. Having so late written by Sir George Carew and writing now to the earl of Ormond and my good friend, Mistress Blanche, I mean not to trouble your honour with any more than the remembrance of my humble duty …'. Blanche is here coupled with affairs of state and it is clear that she was an avenue by which political information was reaching the Queen. Sir Nicholas made this even clearer in a letter to Burghley dated 10 July 1586:

> My singular good lord. I have adventured to send to her Majesty the original whereof this enclosed is a copy … And I thought good first to acquaint your Honour therewith to the end the same may be stayed or delivered as to your wisdom shall seem best and so have I written to Mistress Blanche unto whom I committed the presenting of my letter to Her Majesty …

The following December Sir Richard Bingham, in front of the Lord Deputy and Council for Ireland, accused Sir Nicholas White of writing 'a letter to Her Majesty', claiming that he had a copy of it obtained 'out of Blanche Apparey's chamber ...' which proves that Blanche's position was known and accepted at the highest level of government. This account was signed by the Archbishop of Armagh, the Bishop of Kilmore, the Chief Baron of the Exchequer and the Chief Justice of the Common Pleas. The copy referred to was from Sir Nicholas White to Lord Burghley and included: '... I confess this to be a true copy of my last letter to Her Majesty ... This honest gentleman, Mr. Thomas Williams (whom I favour for Mistress Blanche's sake) hath assured me of the safe carriage of my letter to your Honour ...'.

A further confirmation of her position is found in a letter from Watkyn Vaughan of Bredwardine, a Justice of the Peace in Herefordshire (married to one of the daughters of Blanche's elder brother, Milo ap Harry). In a long letter sent by him to Lord Burghley on 17 December 1584 he includes: '... I have sent instructions for two bills to Mrs. Blanche, good my Lord, the one is profitable to bridle papists. The other touching base captains, who make market of the soldiers ...'.[48] The very commonplace tone of this interpolated note shows that sending material through Blanche Parry was a normal channel of communication and one that Lord Burghley would find quite usual. The outcome can be traced especially for the first Parliamentary bill 'to bridle papists' which was quickly passed. Dated 27 Elizabeth, which is between November 1584 and November 1585, it was entitled An Act against Jesuits, Seminary Priests and such other like disobedient Persons. The second bill, to punish captains who exploited their soldiers, was perhaps designed to strengthen an Act of 1557-1558 (Philip and Mary) entitled An Act for the Taking of Musters, which set penalties for captains corruptly discharging soldiers, withholding their pay or taking bribes. Alternatively, it was the Bill of 31 Elizabeth (November 1589) entitled An Act against embezzling of Armour, habiliments of War and Victuals.[49] It is evident from Watkyn Vaughan's letter that channelling such parliamentary business through Blanche was normal practice and that she had acted in this way before.

The Painting of the Presence Chamber (Plate 5)

This small painting, usually entitled *Elizabeth I Receiving Dutch Emissaries*, is in Kassel, Germany and it is thought the artist was German. It is often used to illustrate Elizabethan interiors as it shows wall decoration, often said to be tapestry but perhaps more likely to be richly painted, with flowers and foliage designs. The floor has matting, with carpet under the red-damask covered chair, the only furniture, beneath a canopy fixed to the ceiling. This is exactly as recorded in the description by Thomas Platter of the Presence Chamber, though the French Ambassador in 1597 pointed out that the Queen would at times receive ambassadors in the Privy Chamber and that she would stand, as she is depicted here, to do so. The two windows each have a hanging bird-cage. The painting depicts the Queen receiving two kneeling emissaries. Five men and one woman stand against the far wall and three girls sit on the floor in the left foreground. Seven of the nine main figures have names written under them: 'Lister, Admiral, Konigin von Schotland, Vestlan, Walsbrun, Konigin, Ambassador'. It has been thought that the painting depicts Queen ('Konigin') Elizabeth's reception of the Dutch emissaries, Vestlan and Walsbrun, on the occasion of the negotiations to support the Dutch against the Spanish. The peculiar presence of Mary Queen of Scots ('Konigin von Scotland') has always been awkwardly explained as being due to her significance in English foreign policy.[50]

An investigation of the dating of this picture presents some problems. The clothes and the appearance of Elizabeth suggest a date in the 1560s, not the 1580s. It seemed possible that tracing the emissaries Vestlan and Walsbrun and their visit to London would help. An approach to the Dutch National Archives resulted in the surprising information that the names were not Dutch and that anyway they were not listed as Dutch representatives to foreign courts. Following a suggestion, a similar approach was made to the Senior Archivist in Stockholm; again the names were unknown, were definitely not Swedish but were possibly German. An enquiry of Staatliche Museen Kassel, where the painting is housed, revealed that it had always been in the collection. Indeed their inventory describes it as an 'old possession' and a note was added that it seems reasonable to suppose that it once belonged to the Electors of Hesse-Kassel.[51] A check on German names from the period showed that the name Walsbrun could certainly have been a German name, though no trace of the individual has as yet been found. Vestlan remains a problem. It is likely that these two were the only persons depicted actually known to the writer of the names.

That diplomatic relations between Hesse and England had existed for many years is shown by the occasional mention of ambassadors. One such contact recorded that the Ambassadors of Saxony and Hesse courteously visited the baby Prince Edward (the future Edward VI), who cried throughout, to the delight of the Bishop of Winchester, Stephen Gardiner. They were checking on the Prince's progress and the Catholic Bishop Gardiner thought the baby showed the correct spirit as the ambassadors were Protestant.[52] As there is no reason to believe that the painting is foreign to its present location, it can be inferred that it depicts the reception by Queen Elizabeth of envoys from the Landgrave of Hesse-Kassel. That this could have occurred is supported by some documentary evidence. On 6 April 1569 Henry Killegrew wrote to Sir William Cecil giving an account of his journey from Hamburg. After Luxemburg and Brunswick he wrote that 'from thence they passed to Cassel … at Cassel, William, the Landegrave of Hesse, entreated him to remain but Killegrew excused himself, on the plea that he had been already over long on his journey but promised to make report to Her Majesty of his good will. The Landegrave sent his dinner to him by his Chancellor and during dinner time Killegrew perceived that they saw the intents of the Catholics and that it was time to prepare for their defence …'. On 12 August 1569 William the Landegrave of Hesse, wrote directly to the Queen that he 'congratulates her on the firm establishment of the true religion in her Kingdom and trusts that she will entertain the same good will towards him as subsisted between their predecessors …'.[53] This correspondence shows that contact with Queen Elizabeth's Court had already been made in the 1560s. Hesse-Kassel was one of the German states most opposed to the rule of the Hapsburgs and Catholic Spain and diplomatic exchanges with England were seen as allying with another Protestant state. Emissaries would have been sent to the English Court and the recording of the visit in a painting was the 16th-century equivalent of filing an official photograph to prove that contact had been made. It is possible that the reception marks the occasion when the letter of 12 August 1569 was delivered.

Francis Walsingham was the Ambassador to France between 1570 and 1573, a period recorded in the surviving pages of his Journal. In 1571 he recorded that the Archbishop of Cassels 'came to speak with me' on four occasions, namely Sunday 25 March, Sunday 15 April, Tuesday 19 April and on Friday 20 April. On 13 May he sent letters to the Archbishop. While in Paris, Walsingham had discussions with the French and ambassadors from Florence and Scotland but these Cassel/Kassel entries are the most numerous for one person and suggest that the Archbishop was taking the opportunity of negotiating. Indeed, further contacts with the Landegrave of Hesse were recorded in 1577.

It is curious that the names on the painting are written, in red, on the matting. As no space was left for the writing they must have been written after the painting was completed. In addition, it seems likely that the names were written by someone who did not know all the individuals or even the scene depicted. The standing figures are drawn so clearly that they can be identified. By the doorway, on the left, is the unmistakable figure of Sir William Cecil, Lord Burghley in 1571, Secretary of State 1558-1572 and then Lord Treasurer, and he is not named. Next to him is Robert Dudley, Earl of Leicester, Master of the Horse, named as 'Lister', who is talking to Edward Fiennes de Clinton, Lord Admiral, named only as 'Admiral'. Next to him is the supposed figure of

Mary, Queen of Scots with just behind her an unnamed figure who is probably Christopher Hatton, Gentleman of the Privy Chamber from the mid-1560s, knighted 1577, Captain of the Guard 1572-1587, Vice-Chamberlain and Lord Chancellor in 1587. On the right is Francis Walsingham, Ambassador to France 1570-1573 when he became a Privy Councillor and Principal Secretary and knighted in 1577; he is named only as 'Ambassador'.

The painter has very deliberately included the men who held power under the Queen, and the earliest that this could have true of the entire group is 1572. At that date Cecil, Leicester, Clinton and Walsingham were all Privy Councillors, while Hatton was the Captain of the Guard and so had a security role. Walsingham had just completed his tour as an ambassador, which would help to date the writing of the names. However, all were at Court in 1569 so that date is just possible. The fact that these men were clearly painted from life means that the depiction of Queen Elizabeth must be contemporary with them. She is dressed very simply, without the huge Spanish farthingale that started to become fashionable in about 1575, with small neck and wrist ruffs. Detailed examination shows that Elizabeth's costume belonged to the 1560s, or possibly the early 1570s. This dating is reinforced by the styles worn by the Maids of Honour sitting on the floor, who are also individually painted.

I am therefore postulating that the writing post-dated the painting, which was a depiction of an actual incident in the Privy Chamber. If so it is impossible for Mary, Queen of Scots to have been included. Queen Mary did arrive in England in 1568 but she never met Queen Elizabeth and certainly never entered her Presence or Privy Chambers. The lady in the painting is shown dressed very simply, indeed far more simply than would be the case for any member of the nobility when sumptuary laws were quite specific about correct apparel. Even in paintings of Queen Mary in which she wished to be relatively plainly dressed, her clothes have a richer appearance than this. It is true that she often dressed in black and white mourning clothes especially between the death of her first husband, Francis II of France, in 1560 and her second marriage to Lord Darnley in 1564 and then again after the death of her third husband, the Earl of Bothwell in 1575 but her style of dress was very different to that in the picture. There was no particular reason to depict her in black and white between 1564 and 1575, the postulated date range for the painting, and as this was Queen Elizabeth's livery for her servants it would not have been politic. (Also Queen Mary's dress would not have reached the neck as her shoulders would have been covered by a lighter material.) The dress and headdress of the lady in the picture is altogether too plain for the Queen. This lady wears no jewellery, not even the crucifix which Queen Mary often wore. The stance of the lady in the painting is also completely different from that of Mary in any other picture. This lady's hands are folded submissively over each other as she watches Queen Elizabeth. Mary, Queen of Scots was born in 1542, Elizabeth in 1533, so Mary was nine years the younger and, according to Sir James Melville in 1564, she was taller than Elizabeth. Here the lady depicted is clearly older than Elizabeth, of a similar height, plainly dressed in the Queen's livery of black velvet or black satin and, moreover, acting as the Queen's chaperone. Thomas Platter would describe (in 1599) how 'as soon as the Queen had seated herself, her lady-in-waiting, very splendidly arrayed also entered the room, while her secretary stood on her right ...'.[54] Here the chaperone is not splendidly arrayed, which suggests that she was not a lady-in-waiting but a Gentlewoman in the Queen's livery. One of the Queen's women was always in attendance, private interviews being conducted out of the chaperone's hearing or even in a language she did not understand.[55] The Maids of Honour as shown in the picture, being only girls, were not considered suitable chaperones, and an older Lady or Gentlewoman would have been required for this duty. Blanche was then the Chief Gentlewoman of Queen Elizabeth's 'Head Chamber', that is her Privy Chamber. She was also the oldest and most trusted of the Queen's women, and she dressed in her livery.

The implication is that this is a portrait of Blanche Parry, who was present at the time the initial drawing was made and that, as the later writer of the names had no idea who she was, he wrote in the wrong name. A comparison with Blanche's Saint Margaret's, Westminster tomb effigy shows a face with similar features. If this is Blanche, and the evidence is compelling, she is painted standing with her friend, the younger Christopher Hatton, in a picture that shows her position in the Queen's life. In her Final Will, Blanche remembered both Burghley, who was her cousin, and Hatton, neither of whom were named in the painting. She included neither Leicester nor Clinton (who had known John Vaughan through his wife, the former Lady Browne), as both had died before her. Neither did she include Walsingham in her Final Will but then he was already ill when she finalised it and he would die in 1590. Presumably the solitary position of Walsingham in the painting may suggest that he had few close associates at Court.

If the painted names are discounted as inaccurate, I am suggesting that this important painting records the power structure at Queen Elizabeth's Court *c*.1569-1573 and that this included Blanche Parry as well as the important and already acknowledged men. She stands, as the Queen's chaperone, confidante and, in modern terms, personal assistant, witnessing the emissaries' presentation of their credentials to the Queen. Blanche held a known, recognised and accepted position at the very centre of the Royal Court.

5 *Preferring Still the Causes of Each Wight* Blanche's Influence

This chapter heading is line 21 in Blanche's Bacton epitaph, which with the succeeding three lines provides in her own words Blanche's summation of how she used her influence. Paraphrased, she is saying that she advanced the causes of many courtiers as well as she could with the Queen, telling Elizabeth what each person had done for her to ensure that they received their just rewards according to the justice of their cause and the service they had given. These four lines suggest that Blanche carefully examined each person's case and their credentials, discussing them with the Queen so that she could arrive at a decision. Blanche's Saint Margaret's epitaph also records that she was 'beneficial to her kinsfolk and countrymen …'.

Although much has been written about the influence wielded by the men at Court there has been little said about the influence of the women. All of the senior Privy Chamber women aided supplicants and such requests were often accompanied by appropriate gifts. King Philip had recognised the ladies' influence for he had given them jewels in his wife's reign. Even the redoubtable 'Bess of Hardwick' (Dowager Countess of Shrewsbury) approached Lady Stafford (in 1600/1601 after Blanche's death) to try to elucidate the Queen's opinion of Lady Arbella Stuart, her granddaughter and a possible claimant to the throne.[1] However, Blanche's position was unique due to her long and constant contact with Elizabeth, her close relationship with Sir William Cecil Lord Burghley and her friendship with other key Court personnel such as Sir Christopher Hatton. Blanche was the Queen's confidante and her influence can be considered in the areas of religion and patronage.

Religious Influence

Henry VIII had placed religion at the centre of politics. A depleted treasury and lack of a male heir had neatly colluded with an attack of conscience over the validity of his first marriage to Catherine of Aragon. His passion for Anne

Boleyn had provided the catalyst for change that resulted in the break with Rome and the Dissolution of the Monasteries in the 1530s. However, Henry VIII's church remained essentially Catholic but without the Pope, for more than ten years. It was in the six-year reign of his son Edward VI that Protestant doctrine took an official hold, principally due to the Regent, the King's maternal uncle. The brief, abortive attempt to continue this through placing Lady Jane Grey on the throne only resulted in Edward's sister being proclaimed Queen to general acclamation, but Queen Mary misinterpreted this as enthusiasm for a return to pre-Henrician Roman Catholicism. This was undermined by Mary's insistence on a foreign marriage to Philip of Spain, home of the feared Inquisition, and the shortness of her five-year reign. She also had little support in reinstating the monasteries from those gentry who had benefited from the lands available. Elizabeth came to the throne as a Protestant Queen but with an attempt to steer a middle way that made extreme Protestants and Roman Catholics political enemies of the State. She was largely successful in that her Court included moderate members from both religious affiliations (and this can be seen in the personnel mentioned in Blanche's Final Will). Elizabeth, growing up through extreme religious changes, was exposed and vulnerable at the heart of politics. She had had to learn caution and her personal views had been influenced by the changing religious precepts. In safely navigating her way through this potentially treacherous quagmire, she must have been helped by her close attendants, who were principally Lady Troy and Blanche Parry. The indications of their religious views are therefore important.

Catholic

Blanche grew up in a Catholic environment where Bacton Church was the focus for parochial activities and she was used to colourful ceremonial. Hereford had its own cycle of the Mystery Plays, a major civic event in the 14th and 15th centuries, performed usually for the Feast of Corpus Christi, in June on the Thursday following Trinity Sunday. Traditionally, each guild performed a play from the religious cycle which had a connection, however vague, to their trade. Guilds vied for the best production and the sets, the best kept from year to year, could be magnificent, some even being embellished with gold-leaf. Most performances took place on elaborately decorated carts or pageant wagons, stopping at designated places and processing to the next venue; sound effects enhanced the performance. Everyone was involved; one estimate suggests that a quarter of York's 8,000 population actually took part, the rest forming the audience. The best surviving evidence for Hereford's cycle of 27 plays comes from the Mayor's Book, where a single, 1503, sheet gives a list of the Corpus Christi pageants for the city[2] and 26 can be matched to plays known from the other, longer Chester, Towneley / Wakefield and York cycles. Hereford's were stories from both the Old and New Testaments, Moses being a particularly popular character. One play concerned Jesse; a tree of Jesse, which was often found in churches to show Jesus' family tree, was depicted in Dore Abbey and there was also one in the Church of Saint Mary, Abergavenny. Indeed, all the stories were familiar from the colourful wall paintings in churches. The one extra Hereford play was the martyrdom of Saint Katherine, reputedly martyred in Roman Alexandria by being tied to a spiked wheel (the origin of her emblem, the catherine-wheel) though eventually beheaded. She was very popular in Herefordshire. In the Mayor's Account Roll for 1533-4[3] Thomas Downe was paid for helping with the procession and performances, so Hereford people were still enjoying the plays in the year Queen Elizabeth I was born. In 1559 Elizabeth's new Protestant Bishop, John Scory of Hereford, described the canons as 'papists' and Hereford Cathedral as 'a nursery of blasphemy, pride, superstition and ignorance'. If the city did not embrace the religious changes, then parts of the outlying districts of the shire were even less ready to do so. People enjoyed the seasonal celebrations and evidently wished them to continue.

Although Blanche's Bacton monument would show that she venerated at least one saint's image (described later), she was not involved with overt Catholicism and she avoided the consequences of the Stradling Icon in the 1560s. Blanche's grandmother, Joan, or Jane, Stradling came from a devout Catholic family and both Joan's father and her paternal grandfather had undertaken pilgrimages to Jerusalem. A descendant of Joan's brother was Damascyn (Damascene / Thomasine), the devoted servant of Jane Dormer, who was the lady Queen Mary entrusted with her jewels and who became the Countess, later Duchess, of Feria in Spain and a supporter of dissident Catholics. On Damascyn's death in Spain, the Countess wrote to Sir Thomas Stradling, her father.[4] He lived at St. Donat's Castle, was a Justice of the Peace and had been Sheriff of Glamorgan and a Member of Parliament. In 1551, in the reign of the Protestant King Edward VI, Sir Thomas was imprisoned in the Tower of London for his Catholicism and in 1558, in the last year of the Roman Catholic Queen Mary's reign, he had been on a commission for the suppression of heretics. So, in Queen Elizabeth's reign, with a daughter in Catholic Spain, he was already religiously suspect, but he became a potential government problem due to a curious incident.[5]

During the night of 20 March 1559 a violent storm split a mature ash tree in the park at St. Donat's Castle. The trunk split about 7 feet above the ground and the lower half further split when the top fell. Inside the standing lower-split trunk a hazel-coloured cross about 14 inches high could be discerned in the pale grain. Not long before this incident Damascyn had sent her father a picture of the Resurrected Christ from Louvain in the Spanish Netherlands so, perhaps to return the favour, Sir Thomas made a paper pattern of the cross and had four pictures of what he evidently considered to be a likeness of the Holy Cross painted in London. He kept one, gave two to friends and sent one to Damascyn, who promptly publicised it on the continent to such an extent that it is possible that even Pope Paul IV came to know of the find. This was particularly unfortunate as this was the Pope who declared Elizabeth to have been illegitimate and so had rejected her claim to the English throne.

In earlier decades this situation would have led to the find's veneration as a sacred icon and perhaps even to the development of a cult. In the reign of Queen Elizabeth such an interpretation of a natural find was subversive and politically dangerous. In 1561 a commission was sent to investigate and the interview transcripts, together with the relevant piece of tree, were sent to the Privy Council. Sir Thomas was committed to the Tower and although he immediately petitioned for his release, he was not freed until 1563 after entering into a monetary bond to appear before the Privy Council on demand. (The local investigations were headed by Sir Roger Vaughan as Justice of the Peace, whose son and brother married the two daughters of Blanche Parry's brother, Milo ap Harry.) Sir Thomas was further investigated at the time of the 1569 Northern Rebellion.[6] He remained a quietly steadfast Catholic, refusing to subscribe to the 1559 Act of Uniformity which was demanded of all Justices of the Peace in 1570. However, his health was failing and he was allowed to live out his remaining months quietly, dying in 1571.

Blanche had no known direct contact with Sir Thomas Stradling, who always posed a risk in matters of religion, and she did not name any Stradling cousin in either of her Wills. However, after Sir Thomas' death she did approach his son, Sir Edward Stradling, who had conformed religiously and was the Sheriff of Glamorgan in 1573, 1581 and 1593 (see also the letters concerning David Morgan described later in this chapter). Sir Edward's loyalty was not suspect in the same way as that of his father and she addresses him as 'loving cousin', again a common description for relatives. Sir Edward wrote a treatise, 'Of the winning of Glamorgan', which he sent to Sir William Cecil Lord Burghley, who seems to have passed it to Blanche. She subsequently gave it to David Powel for inclusion in his book *The Historie of Cambria*, published in 1584. David Powel notes that 'the right worshipful Mistress Blanch Parry' is 'a singular well willer and furtherer of the weale publike' of Wales. She evidently shared an interest in the publication and preservation of Welsh history.

Lollard

The latest scholarship suggests that Queen Elizabeth favoured Protestant doctrine and Catholic ceremonial, largely replicating the Church of England as it was in the last years of her father's reign. These were the religious precepts taught to her under the supervision of Lady Troy and which most of the Household, including Blanche Parry, followed, for although Henry VIII was interested in the new ideas he was inherently traditional in religion.

Elizabeth's mother, Anne Boleyn, seems to have been sympathetic to Protestant ideas, for according to her chaplain (accused of Lollardy) Anne kept a copy of the exiled William Tyndale's English translation of the New Testament in her suite for anyone who wished to read it and she had also introduced Henry VIII to Tyndale's writings.[7] Queen Elizabeth's first Archbishop of Canterbury, Matthew Parker, had been another of her mother's chaplains and in 1554 the Count of Feria had noted that if Elizabeth became Queen she would rule through men who were probably heretics, pointing out that 'all the women around her definitely are'.[8] The inference is that this was true of Blanche Parry through the Lollard influence in her childhood (originating with Gruffudd ap Henry her paternal great-great-grandfather). As the Milborne connections of Blanche's maternal line were also involved, Lady Troy too may have personally preferred some Lollard precepts.

Sir John Oldcastle's family were Lords of the Manor of Almeley in west Herefordshire (a noted centre of Lollardy in the late 14th century) and he had long tolerated Lollardy on his manors. He wanted clerical reform and he helped spread John Wycliffe's writings so widely that remarkably many of these hand-written manuscripts survived the burnings and strictures of the established church.[9] Indeed, in 1526 the then Abbot Thomas Cleubery of Dore incorporated a *Commentary on the Ten Commandments* by John Wycliffe into a composite volume that he owned. In 1415 Sir John was nearly caught near Malvern but was finally captured in 1417 after stiff resistance, in the course of which he sustained severe injuries, by the Lord of Powys, at Broniarth, north-west of Welshpool. Returned to London, he was executed in Saint Giles' Fields.

However, Lollardy continued. Derek Plumb's thesis found that Lollards were 'socially, economically and politically integrated within their communities'.[10] They were 'found at all levels of economic standing within most settlements' associated with Lollardy. Although he researched Berkshire, Buckinghamshire, Hertfordshire, Middlesex and Oxfordshire, there is also evidence of continuing dissent in Herefordshire and specifically in the area of Almeley. Adjacent to and south of Almeley is the Parish of Eardisley. In Bishop Richard Mayew of Hereford's Register two entries, one by John

Croft(e) of Eardisley in English for February 1505 and the other by Richard Wever and William Fylly, both of Eardisley, in Latin for 15 March 1505 (only two years before Blanche's birth), were concerned with abjurations of heresy.

John Croft's declaration gives a vivid picture of Lollard beliefs and practices. He confessed that he had possessed many books containing heresies and errors against the established Christian faith

> and the determination of all holy church, which books I have read and declared often times privately and openly, holidays and feast days, before many diverse persons, reading, declaring and teaching against the blessed sacrament ... also against the sacrament of confession to priests and penance for satisfaction of sin, also against the solemnization of the sacrament of matrimony ... Also, I have read and declared against our holy father, the pope, showing that he has not the power of binding and loosing that Christ gave to Peter but in usurping that power upon him he makes himself Anti-Christ. Also I have read and taught against the veneration and worshiping of images standing in churches ... and again the shrining [placing in a shrine] of saints … in gold and silver and hanging about them the same.

He continued that he foreswore all such errors, heresies and false opinions and that henceforth he would neither read, declare, teach, affirm, believe, nor hold such errors. In addition he would not help anyone else to do so and indeed he would give their names to the Bishop of Hereford or his officers. He asked for God's help in all this and made the sign of the cross at the end 'with mine own hand'.

John Croft's declaration shows the importance the church authorities placed on reading. Croft had been preaching on all possible occasions including the holidays when people would have been able to listen to what he had to say. The Croft family were notable in the shire, some members being government officials (Sir James Croft became Queen Elizabeth's Comptroller of the Household 1570-1590) but there is no evidence of John Croft's connection with them; he must have been self-employed to some extent, perhaps a tradesman. He was evidently not alone in his views. In 1512 George Blythe, Bishop of Coventry and Lichfield, Lord President of the Council in the March of Wales, and five others were commissioned to enquire into insurrections in South Wales, in the six border counties of Herefordshire, Gloucestershire, Shropshire, Worcestershire, Cheshire and Flint, and in the lordships of South and North Wales.[11] The description of the likely rebellions to be pre-empted specifically mentioned Lollards, showing that the sect remained very active in the largely uncontrolled area of the March.[12]

The Almeley area is on the northern side of the River Wye, not far from the lands of Blanche's family along the Golden Valley. However, there was an even closer connection. Sir John Oldcastle's son by his first wife was Henry Oldcastle (1400-*c*.1460) who in *c*.1444 was able to recover much of the entailed Herefordshire family estates, including the area around Almeley. He had been mentioned in two court cases in 1431-1443. He had lived in Hereford but when he was pardoned in 1446, 1456 and 1458 he was described as Henry Oldcastle esquire of Tillington, a manor nearer to Hereford than Almeley. Although he did not attain the same status in society as his father he did try to rehabilitate himself by being a Justice of the Peace for Herefordshire in 1456-58 and by supporting the ruling Lancastrian government. He also represented Herefordshire in the parliaments of 1427-28, 1442 and 1453-54. Henry Oldcastle's wife was Elizabeth Milborne, presumably the daughter of Sir John Milborne and Elizabeth Devereux.

Sir John Milborne was described as holding Tillington and so it appears that Henry Oldcastle obtained this by right of his wife Elizabeth, very possibly as her marriage dowry. However, Henry and Elizabeth had no surviving children and Almeley was definitely inherited by Simon Milborne, presumably Elizabeth's brother, confirmed by his being sued in 1460/65 as 'feoffee of Henry Oldcastle'. Further confirmation of his ownership of the 'demesne of Almeley', described as 'belonging to Symon Milborne, armiger' (esquire), is in Bishops' Registers ordinations of 1476. Simon owned the Herefordshire manors of Almeley, Burghill, Howton, Munsley, Tillington and Wellington.[13] Through Almeley and Tillington Henry Oldcastle can be proved to be connected with Simon Milborne, who was the father of Lady Troy and Alice, Blanche Parry's mother.

So in a family that was only too conscious of its pedigree and affiliations and in which stories would be passed down the generations as a matter of course, there was a possible residual Lollard influence. This aspect of the background of Lady Troy and Blanche Parry has never before been considered and it is certainly worth examining the personal views of these two women who were constantly present in Princess Elizabeth's childhood. At its simplest both women had a family tradition which encouraged reading and very possibly the reading of the Bible in English. They would have appreciated the importance of books and indeed, in the future, Blanche would be given charge of Queen Elizabeth's books.

The Welsh Bible 1588

Although speculative, it is possible that Blanche may have helped with the costs of printing the Bible in Welsh and she may even have been involved in the preliminary discussions about its necessity. The evidence is tentative and not provable but Blanche certainly knew Dean Gabriel Goodman of Westminster for, in her Final Will, she named him as the person to supervise, at his discretion, her bequest of £20 (about £2,500 today) to the poor of the City of Westminster, the phrasing indicating she trusted him.[14] Her Saint Margaret's epitaph says she gave 'money to Westminster and other places for good uses'. Blanche was buried in Saint Margaret's Church, adjacent to Westminster Abbey and she had a house nearby, so it is reasonable to suggest she may have met William Morgan (see below) during his year in London, when he stayed with Dean Goodman.

Blanche was bilingual but she must have considered English to be the language that had facilitated her advancement at the Royal Court. She probably agreed with many of her compatriots that it was necessary for Welsh speakers to learn English. It is too speculative to suggest Blanche was directly involved with the 1563 Act of Parliament, though Watkyn Vaughan's letter to Lord Burghley shows she was a conduit for potential Parliamentary bills. However, it is likely that she knew about this Act, passed within five years of Elizabeth's accession, which ordered the Bible and Prayer Book to be translated into Welsh by Saint David's Day (1 March) 1567. It was thought that if the Welsh could read the Bible in their own language this might aid the spread of Protestantism.

However, the time-scale was too short for full implementation of this Act. By 1567 only the New Testament and the Prayer Book had been translated, both by William Salesbury with the help of other scholars. It was an immense task and the result proved difficult for ordinary Welsh speakers to understand. About 1578 William Morgan, the Vicar of Llanrhaeadr-ym-Mochnant in Denbighshire and a preacher at the University of Cambridge, began the enormous task of translating both the New and Old Testaments. His religious training[15] gave him the skills to translate from the Hebrew and Greek originals as well as to consult English versions and Salesbury's Welsh translation. He was also conversant with the bardic poems and his Welsh was therefore both aristocratic and vernacular.

In 1587 William Morgan accepted an offer of accommodation from Dean Goodman of Westminster, a Welshman born in Ruthin, who was also Chaplain to the Lord Chancellor, the position to which Sir Christopher Hatton was later appointed. William Morgan stayed at the Dean's house for the whole year it took to supervise the London printers who were producing the Bible in, for them, unfamiliar Welsh.[16] The whole Bible was published in 1588 and was a stupendous achievement. The Welsh was readable, readily understood by Welsh speakers, and incorporated words from both North and South Wales. It had the effect of giving the language accepted spelling conventions and was the single most important cause of Welsh surviving as a living, literate language. The Welsh Bible was placed in all Welsh-speaking-area churches alongside the English Bible and some are still preserved.

Blanche must have been delighted when it was published in 1588, although it is likely that her sight was now so poor that she could not read it in detail herself. The official hope was that having the two Bible translations together people would soon learn to speak English as well as Welsh and this is likely to have been Blanche's view. The fact that the Welsh Bible was produced so much earlier than the Bible in Irish and Scottish Gaelic does seem to suggest special pleading for it. Blanche's influential position may have been a crucial factor and it is certainly possible, due to her connection with Dean Goodman, that she could have been at least one of the facilitators of this great enterprise. This would agree with David Powel's description of her.

Patronage

The Royal Court was a hotbed of infighting and jostling for influence, money and position. Tudor society functioned through patronage and connections and it is clear from Sir Nicholas White's letter to Lord Burghley that Blanche facilitated appointments. Sir Nicholas wrote that 'This honest gentleman, Mr. Thomas Williams (whom I favour for Mistress Blanche's sake) hath assured me of the safe carriage of my letter to your Honour…' implying the communication route was through Blanche. Thomas Williams was evidently appointed (he was Master and Clerk of the Check in Ireland) because of Blanche's patronage. She helped a number of people and those traced include:

John Vaughan

John, the son of Blanche's eldest sister, was such a favourite with Blanche that she first tried to help him and then, after his death, asked to be buried near him if she died in the London area. This alone gives him an important place in Blanche's biography. However, John is also important in that his relationship with Blanche can be shown to provide a source of information for the Queen.

Everyone of substance had informants and those who wished to influence the Queen or a minister knew who to contact first. In particular Sir William Cecil Lord Burghley, Robert Dudley Earl of Leicester and later Sir Francis Walsingham, employed agents, or spies, who reported directly to their specific employer. John Vaughan's career provides evidence that the Queen also had her own sources and that at least one of these was via Blanche Parry. Blanche's informants knew their information would be delivered directly and speedily to the Queen.

John Vaughan's appointments included being High Sheriff of Yorkshire in 1559, an M.P., J.P. and a member of the Council of the North from before 1564. He was well placed to make an advantageous marriage in about 1549. His wife was Anne Lady Knyvett, sole heir of Sir Christopher Pickering of Killington, Westmoreland and Escrick and widow of Francis Weston who was executed with Anne Boleyn and then of Sir Henry Knyvett. When Anne and John married she kept her title; even Lord Burghley, in his Parry Family Tree, named them as 'John Vaughan and Lady Knyvit', while in her First Will Blanche wrote 'John Vaughan married to the Lady Knevett'. Such involved nomenclature has the advantage of providing certainty when trying to identify John Vaughan in most documents. Anne had an inherited interest in great estates in Cumberland, Middlesex, Yorkshire and Westmoreland. The difference in rank suggests that Anne's marriage to John Vaughan was a love-match and it endured 26 years. In 1551 John and Anne, living at East Horsley, Surrey, were visited by King Edward VI and in 1559 Anne was a Lady of Queen Elizabeth's Household. Her daughter, Katherine Knyvett, was appointed a Maid of Honour. Anne's sons inherited their respective fathers' lands, though Thomas Knyvett inherited her own manor of Escrick. She and John had Francis and his sister Frances, probably twins, and Sutton-upon-Derwent was inherited by Francis. John had considerable outgoings on this estate for he had to first pay ten annuitants before he could 'take to his own use all the residue of the yearly profit and rents after deduction' of necessary expenses for the repair and maintenance. These monetary difficulties would be inherited by Francis. In 1567 Blanche was granted the manor of Wheldrake for her life and 21 years after her decease, in return for an annual rent and, as it is likely that John administered this for Blanche, it had the practical effect of doubling the size of his estate. Blanche also helped him acquire estates in the Welsh border, giving him the manor of Fawley in Herefordshire. He already owned the manor of Glasbury in Breconshire, and Blanche helped him by clearing his debts and buying this manor from him for a nominal amount.

John Vaughan worked closely with Sir Henry Gate (who was to marry John's cousin) and both were very involved in the Government's response to the disturbances in the north of England that resulted in the Northern Rebellion of 1569-70. This had a religious base as the settlement of the 1559 Act of Uniformity and succeeding Injunctions had had such a shallow hold on the area that in 1566 Sir William Cecil estimated that two-thirds of the Justices of the Peace were still Catholic.[17] People clung to the old ways that had formed a framework and meaning for the seasonal cycle and the important changes in life. This volatile situation had been doubly exacerbated by the arrival of Mary, Queen of Scots, a Catholic claimant for the English throne, who fled to England from the Protestant faction in Scotland in May 1568 and by the appointment of Lord Hunsdon as Warden of the East Marches in August 1568. The Council of the North, which was responsible for security, had been reorganised and made permanent in 1537, following the collapse of the rebellion known as The Pilgrimage of Grace. In 1569 the Council members included Thomas Radcliffe, the 3rd Earl of Sussex (the Lord President), the Dean of York, Sir Thomas Gargrave, Sir Nicholas Fairfax, Sir Henry Gate, Mr. Rokeby and Mr. Vaughan.

On 11 July 1568 Sir Thomas Gargrave, Sir Henry Gate and John Vaughan reported on the developing situation to Sir William Cecil.[18] They noted that many lamented 'the present state of the Scottish Queen in being put from her government' and reported that Mary had set herself to make a good impression for some people in Carlisle, who were not necessarily Mary's religious adherents, had found her 'to be wise, virtuous, eloquent' and generous within the limitations of her imprisonment. Her continued presence in the north they considered a danger to the realm.

On 2 November, 1569, Sir Henry Gate wrote to the Privy Council:

> In reply to your enquiries respecting the troubles and rumours in these parts, I have to state that about the beginning of October, there were dangerous rumours of troubles north of York, which continued for some time. On the evening of the 7th [meaning 'before', i.e.: 6th], being at Mr. Vaughan's house at Sutton, with other gentlemen, we received a letter from the Lord President [the Earl of Sussex], desiring us to repair to him forthwith at Cawood, eight miles distant, which we did. Arriving between 5 and 6 a.m., his Lordship came forth in his nightgown, bare legged and informed us of a rumour that a commotion was intended that or the next night and that he had need to look to himself, lest he should be taken in his own house ...

They debated for an hour and then Sussex went back to bed for another hour, as he had not slept all night. Two hours later Sir Thomas Gargrave arrived: 'When sent for, on 8th October, I found Sir Henry Gate and Mr. John Vaughan with him [Sussex] and he declared to us that he had heard that a commotion was intended in these parts … We consulted what was best to be done …'. It was decided to send letters asking the two potentially rebellious earls (Northumberland and Westmoreland) to meet them in York the following day, Sunday 9 October, which they did, protesting that they knew nothing of any disturbances. John Vaughan was certainly at the very centre of discussions concerning the government response and he was there when the earls addressed the Council in York.

The Earl of Sussex wrote directly to Cecil, on 30 October 1569: 'I am sorry that she [the Queen] is informed that Mr. Vaughan meant to come up on his own business but for a clause in the Council's letter to me. It is true the plague only stayed him, or he had been in London before the bruits [rumours] began. The clause was not in the Council's letters but in the private, whereof Mr. Vaughan had no knowledge ...'. It is evident that restrictions on movement imposed to contain the plague had prevented John Vaughan from travelling south. This letter suggests that someone was trying to make trouble for him and it is noteworthy that here Sussex was giving John his wholehearted support.

On 1 November 1569 John Vaughan himself wrote to the Privy Council from York: 'The rumours of troubles in these North parts were very great and dangerous for the time but who were the authors I cannot advertise ... Touching my knowledge and opinion, you shall understand at my repair to the Court, which shall be speedily, if occasion of service stay me not, having matters of my own weight to deal in.' So John Vaughan was reporting directly to the government through letters and in person. He was not alone in this and Sussex and Sir Thomas Gargrave were amongst those who provided information.

On 2 November, the day after his letter to the Privy Council, John Vaughan wrote directly to Cecil: 'I hope speedily to repair to the Court to declare my knowledge, being an ill-writer. I hear there is some intention to appoint me to serve the office of sheriff; pray prevent it, for it would utterly undo me, as I have written to my aunt more at large. P.S. The Lord President wants me here. If I do not come, I will write at large by a man of my own.' Vaughan did not want the office of Sheriff, an appointment made by the Queen, and to prevent it he wrote not to the Queen directly but to his aunt. Therefore, this letter conclusively shows that the Queen was receiving communications directly from John Vaughan through his aunt, Blanche Parry. Blanche was apparently keeping the Queen well informed.

The letter also demonstrates the importance of John Vaughan's position. Sussex had requested the Queen to: 'Pray appoint a new sheriff in these parts, whose truth you know.' Of his two letters of 16 November, the one to the Privy Council showed that: 'I received your letters of the 13th, with the commission for Sir Henry Gate to be sheriff of Yorkshire and for the discharge of the old sheriff ...'. John Vaughan had been approached, which argues for his probity, but he had already written to his Aunt Blanche by 2 November that he did not want the honour again, imploring his aunt to intercede with the Queen. Blanche's influence can be demonstrated here in that the Queen immediately appointed Sir Henry Gate, on 13 November. The speed with which the Queen acted on Blanche's advice is impressive from the point of view of what it tells us about Blanche's influence. However, Sir Henry was sick and Sussex recommended that 'I think Sir Thomas Gargrave, Sir George Bowes, or Mr. Vaughan the fittest to supply his place'. He reiterated the same to Cecil: 'Sir Henry Gate is extremely sick and not able to serve, so I have written for another sheriff, either Sir Thomas Gargrave, Sir George Bowes, or Mr. Vaughan ...'.

The rumbling discontent in the north broke out into open rebellion on 14 November 1569 when the Earl of Northumberland and the Earl of Westmoreland led their followers to Durham Cathedral for an enthusiastic celebration of the Catholic Mass. The rebellion was largely contained and, among others, John Vaughan reported the events and noted the names of the gentlemen concerned, ending 'My Lord Lieutenant, Lord Hunsdon and Sir Ralph Sadler are assembled to take order herein. The gentlemen here stand dutifully to the Queen.' A letter from the Earl of Rutland to Cecil provides evidence that John Vaughan had operational responsibility: 'My servants, Bamborow and Thomson, are here and bear office; the former is serjeant-major and the other provost-marshal under Mr. Vaughan ...' and on 28 December 1569, Sussex commented that 'I once appointed Mr. Vaughan to be Marshall; if he gave it up, it was not my fault'. However, by the following January, Sussex wrote that 'Mr. Vaughan being gone home sick, I will dispatch Sir Henry Gate, who is at Richmond examining rebels ...'. Being ill may explain John Vaughan's reluctance to re-assume official office, although such an office was also extremely expensive to maintain and his remuneration of £20 for being a member of the Council stayed exactly the same until his death.

Lord Hunsdon evidently disliked John Vaughan's direct access to the Queen for on 13 January he wrote to her noting 'that by the time Mr. Vaughan or any other come from you, I shall understand the Regent's disposition ... You are determined that John Vaughan or some other shall bring up the Earl [of Northumberland] if he is delivered [captured]'.[19] In the aftermath of the failed rebellion, Sussex's letter of 21 January to Cecil has a very ambiguous comment: 'John Vaughan, without any commission, has spoiled and sent away what the other [possibly Mr. Sadler's son] seeks by order to have, so that little is left. The rest of his grant remains untouched and shall do. I will gladly do Her Majesty's command but if all the custodies granted be confirmed, there is nothing left for any gentleman who have served under me, for they have left nothing unbestowed. I would be sorry Her Majesty should be so abused by reports as to conceive they have not deserved as much as any others ...'. It seems John Vaughan had the Queen's permission though not a formal order ('commission') and that he acted with integrity by forwarding the spoils to perhaps London. This left nothing to be divided as rewards between the gentlemen who served under Sussex, who did not appreciate John's getting the credit instead of his own supporters. Lord Hunsdon evidently hated John Vaughan and he certainly wanted to give any credit to Sussex. He knew John Vaughan had sent critical reports on the situation to the Queen. Hunsdon's comments in his letter of 7 April 1570 to Cecil were poisonous:

> I fear when my Lord Lieutenant and others under him venture their lives and do their uttermost, some other John [Vaughan] shall step up to deface our doings, keeping themselves safe enough from peril. It has not furthered her [the Queen's] service sending my Lord of Sussex down with such small credit, it being known how and by whom he was so accused and yet the party not punished. I speak not from affection to the Earl but in respect of the service; for John Vaughan, Her Majesty shall find him but an ox, neither able to serve her abroad nor at home, in war nor in peace but only in words, envying every man that is in authority above himself. My letter may seem malicious but I protest it is on certain knowledge of his doings and I would not have Her Majesty abused by such as he is; but for offending her, I would write no less to herself ...

There is more than a hint of jealousy here! The accusations do not match John Vaughan's twice refusing further office, being described as having operational duties until he was ill and being held in high regard by other members of the Council of the North. That the Queen did not agree with Lord Hunsdon was demonstrated by John Vaughan's remaining a member of the Council, despite the ill-health which would have provided a convenient excuse to retire him. On 24 June 1570, Vaughan was named as one of the three foremost gentlemen in Yorkshire in the Queen's service and Sir Thomas Gargrave wrote to Cecil (now Lord Burghley) that 'I have written to the archbishop to consider the choice of meet [able] councillors in these parts. If Sir Henry Gate and Sir George Bowes, with Mr. Vaughan, would reside here, they would be good assistants, as men of weight and knowledge in the law, for there are none here that meet besides those already placed ...'.

John continued to sit in Parliament, served on at least four committees and by 1573 held the office of Custos / Custodes Rotalorum for the East Riding of Yorkshire. Most counties only had one but Yorkshire appointed three. It meant that John was the official keeper of the rolls, or records (that is the writs, indictments and legal documents) of the East Riding, though in practice his clerk carried out the actual work.[20] It was an immensely powerful local position.

John Vaughan died on 25 June 1577,[21] the Earl of Huntingdon writing to Walsingham, then Principal Secretary: 'I hear God has taken John Vaughan;

if so, the opportunity will serve the better (because his place in this Council will be void) to move Her Majesty for some persons to be added when the commission is renewed ... Mr. Vaughan had a fee of £20 per annum ...'. He died in London, perhaps at Blanche's Westminster house as his burial was recorded in the registers of the Parish Church of Saint Margaret's, adjacent to Westminster Abbey.

Hugh Bethell

It is unlikely that Hugh Bethell was related to Blanche (but see Robert Byddel below). It is tentatively possible that a marriage between Blanche and the previous generation of Hugh's family had been suggested but this is unsubstantiated. It seems that Hugh's closeness to Blanche was initially due to his friendship with John Vaughan and Hugh's own valued abilities. In Blanche's First Will she describes him as 'My friend Hughe Bethell'.

Blanche received her first land grants from the Queen in 1562 but her earliest Yorkshire leases were in 1567. The first mention yet found of Hugh Bethell is in 1563 and he was a witness to a bond dated 15 August 1566 for £1,000 of John Vaughan and Lady Anne,[22] proving that Hugh and John knew each other by this date. In her First Will Blanche wrote that the profit from the woods at Rise and Wheldrake came from the wood sales 'made by Bethell'. It is possible that he began working for Blanche by managing her Herefordshire estates as his family lived just north of the River Wye, and as Blanche's advisor he very probably became the Steward of her Yorkshire estates. His name derived from Welsh ap Ithell and he came from the parish of Mansell in Herefordshire, probably Mansell Gamage, where it is likely his family had farmed in the area below Garnons Hill.

He was a surveyor and a trained lawyer, his name appearing in the Records of the Court of Star Chamber, the Exchequer and Chancery. His first known government post in 1572 gave him a 'Grant for life to Hugh Bethell of the office of Particular Surveyor of lands in the Estridding [East Riding], C. York, in the survey of the Exchequer, void by the death' of the previous holder 'with an annuity of £13 6 8d and expenses'. There is no proof to show why he was chosen but his connection with John Vaughan and Blanche Parry suggests that Blanche was instrumental in his appointment and she was also probably concerned in his further advancement. In Blanche's First Will she declared 'he hath a lease' and her bequest of £20 for him to remit his fine (legal payment) on this suggests that she was involved.

In 1576 he was named as surveyor of the repairs of the castle and military blockhouses in Kingston-upon-Hull, which dated from the reign of Edward VI and 'which are much decayed by the fury of the water and tempestuous weather ...'. This note also connects Hugh Bethell with Sir Henry Gate and strongly suggests that Hugh provided expertise for the Council of the North. It therefore seems extremely likely that it was the connection between John and Hugh Bethell that provided a real and lasting link between Hugh and Blanche Parry. She had probably known his family but it was the friendship between Hugh and John that cemented Blanche's own connection with Hugh. It may also be that, like John, Hugh was providing Blanche with information for the Queen.

Hugh's gratitude and affection for Blanche can be inferred. He was granted a wardship and then lands in Yorkshire and was able to advise Blanche on good financial prospects. Perhaps as a result, in 1582 Blanche was granted tenements and appurtenances in the same area. She was also granted the manor of Rise in the East Riding. In addition, Hugh Bethell had a business connection with Francis Vaughan, who was the Crown's chief Steward in the East Riding.

Hugh would act as Blanche Parry's executor with Thomas Powell (as detailed in Chapter 6 and Appendix 2). He shared Blanche's Yorkshire leases with Francis Vaughan but just over a year after Blanche's death Francis had cash-flow problems and Hugh bought his share.[23] One of the two witnesses was William Garnons, a relative of the John and Robert Garnons of the Garnons Indenture (described later), making a further link between the Herefordshire and Yorkshire personnel. Hugh knew the East Riding extremely well and he took the opportunity that Blanche gave him to build an estate at Rise, where he saw the potential for future development. In his 1610 Will he made provision for the poor who lived in almshouses he had already built at Ellerton, which successfully echoed Blanche's abortive attempt to provide similar accommodation at Bacton in Herefordshire. He also mentioned his servant, George Haxley / Haxby, a relation of John Haxby(e), Blanche's tenant and Thomas Haxbye, the tenant of William Berrowe's farm mentioned in Blanche's Final Will.

It is evident that Blanche's trust in Hugh Bethell was not misplaced. He worked hard, was a skilled administrator and prospered due largely to Blanche's patronage. He was the only person who was not her *known* relation to whom Blanche gave considerable responsibility in her Final Will of 1589.

The Mayor of Hereford

Evidence of Blanche's perceived influence at Court can be found in her correspondence with the Mayor of Hereford[24] who evidently appreciated that she was a powerful point of access. His letter to her has not survived but Blanche's answer was carefully preserved as insurance for the future. It is written by a secretary but signed by Blanche:[25]

To the Right worshipful Mr Mayor and his Brethren of the city of Hereford give this -

My masters I most heartily thank you for your courtesies and good-will, being very glad to hear that you, all my friends, be in good health. Beseeching you to do my commendations to all your wives wishing you and them, with me, to take part of your one [own] gift. If I can, or may stand you in stead, you shall find me ready to pleasure [please] you at all times. This with my commendations, I end from troubling you any further, praying to God to keep you with long lives and health.

Your assured always in that I may

Blancsh Parry

Blanche Parry's signature on the above letter (HRO, BG11/17/6)

Another hand wrote on the outside: 'Mrs blanche parry her letter'. Blanche is saying in her last line that she is their assured friend in anything in which she may be able to help them.

Her courteous tone provides an insight into Blanche herself. She thanks the Mayor and the City Council most politely for their good wishes, extending her reciprocal wishes to their wives, a point that would perhaps have been omitted by a man at that time. She calls them her 'friends', suggesting previous contact if only by correspondence, and agrees to further their interests when she is able to do so. Although undated her letter is likely to be from the late 1560s or 1570s and relates to an administrative problem such as the Mayor's plea of 26 April 1568:

John Maylerd, mayor of Hereford, to Sir Wm. Cecil and the Council of the Court of Wards.

I have lately received two writs, one directed to the Sheriff of the city of Hereford and the other to the Mayor and bailiffs of Hereford. There are no sheriffs in the city, nor is it a county in itself and the writ is no warrant to do execution; I return it for further directions. With regard to the other directed to the Mayor and bailiffs, as there are no bailiffs, I have done execution therein myself in all points and hope my innocence in the matter will be considered if I have erred.[26]

It is absolutely clear that the Mayor and City Council needed a voice at Court to support their interests and had contacted Blanche who (related to important local families) was considered a reliable conduit to the Queen.

Louis Boughton

Blanche was also asked to use her influence of behalf of individuals and she usually personalises such appeals – here with 'a friend of mine'. On 25 April 1564 she wrote from the Court to Sir William Cecil in his capacity as Master of the Wards in London. Although the original letter[27] is damaged the following has survived:

> This poor man, Louis Boughton, a friend of mine, is, as he thinks, wrongfully vexed in the Court of Wards and having urgent business to attend to, I beg you to release him upon bonds for his appearance, until next Michaelmas Term, when he shall answer to all matters objected against him.

She then prayed to Almighty God that his health would be preserved and concluded 'Your assured kinswoman to command, Blanche Parry.' Louis Boughton is difficult to identify with certainty, but he is an example of such supplicants.

Dr. John Dee and Arthur Dee

Arthur was the son of Jane and Dr. John Dee, the mathematician and astrologer who had been asked to work out an auspicious date for Queen Elizabeth's Coronation. His dabbling in alchemy has led to Dr. Dee's having a very bad posthumous press. However, at the time he was considered a learned individual and, over the years, the Queen was recorded as several times coming to the door of his Mortlake house especially to speak to him. He evidently sought to become acquainted with people of influence at Court and hoped for a clerical position which would carry a salary. In this connection Dee noted[28] that in 1571 'Her Majesty's most gracious offer was sent home unto my house by Mistress Blanche a Parry of any whatsoever ecclesiastical dignity ... being then or shortly becoming vacant ...'. However, Blanche Parry 'sent' this offer, which suggests that she did not go to Dee's house herself and also shows that, again, she is acting on the Queen's specific instructions. Dr. Dee would refer to this in 1591 when he noted that 20 years before he had been granted the next available appointment only to discover that another claimant had taken it due to having an advowson. He continued that 'Mistress Blanche a Parry and Mistress Scudamore, now the Lady Scudamore, had obtained her Majesty's grant to me long since'. In fact Mary Scudamore had most contact with Dee, while at least three other ladies helped him. Blanche seems to have had hardly anything to do with him.

Nevertheless, Dee wanted to enlist her support. He asked Blanche to be the godmother of his son, Arthur, on 16 July 1579. Dee wrote in his Diary that 'Arthur was christened at 3 of the clock afternoon; Mr. Dyer and Mr. Doctor Lewys, judge of the Admiralty, were his godfathers; and Mistress Blanche Pary of the Privy Chamber his godmother. But Mr. John Harbert of Estshene [East Sheen] was deputy for Dr. Lewys and Mistress Aubrey was deputy for my cousin Mistress Blanche Pary.' Mr. Dyer may have been the Mr. John Dyer who was yeoman of the Queen's bakehouse and Dr. Lewis is mentioned below. It is clear Blanche was chosen because of her position at Court. She did not attend the Christening, sending a deputy, and she makes no mention of any of the Dee family in her Wills, although she does remember other godchildren. Dr. Dee made a similar attempt to garner a clutch of Court notables when his daughter, Katherina Dee, was christened. On that occasion her godfather was 'of the Court' and her godmothers were the wife of Sir James Croft, Controller of the Queen's household and 'Mistress Mary Skydmore of the Privy Chamber and cousin to the Queen …'.

It is clear that there was no more than a very cursory connection between Blanche and John Dee. He was the one who claimed her as a cousin but, if true, it was a very distant kinship. Blanche does not mention him or his family in her surviving papers. It was evidently Dee who wanted the connection and again this demonstrates the perception current at the time of Blanche's powerful position with the Queen.

David Morgan

David Morgan was the servant of Dr. David Lewis, an influential judge, law officer, MP and first Principal of Jesus College, Oxford. (He used Welsh nomenclature — his father was Sir Lewis ap John.) Dr. Lewis would remember Morgan in his 1584 Will as 'his servant and kinsman', with a bequest of £20. He was buried in St. Mary's Priory Church in Abergavenny where he had commissioned his tomb from John Gildon, the Herefordshire sculptor. Dr. Lewis knew Blanche, his name having been coupled with hers as godparents to little Arthur Dee. They may have been related, for both claimed kinship with David Morgan (who may have been related to the John — probably Blanche's Steward — and Walter Morgan mentioned in Blanche's Wills).

The Stradling Correspondence, 267 letters written to Blanche's cousin, Sir Edward Stradling (Sheriff of Glamorgan in 1573, 1581 and 1593), includes five letters concerning David Morgan, one of which was written by Blanche.[29] The first, from Dr. Lewis on 18 July 1578 to Sir Edward said '… Understanding that your shire doth want a convenient gaol to serve the

Sheriff … I am minded to cause the Queen's Majesty to be moved to grant the keeping thereof to my servant David Morgan, bearer hereof, by patent for term of his life …'. He evidently had access to the Queen as he was eventually successful, obtaining the patent from her on 9 April 1579.

Three years later Blanche was writing to Sir Edward, requesting his help (as he was then Sheriff) for David Morgan whom she denoted her 'kinsman'. It suggests that the Queen's grant was made at Blanche's instigation and that Blanche was checking on the present situation, although it may be that Blanche was acting on the Queen's behalf. Blanche goes as far as saying that she would personally return any favour shown to David Morgan.

> To the right worshipful, my very loving cousin, Sir Edward Stradling, knight.
>
> After my very hearty commendations to you. Whereas the Queen's Majesty, of her gracious favour, has heretofore granted a patent of the gaolership of that county to my kinsman David Morgan, which he has ever since enjoyed: for that he is a younger brother and has no other way of living, I have thought good to pray you most heartily that he may, with your favour and liking, enjoy the same by himself or his deputy without trouble; and you shall have sufficient sureties to save you harmless, according as her Majesty's said grant does purpose; and what favour you shall show him I will be ready to requite. And so, trusting that he shall need no other help herein beside my request, I bid you heartily well to fare. From the Court at Windsor, the 12th of December 1582.
>
> Your assured loving cousin,
>
> Blanche Pary

Blanche was at pains to explain her motives clearly. However, her power is evident in her assertion that her request alone would be sufficient to help David Morgan, although she reinforces this by mentioning the Queen twice in only a short letter.

On exactly the same day Thomas Perrot, son of the Sir John Perrot mentioned in Blanche's Final Will, also wrote to Sir Edward and his letter was almost identical to Blanche's though he does add that David Morgan was '… a gentleman of good parentage and servant to Mr. D. Lewis, a very good friend …'. He requested Sir Edward to show David Morgan his lawful favour in the exercise of his said office and also signed himself 'loving cousin'. On 11 January 1583 the diplomat Sir Valentine Dale wrote privately to Sir Edward, his 'old friend', advising him that 'I understand there is a matter in variance like to arise between you and David Morgan touching the keeping of the gaol in the county of Glamorgan. The truth is that her Majesty granted him that office upon such special suit and upon such substantial information, that it is very like she will see her grant maintained and will mislike that it should be in anywise impugned...'. A letter from Dr. Lewis and Sir Valentine Dale (and one other, all Doctors of Civil Law and Masters of the Court of Requests) dated 15 January 1583 further explains the situation. David Morgan had been granted the gaolership 'with all fees and other commodities incident thereunto', which he had quietly enjoyed until Sir Edward became Sheriff. David Morgan had made complaint against Sir Edward in the Court of Requests and Sir Edward was asked to allow David Morgan to continue in the said office.

It is interesting that David Morgan was granted the office on 'such special suit' and it seems reasonable to conclude that Blanche was responsible for the special suit to the Queen. She had evidently provided a dossier of information to support the case, demonstrating her meticulous attention to detail.

Elizabeth Bourne

Elizabeth, daughter of Sir John Conway, had been the ward of Sir Henry Jerningham, Master of Horse to Queen Mary. He had married her to Anthony Bourne the son of Secretary of State Sir John Bourne. Anthony deserted his wife for another woman, the resulting debacle culminating in a fine of £1,000. Elizabeth was left in such difficult circumstances that she appealed for help:[30]

> Mrs. Anthony Bourne to the Worshipful Mrs. Morgan at Westminster.
>
> Good Mrs. Morgan with my hearty thanks for your great courtesy showed me. I commend myself to you most heartily praying you amongst the rest of your friendships towards me that you will wyttsafe [vouchsafe] to deliver me a letter to good Mrs. Blanche Parry and that you will entreat her most earnestly to move her majesty for me in a reasonable suit, that is, that her Highness will show Mr. Bourne and me that gracious favour as to accept her thousand pounds which we must pay her by one hundred pounds a year until the whole sum of a thousand pounds be paid. And we will put in such good sureties therefore to her majesties use as my Lord Treasurer [Lord Burghley] shall allow of. I pray you, good Mrs. Morgan, be earnest with Mrs. Blanche in this for God he knoweth if I cannot obtain this favour I and all mine shall presently beg and be undone.
>
> Our whole state is but three thousand two hundred pounds, her majesty must have one thousand, Mr. Bourne's debts and his mother's legacies be an other thousand which must be presently compounded or he shall be imprisoned and I undone. The rest remaineth in the hands of several debtors which will not be recovered but by time and charge,

> so that it is an impossible thing for us to pay her majesty the thousand pounds in any other sort than by £100 a year and live well. Therefore I pray you be earnest in this case for your poor unfortunate friend. I will requite any good you shall do to the uttermost of my power. If you can get Mrs. Blanche to obtain the favour to pay it by £100 a year till the £1000 be paid I will give you 200 marks. If you cannot obtain that, increase her Majesty's £1000 and make it £1200 to pay it by £100 a year and give you 100 marks and your money shall be presently paid you upon either of these ends obtained. And so I commend your health and Mr. Morgan's to God and the consideration of this cause to your friendly remembrance.
>
> Your loving and unfortunate friend,
>
> Elizabeth Bourne

This undated letter, quoted here in full, mentions Blanche three times. It reinforces that Blanche was a person through whom suit could be made to the Queen and that she required full, precise information if she was to do so. The practical points delineated demonstrate the procedure to be followed in using Blanche as the Queen's conduit. Bradford, in his book *Blanche Parry, Queen Elizabeth's Gentlewoman*, suggests that Mrs. Morgan was the wife of Hugh Morgan the Queen's apothecary, a beneficiary of Blanche's Final Will but it is also possible that she was Susan Morgan, the wife of John, Blanche's Steward.

Robert Byddel / Bethell?

A letter[31] has survived which couples Blanche's name with those of Lord Burghley and the Earl of Leicester. Written from the Court, dated January 1583, it was sent to George Talbot, 6th Earl of Shrewsbury asking him to ensure that Robert Byddel, described as a relation of Blanche Parry, was able to take possession of the demesne lands of Bampton for the time outstanding on the lease which he had recently bought. Robert's surname could have been a Welsh spelling of Bethell and, if so, he was perhaps also a relative of Hugh Bethell (in which case Blanche and Hugh would have been related).

One of Lord Burghley's secretaries had appended a note to this letter to the effect that the signatures of Burghley and Leicester were counterfeit. This obviously troubled Shrewsbury as some days later, on 2 February 1583, he wrote from Sheffield to his man, Thomas Baldwin, at Coldharbour, Shrewsbury's London house,[32] requesting an investigation. The interesting points are firstly that Blanche's name was in company with those of the two most powerful men in the government and secondly that no-one was surprised. Whether the signatures were genuine or forged, it is still absolutely clear that Blanche herself was also sufficiently powerful for her name to be used.

Jane Shelley

In the late 16th and 17th centuries South Herefordshire and North Monmouthshire had large numbers of recusants, people who adhered to the Roman Catholic rites as opposed to the official Church of England. Two of these were William Shelley and his wife Jane Shelley (née Lingen).[33] William, distantly related to Lord Burghley, came from Sussex. Jane, his second wife, inherited extensive properties around Sutton in Herefordshire; her mother was Blanche's cousin.

Although William Shelley, denounced as a suspected recusant in 1564, 1569 and 1576, served as Sheriff of Herefordshire in 1567, he was finally committed to the Fleet Prison in 1580 by the Clerk of the Privy Council. In response to Jane's petition to the Council he was granted bail in 1581, with a second bail term in November 1581 to visit Jane, who was ill at Sutton. He found his mother-in-law on her death-bed and had to restore order as his servants had ejected Jane. This pattern of imprisonment and temporary releases continued until he became involved in the secret manoeuvres to rescue Mary, Queen of Scots and instigate an invasion of England.[34] Many of these machinations were disclosed on the rack by Francis Throckmorton in 1583 and while others escaped, William was imprisoned in the Tower on a charge of high treason. He was probably also racked as he pleaded guilty before Sir Christopher Hatton and was sentenced to be hung, drawn and quartered. He was returned to the Tower but evidently agreed to be a double-agent for the sentence was not carried out. Instead, he gave evidence in 1588 against the Catholic Earl of Arundel.

Although his life was saved, William was attainted, his property being forfeit to the Crown. On 20 June 1586 a warrant was issued to the Receiver-General of Herefordshire and Shropshire to pay £200 annually to Jane from the rents William held in right of his wife. It is clear that this £200 annuity was Jane's inheritance from her father which she could claim with the correct procedure: 'In this account the annuity of Jane Shelley with others mentioned under the title of annuities granted for the term of life by the last Will of John Lingen (who was father of the said Jane Shelley).'[35] This annuity is referred to in a letter she received from her cousin, James Parry (see below). James pointed out that as 'all her greatest kinsmen in Herefordshire' had refused to help, he himself had found Catholic gentlemen to aid her and they had approached 'Mrs Blaench Parry to procure you maintenance of £200 by year'. Subsequently Jane had been convicted of harbouring a priest, which resulted in a sentence in Worcester Gaol. Then she began consulting astrologers about her husband's fate and was accused of seeking to know the date of the Queen's death, which resulted in imprisonment in the Fleet in London in 1593. Imprisoned with her, as an *agent provocateur* to incite Catholics to incriminate themselves, was Benjamin Beard (her husband's cousin) who worked for Sir Robert Cecil (Lord Burghley's son). Beard was so successful with Jane Shelley that Joachim Newton, Warden of the Fleet wrote to him accusing him of acting 'to take a simple and silly gentlewoman into your company and make her drunk ...'. James Parry wrote[36] to her two days later on 13 November 1593 stressing that she should reform and reiterating how Blanche Parry had helped her in the past, and he warned her against Benjamin Beard. Beard himself wrote several letters to Sir Robert Cecil complaining that the Fleet Warden was preventing his fifth-column activities. Incredibly, Jane herself wrote to Beard on 9 December saying how sorry she was that the Warden treated him as he did. Beard must have found her a very easy target. The saga[37] continued and after William's death Jane recovered most of her lands. Despite her naivety, she was a generous lady, supporting various charities and founding an almshouse in Hereford.

The evidence suggests that Blanche facilitated the presentation of Jane's petition in 1581 and James Parry's evidence shows that she helped Jane by arranging, in 1586-1588, for her to have the £200 annuity she had inherited from her father, which was no more than Jane's legal due. Blanche must have been acting on the Queen's behalf as none of this would have happened without her approval. Jane was unreliable and her husband was accused of treason. Blanche, a cautious lady, provided help that was legally fair but that was all. There is nothing here to suggest she sympathised with the Shelleys' religious stance.

James Parry

This case illustrates very clearly that even relatives could not simply ask Blanche for help and assume that she would give it unconditionally. James had to explain in great detail exactly what was wrong and he provided detailed evidence to justify the awkward questions he evidently expected her to ask. His politeness to her in his letter supports her status at Court. The date of this is of particular note as in 1587 Blanche was already 80 years old, near the end of her life and yet obviously still mentally alert and influential.

James Parry of Poston, Blanche's cousin, was a Huntsman to the Queen and his son, Blanch, was Blanche's godson and as such remembered in both her Wills. James Parry himself was only mentioned in her First Will so perhaps Blanche felt she had helped him sufficiently when she agreed to investigate a third surety for him as recorded in James' letter. James' brother John was a Clerk of the Green Cloth in the Queen's Household, working in the spicery. When James was imprisoned in the Fleet Prison, on 23 April 1587 he wrote to Blanche for help, sending his letter via his brother John. 'To the right worshipful Mrs. Blaunche Parry attending her Majesty at Court ... .Although loath yet enforced to trouble you or stay in prison ... by the unchristian dealings of the Lord Chief Baron and my adversary Shepham [a moneylender] ... and for my relief am enforced to crave your aid towards the right honourable the Lord Treasurer [Lord Burghley] ...'. He describes his case in nearly three pages of close writing. He had stood surety for payment to a goldsmith, the Queen had become involved over the bond and the mounting interest had led to the sequestering of his Herefordshire manors. He mentions another son, John, and his cousins Roger Vaughan and John Morgan. James concluded with the hope that Blanche would not refuse 'my reasonable request herein ...'.[38] Despite Blanche's age James Parry evidently considered she would still be able to help him.

James' letter to Lord Burghley was dated 11 August 1587.[39] Richard Shepham agreed that James Parry had repaid £146 2s 5d, which James maintained was £41 2s more than he owed the government. Although briefly interviewed (the official not staying 'to hear any part of my cause'), James offered to find, within two days, people who would stand surety for his repaying any other outstanding money. He begged for his freedom and for his land to be freed so that he could extricate himself from his other troubles. Because he was in prison he could not find out who was in London who could help him. 'Whereupon I have entreated Mrs. Blaunche Parrye to help me to one surety wherein she has signified her mind to your Honour by letter ...'. He continued that he had also secured the help of Blanche's cousin, Mr. Thomas Games of Aberbrane, Breconshire, 'who is the best man of living in that country', as another surety. He said the auditors were Mr. Broughton and Mr. King.

Blanche's letter to Lord Burghley, written by a secretary, shows that Blanche's blindness now caused her to write a very unsteady signature. Despite this, the letter is written in such a personal style that it was clearly not simply written for her but was dictated by her.[40] It is lucid and logical and is worth quoting to show her grasp of detail only months before her death. Indeed the last sentence reveals that she did not think she had long to live:

> Right Honourable: I do understand by poor James Parry that your good lordship has very charitably granted his long suit, to release his lands taken for the Queen's Majesty's debt, upon bonds to pay so much as shall appear not to be already levied by the sequestrators and sheriff. If any happen to be behind, or to answer the profits of the lands and for that Mr Osborne (as he says) did deal very partially against him, for that he could not (in this time of vacation) [of the Inns of Court] name sufficient sureties on the sudden but requested time of two or three

days to send and enquire, what gentleman of his friends were about the town, which Mr Osborne denied, saying further that the sureties must be presently named. Whereupon my cousin Thomas Games of Brecknockshire (the best of that name) offered his bond with him and for that he could find no other fit in the town, has requested me to help him to a third surety, which I am contented to procure him, hoping that having his lands freed from her Majesty, he will with the continuance of your lordship's favour the rather work his liberty from the rest of his troubles, which in truth he could not procure so long as his lands was from his possession. For want of ability, beseeching your good lordship to perfect that which you have so charitably begun and to allow of his assuraunce which are sufficient for a far greater sum then the remainder of her Majesty's, as the case rests. For he affirms that upon the foot of Mr Auditor King's account taken, which he has certified to your lordship, it do appear that by Mr Shepham's own confession, the sequestrators have received Cxlvi li. Ii s. v d. [£146 2s d], which is more than her Majesty's debt, which being true, easy sureties may serve to pay the remainder. Therefore, good my lord, allow of the sureties, otherwise if your lordship, do refer the allowance of them to the masters of the Exchequer (who James Parry says do all they may to shadow the truth of the cause from your knowledge) they will not allow of any sureties by him named, only to delay him, or rather to weary him. All which, with my humble duty to your good lordship for your manifold goodness, I commend to the further consideration of your grave wisdom.

From Greenwich the xixth [19th] of August
Your lordship's high humble
during life Blaunch A Pary

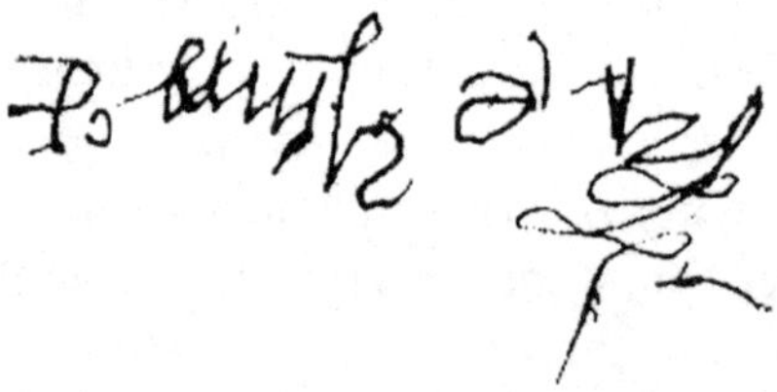

Blanche Parry's signature on the above letter (NA SP 46/18)

6 *Not doubting Want*
Wardships, Lands and Wills

As far as can be ascertained Blanche had made no attempt to accrue wealth before the Queen's accession. In her Bacton epitaph she stated she was 'uncareful of my wealth ... not doubting want whilst that my mistress lived ...'. She had no need to acquire lands and revenues for initially her parents, then Lady Troy and finally Elizabeth's Household provided for all her needs. She was not an acquisitive person, contrasting with Kate Ashley who evidently felt impelled, with her husband John, to acquire a portfolio of lands and manors. Such grants, as was usual at this time, tended to be former monastic property and were facilitated by confiscations resulting from the Dissolution of the Monasteries. Queen Mary had attempted to refound monasteries, notably at Westminster but under Parliamentary pressure she had had to agree not to repossess the monastic lands. Too many gentry had been able to enrich themselves and even staunch Catholics were notably reluctant to relinquish these pickings. Nevertheless, the walls of many monastic buildings still stood as new owners were obviously not certain of the durability of their tenure. It was only in the subsequent peace of the later 16th century that the fashion for restructuring them as new mansions became feasible.

Gifts of land, used as a method of patronage for the benefit of the Crown, were rarely made by Queen Elizabeth, whose parsimony extended to unchanging wage levels for the paid members of the Royal Household. It is extremely significant, therefore, that one of the earliest grants of the new reign, in 1559, was made to Blanche, especially as favourable grants were particularly rare for women.[1] Blanche was granted gifts, partial gifts and leases on favourable terms which clearly demonstrate the Queen's continued regard for her.

Blanche's Wardships

The first grant[2] to 'Blanche Apharry gentlewoman of the privy chamber' was the wardship and marriage of William Warren, the son and heir of Lawrence Warren, citizen and goldsmith of London, an assay master at the mint, who owned a house at Bygrave in Hertfordshire. Dated from Lawrence Warren's death on 4 August 1557, this was valuable as the revenue, which is not enumerated, would have been considerably more than the annual payment of 20 marks. It may be that Blanche's friendship with Margaret Dane brought this wardship to her notice. Four years later, in 1563, Blanche was granted the wardship and marriage of Thomas Buckingham, the son and heir of Stephen Buckingham of Follyfaunts in Essex, with a similar annual payment of 20 marks from 10 December 1558, when Stephen had died, until Thomas reached the age of 15 years and thereafter of £20. This wardship ended on 13 February 1570 when Thomas became 21.[3] Both wardships[4] provided Blanche with an income.

Blanche's Property

It may be that the acquisition of her first wardship inspired Blanche to begin to accumulate a land portfolio. The impetus seems to have been her perceived necessity to provide estates for John Vaughan and William Vaughan.

Herefordshire

Between her two wardship grants, on 4 January 1562, Blanche purchased her first land, paying £942 2s 6¾d into the Exchequer. This considerable sum must represent her savings, some perhaps originating from family bequests. The land, in Herefordshire, comprised the manor of Fawley (originally the property of the Augustine Canons of Llanthony Secunda in Gloucester), Wistaston Chapel and income from Bowley, Marden and Wellington (originally of the Knights Hospitallers of Dinmore Commandery).[5] That Blanche's 1562 patent had a mistake is clear from its replacement on 3 July 1565.[6] It was typical of Blanche to make sure that the documentation was correct and this copy was Blanche's own for, on the dorse, she wrote herself 'purchase of my woods at Fawley'.[7]

'The Queen to all etc. greeting. Know that we, for the sum of £942-2-6¾ paid into our Treasury ... for our use by our beloved Blanche Aphary one of the gentlewomen of our Privy Chamber, with which payment we acknowledge ourselves satisfied, of our special grace ... do give and grant to the said Blanche Aphary all that lordship and manor of Falley [Fawley] ... and all the demesne lands belonging thereto ... And all the stock of 360 sheep with their pasture. And all the customary messuages in Falley late in the tenure of John ap Williams ...'. Nothing can be inferred from Blanche's being described as 'our beloved' as this was usual in such documents. Fawley, a detached chapelry of the parish of Fownhope (now in Brockhampton, Ross, parish) is situated in a bend of the River Wye. The river, usually tranquil and picturesque, can become a rushing torrent in the winter and spring floods. The ground is fertile,

Map showing Blanche Parry's Herefordshire and Welsh lands (Geoff Gwatkin)

gently undulating and just high enough to avoid serious flooding. The field-names,[8] although recorded at a later date, are indicative of the use traditionally made of different fields and so can be used to locate the exact area referred to in this grant. Richard Cox / Cockes lived at Little Fawley, the timber house that pre-dated the 1627 Fawley Court.[9] Fieldnames indicate use for sheep (1037 Sheepcot field) and these would have interested Blanche as they were probably the same breed as the Dore Abbey sheep (the superb clip had fetched the highest price in Europe in the 13th-14th centuries), the ancestors of the Ryeland, that her father had managed in her childhood. It is likely that John ap Williams' family remained tenants, paying their rents to Blanche's steward.

She also had the farm (lease) of 'a certain water or river of Wye with all the fishery there and the watermill on the river with all the produce and profit ... lately granted to Roger Cock for the term of certain years'. The watermill, which was grinding corn before 1250, was sited on the south bank of the River Wye on the northern stretch of the river at Fawley. In 1528 Roger Cox (Richard's father) had a lease from the Prior of Llanthony Secunda of 'two water mills constructed under one building called Cary mills with the weir and fishing there ...'.[10] The area is identified[11] with the Carey Islands and the fields in the tenancy of the Cox family can be traced.

'And the weir and the meadow adjoining it in Mordiford called Old Rye Mill with a water course lately granted to William Hereford gent.'. William Hereford lived at Old Sufton, Mordiford (pre-dating the 1788 Sufton Court). A large mill ('Corn Mill' on the first edition of the OS map) stands by the bridge over the Pentaloe Brook, used as the mill leat and serving as the parish boundary. The mill stands in the north corner of an area bounded by brooks and two minor roads which, in the 1560s, was 'the meadow adjoining', the fieldname surviving in many of the small subdivided plots of 1843. There is a weir on the Pentaloe Brook east of the mill. 'Old Rye Mill' was such a valuable asset that it occasioned a law suit with William Hereford's widow, Margaret.

Blanche also had 'the free chapel of Wistaston alias Westerton ... and 7 acres of meadow there called Saynt Jones grounde [Saint John's Ground] lying in Whitwarden in the parish of Marden ...'. Wisteston Chapel (demolished 1909), field 117,[12] stood just above the flood-plain of the River Lugg. It was a free chapel, not subject to the Bishop's jurisdiction and only answerable to Dinmore Preceptory, with a chaplain and full sacramental rights including a graveyard (field 118). As the Hospitallers used Saint John in naming their fields ('Great St. John's Meadow' was near Dinmore Preceptory), 'Saint John's Ground' was one of their fieldnames. 'Whitwarden' (preserved as 'Whitterday' in ten adjacent subdivided fields in Marden parish and one in Bodenham) was sited just north of the ruinous Wisteston Court (north-east of the chapel). Lying on the east bank of the River Lugg, this was a very productive and valuable meadow group in the flood-plain.

However, Blanche only kept Wisteston Chapel until 1566 as it was then granted to Hugh ap Harry, a cousin from the Poston branch of the family, who had already bought the adjacent property.[13] (She also sold him 'the patronage of Gylles of Shorden' which she had bought in 1565.)[14] As Blanche had had to defend a lawsuit concerning the tithes in the Court of Requests in 1566[15] she was probably pleased to relinquish the property.

'And ... all lands, meadows, feeding grounds, pastures and appurtenances ... in Boowley ... And all the rent of free and customary tenements in Wellington ...'. Bowley is a township of the parish of Bodenham. The meadows lay along the east bank of the Humber Brook. The village of Wellington is a part of that parish situated on the west bank of the River Lugg. Blanche's holdings in Bodenham, Marden, Sutton St. Michael and Wellington form a reasonably compact area. She may well have known that her grandfather, Simon Milborne, had held lands, tenements with gardens, a part of an orchard and a dove house in 1505 in Wellington from the Hospitallers.[16] Wellington's relation to Dinmore is preserved in fieldnames such as '85 Saint John's Orchard', which may well be the site of 'St. John's Land', Blanche's holding. It featured in a 1566 lawsuit[17] that she fought in the Court of Requests against John Haworth, whose family had been named as tenants in the 1505 Rental.

She was granted every source of revenue in the '... hamlets of Falley, Wistaston ... and in the parish of St Michael and elsewhere. We give also to the said Blanche Apharry all woods, underwoods and trees growing in and upon the said lordship, manor, free chapel and other premises ... in the same manner that the Prior of Llanthony and the Governor of the Preceptory of Dinmore held them and enjoyed them and as they were granted by our predecessors.' Many of the structures, such as mills and dovecotes may be physically traced or sites indicated by fieldnames. Although Blanche's patent had cost her a considerable amount of money, the terms were favourable, an indication of the Queen's regard. However, as these holdings are not mentioned again by Blanche she must have surrendered them during the later 1560s or 1570s.

Of the several lawsuits that resulted from these properties, the two Fawley cases have a wider interest as they illustrate the difficulties that ensued when long-standing agreements with monastic houses were summarily overthrown. These two 1566 lawsuits were brought by Blanche against Richard Cox in the Court of Requests.[18] Blanche's initial petition provides a brief job description for her: '... your most excellent Majesty your subject and servant Blanche Aparrye attendant upon your Highness as to her duty appertaineth'. The documents also show that Blanche had an 'officer' or 'bailiff' to collect rents and that her brother Symond and cousin John ap Harry of Dulas (mentioned in her Final Will), were both involved in administering her estates. The speed with which Blanche was able to communicate with her brother and cousin between 6 and 22 June 1566 is certainly noteworthy.

It is clear Blanche had been given the Prior's copy of the lease of the Fawley property and she requested that Cox's copy be examined to check it was the same. In dispute was Cox's encroachment on the manor of Fawley and his spoil of timber on leasehold premises. Cox had entered the mill, 'Cary Wood' (field 1029), 'Byfelde' pasture (1024) and 'Range' field (1023) and he had felled valuable timber. Blanche pointed out that the Prior's lease had contained a condition stating that trees could only be felled in 'Carey Wood' to repair and maintain the watermill. She then asserted that within the last two or three years, since 1564, Cox had felled 30 great oaks for use elsewhere (perhaps to build his house). She requested that Richard should be ordered to leave the property so that she, Blanche, could take possession.

Blanche, or her lawyer, realised that the case hinged on comparing the wording of the lease copies. Although Richard Cox said he had delivered a true copy to Symond ap Harry (here spelled Apparye) Esquire, her brother, to forward to Blanche, he also maintained that Blanche had sent John Apparye of Dulas to write out a true copy — which Richard allowed him to do as he was 'desirous of being quiet' and wanted Blanche's 'good will'. He also said that Blanche's officer had many times accepted the yearly rent. Although the result of the case is not known, it seems likely that Blanche, especially with the Queen's influence, which Richard tacitly acknowledged, won her case. Certainly she was able to make bequests in her First Will of one tenement in Fawley to William Vaughan and the manor of Fawley (valued at £26 in 1578, an increase of about £3 less the tenement since 1566) to John Vaughan.

These lawsuits provide an insight into Blanche's character. She had not acted precipitously, for she waited two or three years before lodging her complaint. Many of the Privy Chamber women, including Blanche, understood the tenets of the law, especially as they were asked to intervene on behalf of various suitors. They also knew from whom to obtain the best advice. Blanche evidently knew enough law, or had obtained sound legal advice, to note the condition in the lease and its implications. Indeed the course of events shows her to have acted intelligently and with deliberation. Her estate was well-managed and she could trust her brother and cousin to oversee it on her behalf, showing that she was a good judge of personnel. There is no violence involved and even Richard Cox does not bear Blanche any ill-will. In the last resort Blanche also knew that she had the Queen's ear and her plea was measured and accurate.

However, there is further elucidation of Blanche's relationship with Richard Cox which comes from the remarkable survival of the Indenture between Blanche and Francis Vaughan (John's son and heir) of Sutton-upon-Derwent and Richard Cox of Little Fawley.[19] Dated 24 January 1589, exactly a year before Blanche's death, it is further evidence to show that Blanche retained all her intellectual faculties until her death and that she was not a person to bear grudges. It is clear that she shared the ownership of Fawley with Francis, Blanche owning the manor for her life and Francis Vaughan for the following 21 years. Richard Cox was to pay £100 for himself and his heirs to lease Cary Mill with its attendant rights, the pasture called 'Byefield' and the long parcel of land called 'Le Range' which included 'Cary Wood', precisely the area he was occupying. He agreed to keep the mill in good repair and was allowed to use sufficient timber from Cary Wood for the purpose. He could also use the wood to mend necessary hedges, fences, ditches and enclosures but for 'no other use or uses'. Blanche had not forgotten his earlier removal of timber for other purposes. His rent of 16s 8d was to be paid twice a year, in two portions, on 25 March, the feast of the Annunciation of the Virgin Mary (Lady Day), and 29 September, the feast of Saint Michael the Archangel, two of the traditional payment days, or within 30 days of either feast, in the Hall of the Inner Temple in London. Evidently making payment in London presented no difficulty for Cox personally or through an intermediary. Richard Cox signed and sealed the document, giving it to Henry Caldicot / Cauldycotte, who was acting as Blanche's local Steward. There was other litigation after Blanche's death but Richard Cox's descendants did inherit the occupancy of the site.

Blanche was involved in other court cases whose defendants included Thomas Berington, John Breynton, Richard Hancocks and George Keinsham. Of these John Breynton was probably a relative of Blanche, as one of her mother's sisters had married a man of the same name and it is possible that Thomas Berington was related to Blanche's own sister. All seem to have been cases concerning the terms of occupancy similar to that of Richard Cox, the type of case that was all too prevalent at the time. They demonstrate that Blanche kept a close administrative eye on the lands she was granted and that she was an efficient landlord.

Wales

Blanche's land grants in Breconshire were the result of her wish to provide estates for her nephew John Vaughan, son of her sister Elizabeth, and for her great-nephew William, the only son of her brother Milo ap Harry's elder daughter Elizabeth. As such they were probably the eldest males of the next two generations in Blanche's family. The area she wanted for them was where their ancestral lands were located and initially this seems to have been facilitated by Sir Roger Vaughan (William's paternal grandfather and eldest son of Sir William Vaughan of Porthaml). Sir Roger had immense local influence as by 1558 he was Custos Rotalorum for the county of Brecon.

The story really started in 1553[20] when Sir Roger acquired two manors in Breconshire, spelled phonetically as Schetrock / Scethrog and Moote. In 1562 he sold these to Edward Jones, a merchant tailor in London. In turn Jones sold them to David Jones, a fellow London merchant tailor, in 1570. Two years before this, in 1568, Sir Roger had sold David Jones the lands and tenements of Charles Farm in Brunktles / Bronllys just north-west of Talgarth. In 1574 Blanche negotiated with David Jones to buy both the manors and farm and a sale was concluded for £600 to Blanche and John Vaughan, who had joined his aunt in the enterprise. Through these transactions Blanche had settled land from his ancestor's area on John, land that was not entailed and could be used to settle debts. She had been astute enough to take the best legal advice (probably from Lord Burghley) to ensure that she acted in a responsible financial capacity to benefit her family. However, in this instance David Jones did not immediately enrol the transaction and Blanche had to ask him to do so in the Court of Chancery, which he finally did on 29 November 1579. Sadly, by then John Vaughan had died, in 1577, necessitating different arrangements. Blanche was about 72 years old and it may be that her age and perhaps depression following John's death exacerbated the illness she contracted in November 1578. In her nuncupative First Will made at that time, the holdings were to be placed in the care of trustees, Lord Burghley (Lord Treasurer of England) and John Morgan esquire of Westminster, who was probably her Steward, agreeing to act for her. Blanche evidently did not expect to survive long and she wanted the trustees to use the holdings as an estate for her great-nephew, William Vaughan.

Meanwhile, in 1566, Sir Roger Vaughan had been granted two letters patent on Crown lands in Breconshire to run for 21 years. The first patent concerned the named demesne lands (that is the lands not let out to tenants but held directly by the lord) of the lordship of Dynas with herbage (the right to pasture animals) and pannage (the right to pasture pigs) in the forest of Dynas. In addition Sir Roger was granted a part of a pool called Brecknock Pool or Mere (now Llangorse Lake). The annual rents totalled 103s 4d. All the property was in Talgarth and Llangorse in an area which had once belonged to the Earl of March and which had come to the Crown when he became King Edward IV, Queen Elizabeth's great-grandfather. The second patent grant on the same day was the result of a payment of £6 19s 4d to the Exchequer. This concerned the fishery at Lacne and Mere (Llangorse Lake), with annual rents of 36s, which had belonged to Edward Stafford, 3rd Duke of Buckingham, executed 1521, whose possessions had been forfeit to the Crown on his attainder. (He had been the patron of Sir William Herbert of Troy.)

However, Sir Roger Vaughan seems to have had a cash-flow problem in 1569 as he had to mortgage both the fishery of Brecknock Mere and the demesne lands of Dynas to Francis Myn, gentleman of the City of London for £80. This was just after he had sold the Bronllys farm to David Jones. It is likely that his main estates were entailed and could not easily be sold or mortgaged. Indeed, matters deteriorated, as Sir Roger defaulted on the interest payments, perhaps due to illness preceding his death in 1571, and Francis Myn took possession. In 1572 Blanche paid the entire sum owing to Francis Myn and so became the owner of the fishery and the lands. If she was deliberately acquiring land that could be sold to service debts, it argues for financial forethought but it may be that she was simply amassing an estate. She obviously wanted to regularise the situation so on 16 June 1575[21] she surrendered her said several interests to the Queen, paid the fee of £6 13s 4d and had a new 21 years letters patent in her own name, to 'Blanche Parry chief gentlewoman of your majesty's most honourable privy chamber', for Brecknock Mere and the demesne lands in Dynas. This estate Blanche then re-assigned to William Vaughan, Sir Roger's grandson, probably to help him repay debts which had perhaps accumulated since 1571 and which William had been unable to pay before he reached his majority. However, her plans only functioned for two years as William died in 1584 leaving his estate to Blanche and entreating her, probably on his death-bed (in his own nuncupative Will), to pay his debts. In this sad way the fishery and lands had returned to her and she took her responsibilities seriously. Perhaps as an interim measure, she let the holdings to Robert Vaughan the younger brother of John Vaughan, who was also given a lease for life of the manor of Glasbury and was mentioned with his children in her First Will.

In about 1584 she commissioned a map[22] of the Mere / Lake and its surrounding land (Plate 9) to help counter the difficulties with local landowner Hugh Powell of Ty Mawr who, by scouring ditches and erecting (or repairing) a weir and banks, was accused of interfering with the free flow of lake water to the River Llynfi allowing him to purloin the valuable eels. Blanche herself may have initiated the production of this map '... drawn and confessed to be true on both sides ...' or if made at the suggestion of her lawyers she agreed to pay for it. It is drawn from a northern ground level vantage point, a position from which the map still appears to be surprisingly accurate. Such a map, the first known of the area, was typical of Blanche's practical approach, setting out information in a clear order, and was essential in understanding the tangled local politics of the area. This hearing before the Court of the Exchequer had to be deferred by a day due to the non-appearance of Hugh Powell and he was ordered to compensate Blanche '£5 for the fees disbursed to three of her Majesty's learned counsel and to the solicitors and attorneys of the said Blanche Parry' which gives clear information about the legal costs (about £690 in today's value per day) involved.

However, William Vaughan's death had changed everything. Blanche had tried to settle the debts of one nephew and then to help her great-nephew but now it was no longer necessary to retain the land. She decided to sell Scethrog, Moot, Bronllys, Brecknock Mere and Dynas, and invited offers. David Williams of Gwernyfed tried to buy at a reduced price and was refused, as was Robert Knollys, who had married Katherine, William Vaughan's elder sister and who obviously thought family ties might bring him a bargain. Knollys seems to have been angered that another branch of the family now enjoyed the Breconshire leases and was particularly upset that Blanche had refused his offer, especially as she specifically said he could not afford them. Finally Blanche agreed a sale with Hugh Powell of New Sarum, MP and Registrar of the diocese of Salisbury, who already owned the neighbouring manor of Tallyllin. Lord Burghley came to Blanche's aid and he and John Morgan made a conveyance of Scethrog, Moot and Charles Farm to Powell while Blanche assigned him Brecknock Mere and Dynas.

Blanche's difficulties with this property were compounded, resulting in a series of law suits attested by at least 13 bundles of evidence and depositions.[23] This was a litigious age and nearly everyone who could afford to resorted to the courts. In such company Blanche appears to have been rather reluctant to address legal problems, though if she had to she did so intelligently. Much of the trouble seems to have originated with Robert Knollys. He claimed that the mere and demesne lands still belonged to the Vaughan family and that Blanche Parry had no legal right to them. As Sir Roger had died intestate Knollys had also arranged for Sir Roger's cousin, Robert Prosser of Talgarth, to procure Letters of Administration.[24] Prosser then assigned his interest to Knollys, which was evidently the point of the exercise. Furthermore, Knollys stated that Blanche was only able to let the holdings to Robert Vaughan because at that time Katherine Knollys was Blanche's gentlewoman as she 'lived with her and attended upon her',[25] the implication being that the lease to Robert was made on Katherine's behalf. Blanche was obviously very fond of Katherine as she made her handsome bequests in her Final Will.

Local politics now violently intervened. Force was used to take possession of the crannog (the largely artificial island) in Brecknock Mere /

Llangorse Lake, which was then fortified. The situation was further exacerbated by Robert Knollys' instigating a riot which meant that an intimidated court at Brecon Assizes found in his favour, after which he proceeded to pay the Crown rents to the Queen. In the course of the disturbances a night attack by 40 men armed with guns was made on Hugh Powell's house. Apparently Prosser went so far as to drag a ferryboat nearly seven miles from the River Wye, presumably to attack the crannog. All the local householders seem to have been asked to whom they paid rent to try to establish ownership. As litigation continued Blanche asked for the case to be transferred to the Court of the Star Chamber as she maintained, with good cause, that she could not have a fair hearing at Brecon. She said that her case was that her purchase was entirely legal and that she was using the leases to pay William's debts, as she was the executrix of his Will and according to the terms of these leases she was absolutely entitled to do so. Again she stressed her constant attendance on the Queen which also made the transfer to the Star Chamber in London suitable for her. In fact there were at least four cases[26] in the Court of Star Chamber and in each one Blanche was associated with Hugh Powell against various defendants. David Williams and Robert Knollys were both so aggrieved over this course of events that matters were protracted to 1596, long after Blanche's death. By then, in 1594, Robert Knollys had managed to be appointed Custos Rotulorum for Brecon, giving him the influence Sir Roger Vaughan had enjoyed. Despite his claim to wish to help Blanche, it is not surprising that there was nothing in either of Blanche's Wills for Robert Knollys. Katherine's views are not recorded but it cannot have been a happy situation for her. It is clear, however, that she retained Blanche's regard which adds to the evidence that Blanche was not a vindictive person.

According to Robert Knollys he had never intended to offend Mistress Blanche, who was his wife's great-aunt. In a summary of a part of his case he claimed that he held a lease due to expire in 1587, which was the 1566 lease of the Mere / Llangorse Lake and the Dynas demesnes granted to Sir Roger Vaughan. However he said that he was willing to put aside his own claim during Blanche's lifetime 'to benefit her and avoid her displeasure'. He complained that Lord Burghley had refused to accept the surrender of this lease, which would have led to a renewal in Knollys' favour. Burghley's refusal was not surprising as this 1566 lease had already been surrendered to the Crown by Blanche in 1575 before he himself had issued her with her new lease. Knollys maintained that Burghley was causing a deliberate delay so that the complete expiry of the old lease would allow a totally new lease to be granted to Mistress Blanche. Very obliquely but clearly, Knollys is saying that Burghley was favouring Blanche in the matter, which gives an interesting insight into the relationship of these close friends and cousins. Burghley, 13 years younger than Blanche, had known Blanche since her first years at Court and theirs was one of the most enduring friendships of the period.

At some point Blanche was granted the manor of Ketherogh (probably Cilgwrrwg / Kilgwrrwg Common) and Usk which must have delighted her as this was an area where her family had had considerable and long-standing influence. Her grandfather had been steward of Usk and Caerleon in 1453 and her brother still held Trostrey in the lordship of Usk in 1542. She bequeathed the manor to William Vaughan in her First Will and seems to have disposed of it after his death in 1584 as neither name re-appears in her Final Will. It may be that she had already passed the manor to another member of the family.

John Vaughan had been granted the manor of Glasbury, again in the area of family influence, and given it to his mother, Elizabeth (Blanche's eldest sister). On 1 June 1577 he was granted a licence to alienate / transfer it for the use of his Aunt Blanche, who bought it from him for a considerable sum. The date is poignant as he died just 24 days later. He was regularising his affairs knowing that he had only a little time left and Blanche acquired the manor to pay his debts (a massive £700) from unentailed land. Perhaps John had found it expensive to maintain the style of life his wife, Anne, formerly Lady Knyvett, expected, and he must also have found being a member of the Council of the North costly. He also had to pay the annuities entailed upon his manor of Sutton-upon-Derwent. This transaction suggests that Blanche was used to financial responsibility. She helped John, as later she would help his cousin, William. Having bought the manor she then leased it, for an annual rent of £20, to John's brother Robert Vaughan for the term of his life. The clause in the license 'wishing that the said Blanche should not be troubled, vexed, molested or injured in any way' by related matters has a particular poignancy when the later Breconshire situation is considered.[27]

On 25 June 1577 John died. This necessitated further discussions, especially as Blanche felt that she would not survive long herself. It may be that she also wanted to raise funds to pay John's debts. Lord Burghley and John Morgan of Westminster, again came to her rescue. On 1 November they bought, or mortgaged for her, the manor of Glasbury, probably as a surety, and she was granted a licence to alienate it on 27 November 1578. Between these two dates, in her First Will of early November 1578, Blanche requested that if she died, Lord Burghley and John Morgan make an estate from the manor for William Vaughan, presumably adding to the other Brecknock holdings. Presumably Robert Vaughan continued as tenant. It is an interesting point that Blanche was concerned about the fortunes and debts of elder sons, the heirs, namely William Vaughan, grandson of her elder brother, John Vaughan, possibly the eldest surviving son of her eldest sister and later Thomas Powell, again probably the eldest surviving son of another sister. This was English primogeniture in operation rather than the Welsh equal division amongst siblings and illustrates Blanche's anglicisation in this regard. However, none of Blanche's lands in the March were in her possession when she died. She had disposed of them before 1589.

Yorkshire

The former owners of the lands Blanche was granted in Yorkshire had also been monastic houses and the Crown. Her earliest known grants, on 14 June 1567, were two years before the Rising of the Northern Earls. Blanche had already been granted the tenements in Wheldrake[28] and she received the manor in her second, June 1567, grant. John Vaughan was established at Sutton-upon-Derwent and it is reasonable to suggest that he recommended the lands to his aunt. The area is flat, extremely fertile and at that time had hedges and woods primarily of oak. The parish of Sutton borders Wheldrake, adjacent to Escrick and Thorganby, which adjoins Ellerton and then Aughton (the home of Robert Aske, leader of the ill-fated Pilgrimage of Grace in 1536).[29] One can almost hear John assuring his aunt that he could easily 'keep an eye' on this estate for her. Rise too was not very far distant, being north of Hull in the East Riding. Blanche's affection for John was such that she would have been only too delighted to take his advice in the matter.

Wheldrake had belonged to the Cistercian Fountains Abbey and its ownership was preserved in the 'Fountance Dyke' mentioned in Blanche's grant.[30] Blanche would certainly have understood the great sheep ranges of which the grange (monastic farm) at Wheldrake was one. In the 15th century the abbey had found the lush grassland ideal for dairy farming. The parish, partly bisected by the River Derwent where it has changed course, includes an area of the ings, the flood meadows of the river, now protected and rich in flowers and wildfowl. Huge numbers of wading birds flock to the swollen river and then, when the water subsides, the silt allows for herb-rich vegetation. Traditionally hay is cut from the meadows in high summer and then cattle and sheep are run on the ings until the river floods again.[31] Wheldrake village, lying on the Escrick moraine, is south of a surviving portion of Wheldrake Wood.

Blanche also received property and rights of Thorganby Church (formerly a chapelry of Aughton Church) that had belonged to Ellerton / Elreton Priory, a Gilbertine monastery. (The almshouses endowed by Hugh Bethell, now two cottages, are adjacent to Ellerton Church.) Thorganby Church (largely rebuilt in brick in the 18th century) stands in a peaceful location on rising

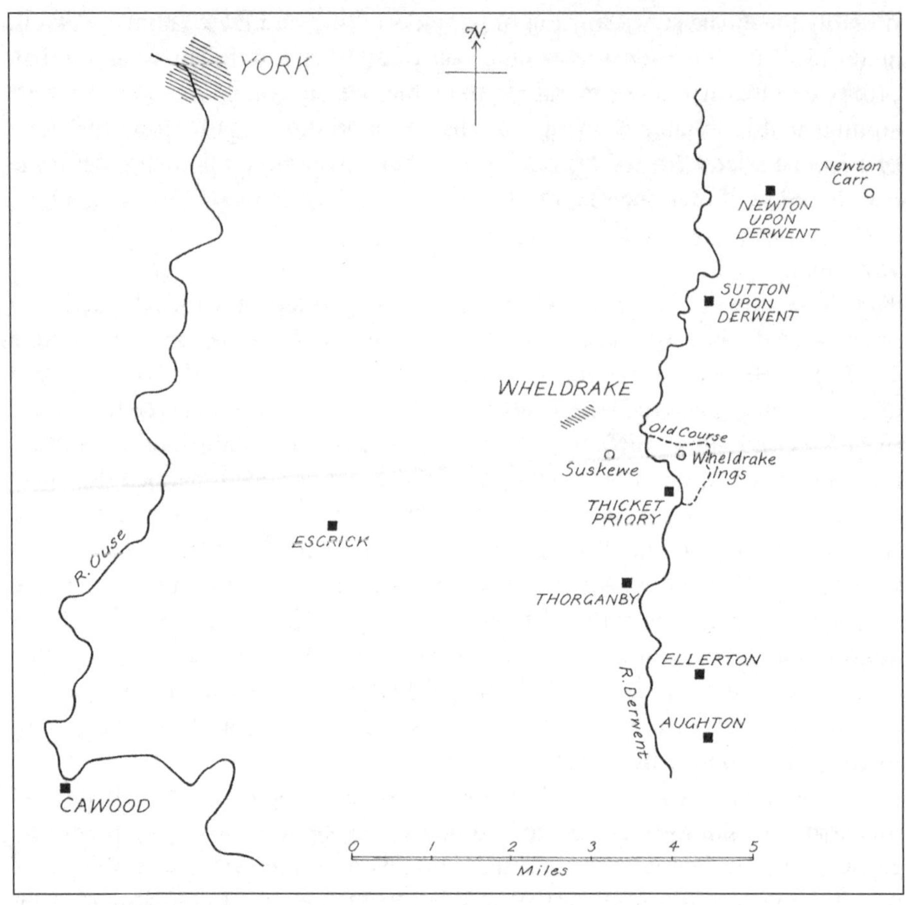

Map showing Blanche Parry's Yorkshire lands (Geoff Gwatkin)

ground above the ings of the west bank of the River Derwent. The oldest remaining parts are the 45ft stone tower, dating to the 12th-15th centuries, and the 14th-century segmented chancel arch. In 1481 bricks, tiles and £13 had been bequeathed to repair the fabric so the Church, as John Vaughan would have known, was in reasonable order when Blanche owned it. In 1527 the chaplain of Thorganby Church received £4 a year and it would have been little more when Blanche had to find and pay for a priest and maintain the chancel of the Church, houses, buildings, fences and enclosures.[32] She was granted the priest's house, 'Holde / Olde House Garth', with the tithe barn and garth. As land which had been given to support a priest was granted away in 1570, Blanche had to find the necessary funds herself. In 1582 the priest house still existed as it was let to Blanche with the rectorial estate. However, she does not mention it in either of her Wills.

Blanche's other manor was that of Rise / Ryse, located about ten miles north-east of Kingston-upon-Hull and about five miles from the east coast. The manor had belonged to the Earl of Warwick, 'the Kingmaker' and after his defeat was granted to Richard, Duke of Gloucester (King Richard III), as a part of the lordship of Sheriff Hutton. Hugh Bethell used the mediaeval manor house (now an earthwork) and his brother's descendants still live in its replacement (the 1820 Rise Park, now Rise Hall) north-west of the old site.

Blanche's first, 14 June 1567, patent,[33] a 'grant for life to Blanche Parie, the Queen's servant, for her service', was in fact an outright gift of the rents of the holdings not reserved to the Crown, which eloquently shows the Queen's regard for her. Where she was to pay rent it was on very favourable terms. A second grant on the same day reiterated that this was for Wheldrake manor and its lands, with named tenants, Thorganby Church and the manor of Rise. It is noteworthy for the reason that is given for the grant: 'Now know that we in consideration of the good and faithful and acceptable service done and devoted to us before this time in many ways by our beloved servant Blanche Parie, of our special grace' and also for the trust placed in her, namely, 'to have and to hold and to enjoy the reversion of all the said properties for the term of her natural life by our gift without any account being made or paid' As the details include a number of field and place names the exact area may be traceable. Many fieldnames arise from the shape of the field, location, agricultural potential, ownership or use.[34] 'Round Acres' may have been the site for staging the local mediaeval mystery plays.[35] These fieldnames, except 'Ingemershe' (ing marsh), 'Westbancke' and the seven closes are repeated in the grant.

As tenant lists are included for both 1551 and 1567 comparisons can be made.[36] The 1551 tenants represented 40 families and 34 of these were still represented in 1567, suggesting remarkable continuity. The wealthiest of the tenants was undoubtedly John Haxbye who lived in a named property, 'Suskewe' (which became Susscars), valued at £4 13s 4d, and who also rented a windmill worth 16 shillings. It seems likely that his sons were George Haxley, Hugh Bethell's servant who moved to the Rise area, and Thomas Haxbye, the tenant of William Berrowe's farm in Blanche's Final Will. The houses mentioned would seem to have been scattered across the parish as only one is described as a 'cottage in Wheldrake', presumably the village. The 1567 list shows the tenants of 26 tenements, 5 messuages and 20 cottages, all legal terms indicating different types of dwelling. All this property and these tenants were now Blanche's responsibility and it seems likely that John Haxbye was given an administrative role by John Vaughan in his aunt's name. As Blanche was assigned Wheldrake 'for 21 years after her decease (paying a rent of £67 17 1¼ per annum)' Wheldrake was not only Blanche's for her lifetime, she was also able to use it for bequests in her Wills.

The Crown here retained 'large trees, woods, underwoods, mines and quarries' as well as legal perquisites, but on 13 December 1572 four woods were added to Blanche's grant for a negligible fine 'paid at the Exchequer'.[37] The surveyor of the woods was very probably Hugh Bethell, who had found a valuable resource for Blanche. One wood was in Wheldrake and two in Rise. The fourth wood, 'in Lawghton in Limracke' and described as surrounded by a ditch, was probably in Laughton-en-le-Morthen (however, 'Limracke' may be Lindric). It was within 15 miles of the former owner, the Cistercian Abbey of St. Mary of the Rock, or Roche, as all this abbey's property was within this radius.

Blanche's patent of 14 June 1567 was presumably superseded by the patents of 13 December 1572 and 7 July 1574, and these lands were a prime concern for her when she became so seriously ill in November 1578 that, with the help of Lord Burghley, she made a nuncupative Will (and they also formed a part of her Final Will). On 1 July 1582 Blanche surrendered a patent to be replaced, on 16 July 1582, when Blanche was 75 years old, by a new grant, which included a 21-year lease of the rectory of Thorganby with its named tenements and appurtenances.[38] The Crown kept the woods and quarries. Such complicated transactions suggest that Blanche's interests were being carefully overseen by her friends, notably Lord Burghley and Queen Elizabeth herself, both of whom Blanche trusted implicitly. Blanche's intelligence was such that, despite her advancing age, it is likely that she was sufficiently financially aware to comprehend the grants the Queen was making available for her.

The Lady Burgh Indenture

Blanche bequeathed Frances (John Vaughan's daughter) the manor of Wheldrake in her First Will of 1578 (in which she had also forgiven a debt Frances owed her). Then Frances, 'the Queen's maid' at Court in 1579, married Thomas Burgh(e) (who would become 5th Baron Borough / Burgh of Gainsborough in Lincolnshire in 1584). This match was extremely advantageous for Frances, who had few lands of her own. A marriage settlement was drawn up on 20 April 1580 which was amended by an Indenture dated 15 December 1583.[39] The parties to the 1580 deed were Lord Burgh and Lady Katherine Burgh (Thomas Burgh's parents), Lord Burghley, Lady Katherine's father Sir Edward Fiennes de Clinton Earl of Lincoln, Lord Burghley's son Sir Thomas Cecil, Dame Anne Knyvett widow of John Vaughan (Frances' mother), Blanche Apparay Gentlewoman of the Privy Chamber, Sir Richard Buckley, Sir Henry Knyvett (Anne's son by her second husband), Thomas

Burgh himself (Frances' husband) and his brother John Burgh — a list which demonstrates the circles in which Blanche moved.

It is apparent that Blanche's involvement was merely as a party to the 1580 Indenture, her name being appended according to rank, and was perhaps essential if she had been a trustee of the settlements previously made by John Vaughan. The land in question belonged to Lord Burgh (not to Blanche as Bradford thought), though Blanche's position at Court may have mollified Thomas Burgh's parents.

Blanche's Wills

Blanche's First (nuncupative) Will of November 1578

Internal evidence in the surviving notes for this Will (see Appendix 2) shows that Blanche was seriously ill between 2 and 26 November 1578. As she was now 71 years old, considered a venerable age at that time, she certainly thought that this would be her last illness. A Will, considered the last testament of a person who was imminently entering the presence of God, was rarely made long in advance of death. Lord Burghley was notified and he personally sat with the old lady, writing out her Will from her dictation. The style and changes make for a real and fascinating immediacy as Burghley attempts to obtain clarity from the ailing Blanche. Blanche started with a religious declaration, a short preamble that includes the word 'declare' which, with her mention of the single word 'Jesus' (also on the dorse), indicate that this was a nuncupative Will, a formal oral statement which was made because the testator was unable to sign it and which had to be sworn by witnesses, here William Vaughan, his two sisters and his two cousins (children of John Vaughan). Indeed, Blanche may have simply discussed matters with Burghley and provided a list of relatives and friends to which he later added the bequests she had mentioned. It was evidently thought that there was no time to produce a properly written Will, for Blanche says that 'there are many things requisite to be devised by me that can not for lack of time at this present be put into writing', but Burghley did his very best for his old friend and cousin.[40] He even noted what should happen 'if God shall call the said Blanch out of this life before any redemption'.

The most poignant moments are the changes of tense indicating where Blanche was finding it difficult to concentrate. At one point William promised her to provide a house for the vicar of Bacton and she roused herself to remember that he would need ready money. Blanche is still meticulous for she asks that only proved debts be paid and that a discharge certificate for her heirs be obtained. Her thoughts are with her family and she focuses on the tomb which she had already prepared at Bacton Church, her family's mausoleum. Such considerations of close relatives and of her tomb are typical of the very sick and further support this being a nuncupative Will.

However, remarkably, Blanche recovered and this indomitable old lady resumed her duties. She remained in good health until July 1587 when she handed over the care of the Queen's jewels to Mary Radcliffe. By this time Blanche was blind, perhaps with untreated cataracts, and she was evidently being regularly examined by Mr. Hugh Morgan, the Queen's apothecary. However, it was another two years before she felt the need to finalise her Will. Although she knew she would not need to retire from Court as she would not now outlive the Queen, Blanche was still active, recording her wish in her Final Will 'to be buried in the parish Church of St Margaret's within the City of Westminster, near unto my nephew John Vaughan, if it please God to

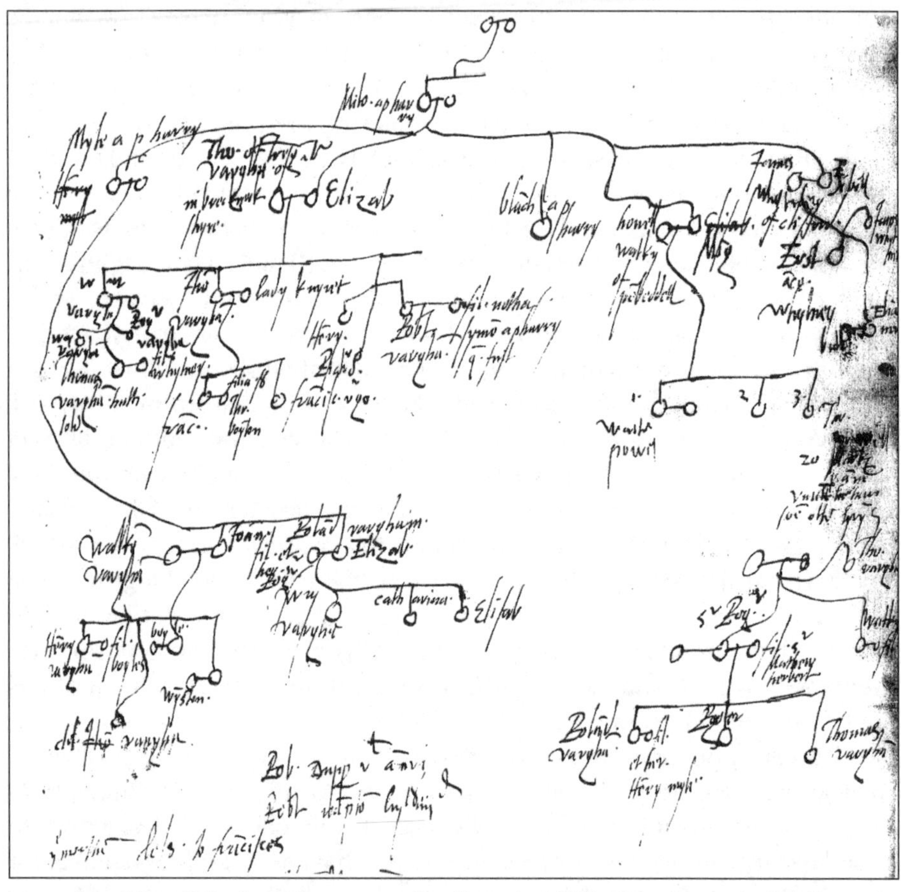

Lord Burghley's rudimentary family tree of Blanche Parry's family (BL Lansdowne 109 no. 90)

call me near London'. It is clear that Blanche was even now able to accompany Queen Elizabeth on the round of her palaces and on her regular summer progress. Although Blanche's total estate was not comparable to that of the Earl of Leicester or of Burghley himself, the incomplete totals available indicate that, with some financial acumen, she had nearly trebled the amounts at her personal disposal, probably from her estate rents and possibly from investments, and in addition she had acquired some lovely jewellery.

By 1589 Burghley, now formally named as Supervisor of Blanche's Will, evidently had as much difficulty in identifying Blanche's relations as we do now and so, as an 'aide memoire' for fulfilling her final bequests, he wrote out a rudimentary family tree.[41] The whole business of listening to Blanche's bequests must have taken a great deal of time, which graphically illustrates Burghley's regard for her. Already in his 60s, in 1590 he would become deaf so it is likely that he was already somewhat hard of hearing. In addition Blanche knew that he was becoming forgetful at times, hence her poignant bequest to Burghley's son, Sir Robert Cecil, to remind his father to carry out her instructions, although in the event this was unnecessary.

Blanche's Final Will of 1589

Blanche's Final Will and Testament of 1589 (see Appendix 2) was written to her dictation and this time she was able to sign it, albeit shakily. It is a more considered document. Blanche was now 82 years old and realising that her death could not be long delayed, she put her affairs in order, again with the help of Lord Burghley. An analysis demonstrates that the document's structure is determined by religious considerations and the frequency of contact, or close relationship, Blanche had with beneficiaries. It also shows the very special regard she had for Hugh Bethell. Blanche's main beneficiaries were Francis Vaughan and Hugh Bethell, while her executors were Thomas Powell and Hugh Bethell. Hugh was the only one so favoured who was not a close relation, the reason probably being his friendship with his contemporary, John Vaughan.

Blanche bequeathed her soul into 'the hands of God, Father, Son and Holy Ghost …' for, while belief in Purgatory was no longer acceptable, it was still thought that a person dying in a state of grace had a better chance of a place in Heaven. One way to achieve this, which was popular throughout the 16th century, was to give alms to the poor. In her First Will Blanche tried to resurrect a Parish Store in Bacton and to arrange for a house to be used by the vicar. By her Final Will provision for the poor had crystallised into building an almshouse and providing funds to repair the highways from Newcourt to Morehampton and Newcourt to Dore, showing that Blanche knew of the deplorable state of the local roads, which demonstrates how closely she kept in touch with the area. By 1589 she had realised the impossibility of re-establishing a Parish Store so she bequeathed money to the poor of Bacton and to the poor of Newton on the perimeter of Newcourt Park. As she was also now more involved with the City of Westminster, the poor here were also remembered and Dean Gabriel Goodman was asked personally to oversee the gift.

This was how matters stood until 2 December 1589 when Blanche found that her plan for an almshouse in Bacton was also impossible and she was forced to change her bequest. In 1587 there had been a severe harvest failure and so, evidently being apprised of the local situation, she made an alternative arrangement to be overseen by the Dean and Chapter of Hereford Cathedral. She obviously considered a Dean suitable for dispensing such alms, perhaps because she knew and admired the work of Dean Goodman (at Westminster 1561-1601) who actively promoted learning, had encouraged the investigations of the antiquarian William Camden and had helped with the publication of the Welsh Bible in 1588. However, Blanche may have met John Watkins, the Dean of Hereford 1574-1593, when his quarrel with Bishop John Scory was investigated by the Privy Council in 1582, and it may have been this discord, plus her local knowledge, that caused her to couple the Chapter with the Dean of Hereford in her bequest. A small point perhaps but one that may demonstrate the meticulous care she showed in her business affairs. The saga also demonstrates the importance Blanche placed on the religious duty of aiding the poor.

Blanche's friends at the Royal Court were only listed in full in her Final Will. Apart from the Queen and Lord Burghley himself, few of the Royal Household were mentioned in her First Will, though bequests were made to the Grooms and Maids of the Privy Chamber. This is entirely understandable, as Blanche was otherwise concerned with family and servants. The closest group around the Queen had been Burghley, Hatton, Blanche Parry and Robert Dudley, Earl of Leicester and, of these, Leicester had died in 1587. (His Will mentioned only two women, the Queen and his wife.)

Queen Elizabeth I was the most important person in Blanche's world. In her First Will Blanche described her as 'my dear Sovereign lady and mistress'. However, her affection did not blinker her to Elizabeth's possible parsimony and the need to take necessary precautions. Blanche directed that a discharge certificate be obtained for her heirs so that 'all jewels and other things belonging to her Majesty' were properly accounted. Otherwise, Blanche's heirs would have had to make good the monetary value. She was also anxious to ensure that the fine for William Berrowe's farm was paid (deducted from the annuities accruing from the Wheldrake estate).

Blanche bequeathed the Queen 'a pair of sables garnished with 8 chains of gold'. These furs were very probably the ones given to Blanche by the Queen in 1569, rather than the ones from 1579 which were described as 'old'. If so, Blanche had added the chains herself. Jewels were left to William Vaughan, to his two sisters and to Francis Vaughan and his sister. Presumably Blanche did not acquire jewels of note as her personal property until near the end of her life. Then, in her Final Will, she was in a position to leave the Queen her 'best diamond', with no reference as to its setting, though it is sure to have been sufficiently striking to please the Queen, who loved jewels.

In formulating her Final Will Blanche had the time to ensure that she always used correct titles and designations. For example, she referred to Sir Christopher Hatton (*c*.1540-1591) as Lord Chancellor, a post to which he was appointed in 1587. Hatton had been on daily attendance at Court since becoming a Gentleman Pensioner in 1564, his subsequent promotions only bringing him closer to the Sovereign. He was a generation (at least 33 years) younger than Blanche but that they were friends within the Queen's close circle is suggested by his position in her Final Will and by the picture of the Presence Chamber which shows them standing together. Hatton never married but he may have had an illegitimate daughter, Elizabeth, who seems to have had an association with the much older Sir John Perrot. Hatton's biographer[42] noted that the evidence suggests that the two men thoroughly disliked each other. If that is true, the fact that Sir John Perrot (*c*.1527-1592), a Protestant, was also Blanche's beneficiary demonstrates that she took no part in such discord. It may be that she was grateful for his influence in helping her great-nephew Rowland Vaughan, as Sir John had responsibilities in Ireland in 1570-1573 heading the newly created presidency of Munster and again in 1584 when he was appointed Lord Deputy of Ireland.

Lady Cobham was a close friend, known to Blanche since the troubled times of Queen Mary, and Blanche's very handsome bequest to her was similar to Queen Elizabeth's own chain of gold enamelled green with 101 gold knobs, which was listed in the July 1587 Inventory of the Queen's Jewels. Of Lady Cobham's seven children only one of her twin girls was remembered and the bequest was to provide her with a wedding present for her marriage to Robert Cecil on 31 August 1589. The token ring given to Mr. R. Williams, Lord Cobham's steward, suggests that Blanche had used his services and shows her care to remember anyone who had been helpful to her. Blanche's other great friend in the household, Lady Dorothy Stafford, was bequeathed a diamond set in gold with a broad hoop.

Blanche remembered several of her godchildren, of whom the 6-year-old Lady Blanche Somerset was one. Although her father, the 4th Earl of

Worcester, was a convinced Roman Catholic, he was also a favourite of the Queen. Despite her age, Blanche (then in her 70s) was still considered sufficiently important to be asked to be godmother, presumably in an 'official' Church of England ceremony. (Lady Blanche would become famous for her spirited defence of Wardour Castle during the Civil War.) Another Roman Catholic and close friend was Lord Lumley, a great collector of paintings and sculpture some of which he may have displayed at Nonsuch, which he had bought and where the Queen regularly visited him. Perhaps it was here that Blanche acquired her interest in sculpture.

Sir William Cecil, Lord Burghley, 1520-1598, was not only a prominent member of the government but also, as he said himself, Blanche's 'cousin'. Their kinship was a relationship that both Blanche and Burghley considered important. Blanche certainly knew the Cecil family home of Alt yr Ynys, about seven miles south of Newcourt. In her First Will Blanche calls him 'my friend'. He agreed to oversee the legacies and bequests to be made in both her Wills, continuing steadfastly in this role, and Blanche left him her second diamond and £50 to compensate him for acting as her Supervisor. Burghley's steward, Mr. Coppe, 'my Lord Treasurer's man', was remembered and so is likely to have helped Blanche and the three witnesses to her Final Will were also connected with the government.

Blanche's Final Will is unusual in providing bequests to more women than men; women are notoriously difficult to trace through documents and family pedigrees at this early period. By the time Blanche died her nearest surviving relations were descended through the female line. Two of her cousins were connected with the Court, John Parry (descended from the Parrys of Poston) and his brother James, who had considered the connection with Blanche to be so important that unusually he had named his son Blanch and asked her to be his godmother. Blanche's brother, Symond, had died in 1573 but his daughter Maud Berrowe was remembered. Her son William Berrowe, described by Blanche as her servant, was initially bequeathed money and then left Suskewe Farm in Wheldrake.

The Powell family were the descendants of Blanche's sister Margaret, who had died before 1589. Interestingly, her unmarried daughter was bequeathed twice as much as her sisters, so it is likely that she was Blanche's goddaughter and so was named Blanche too. The sum could even have been intended as a dowry but it may just be that Blanche knew only too well that an unmarried girl needed more support than one who was married. The provision for redistribution if any child died before Blanche meant that the family's portion remained the same and is indicative of Blanche's care for fine detail. However, by 1589 Thomas was singled out, perhaps because he was the eldest surviving son. Described as 'of the City of London, gent.', he was Blanche's joint executor and bequeathed not only his unchanged annuity but also, with Hugh Bethell, the 'rest [of her] goods moveable and unmoveable not bequeathed'.

There were at least four Vaughan branches in the family so it was no wonder that Lord Burghley felt the need to scribble down a Family Tree in 1589 to work out to whom he had to pay bequests. Of these, the most valuable were made to the descendants of Blanche's sister Elizabeth, Blanche's favourite being John Vaughan, and it was his son Francis who, jointly with Hugh Bethell, was given the Rise and Wheldrake leases, as well as plate. His sister Frances, designated 'the Right Honourable the Lady Frances Burghe my Niece', was the chief mourner at Blanche's funeral. This was not only due to her evident and continued closeness to Blanche but because her rank of baroness was commensurate with the rank accorded Blanche at her funeral. Blanche also remembered the family of her elder brother, Milo ap Harry, whose two daughters (Joan and Elizabeth) and joint heiresses had married Vaughans. Joan's eldest child was Harry / Henry Vaughan of Moccas, for whom Blanche is said to have obtained the Stewardship of Brecon Castle[43] but he had died by 1589. His sister Catherine was connected by marriage with Sir Francis Walsingham (the brother of her second husband, Sir Henry Gate, married Walsingham's sister). Her surviving brother was Rowland Vaughan and it is perhaps significant that Blanche's bequest to him came before her admonition that if any beneficiary tried to contest her Will, or troubled her Executors, then that person would not receive anything.

Elizabeth's (Joan's sister) son was William Vaughan, whom Blanche intended to be a very significant beneficiary, probably because he was to inherit Newcourt. However, William's death without heirs in 1584 changed the situation and Blanche had to alter her intentions in 1589. It must have been very hard for her to lose first John Vaughan and then William Vaughan, both of whom could have been expected to outlive her.

William's elder sister was Katherine Vaughan whose mention in Margaret Dane's Will of May 1579 suggests that she married in 1579-1580, her husband being Robert Knollys / Knowles, son of Sir Francis Knollys, a convinced Protestant and Lord Hunsdon's nephew. Sir Francis held various posts at Court including, in 1566, that of Treasurer of the Queen's Chamber. All the Knollys brothers were prominent courtiers, so although Robert was only the fourth son, such a marriage with Katherine Vaughan may only have come about because of the proximity of Blanche Parry to the Queen. Katherine was Blanche's waiting gentlewoman[44] and this was certainly the reason she received such personal bequests in Blanche's Final Will. Her two daughters,

Lettice and Frances, were remembered and Blanche evidently saw them often at Court. Lettice was a family name and Robert Knollys' sister, also Lettice, was the mother of the Earl of Essex and later married the Earl of Leicester.

The Whitney family of Clifford[45] were relations of Blanche's sister Sybil who married James Whitney of Clifford and although both had died before 1578, several descendants were remembered. A granddaughter had married one of Blanche's servants and another was Elinor Bull (in whose house in Deptford the playwright Christopher Marlowe was stabbed in 1593). Many of the Whitneys moved to the London area and several of these were the descendants of the other branch of the family, that of Robert Whitney of Whitney, the son of Lady Troy. The senior Whitney family in the United States are descended from Thomas Whitney, gentleman, of Lambeth Marsh, who was married in St. Margaret's Church, Westminster in 1583, where his son John, the Puritan emigrant, would be baptised in 1592. This continued the family connection with St. Margaret's Church where John Vaughan and Blanche herself were buried. Anne Whitney (Blanche's cousin) was Blanche's 'waiting gentlewoman' in 1589.

John Morgan of Westminster, married to Susan, was another kinsman, probably Blanche's first Steward, or man-of-business, a position later filled (at least in Yorkshire) by Hugh Bethell. John and Susan Morgan evidently lived in a house in Westminster which was either owned by Blanche or where she kept her own furnished rooms. When her First Will was made Blanche had a further five male servants, of whom Robert Haxby seems to have been a member of the Yorkshire family who were her tenants, showing that Blanche's patronage was not just confined to the Welsh border. In addition, her great-nephew Rowland Vaughan served her for some years, while her brother Symond and cousin John ap Harry of Dulas were her Herefordshire agents. Blanche's Final Will of 1589 shows that at the end of her life her complement of personal servants had increased. Her reference to William, her chamber keeper (in charge of her rooms) proves that Blanche had a separate staff of her own and her establishment then included William Berrowe, Anne Whitney, three other women servants, several yeomen and Mark Stanburne, 'her boy'. However, she must also have been served by members of the Queen's household for she comprehensively remembered each Lady, Gentlewoman, Groom and Maid of Honour and the six pages in the Privy Chamber, as well as particular servants.

7 *A Maid Did End My Life*
The Meaning of Blanche's Monuments

Blanche died, aged 82, on Thursday, 12 February 1590, almost certainly at the Palace of Westminster. On 17 February 1590 Thomas Markham wrote to the Earl of Shrewsbury from Westminster. Halfway through his letter he mentions that 'Thursday last Mrs Blanche Aparrye departed, blind she was here on earth but I hope the joys in heaven she shall see. Her Majesty, God be praised, is in health. My Lord Treasurer … keepeth his chamber, the gout and wind in his stomach is the cause …'.[1] Lord Burghley may have felt unwell but he still opened Blanche's Will on 17 February, the same day as Markham wrote his letter. Markham's affectionate remarks surely show that she was a much loved lady who was much mourned.

Blanche's funeral, which took place in the late evening of 27 February, was of the degree of state accorded a baroness and the burial register shows that hers was the only one that day. Blanche had intended for her 'funerals' (the procession, Church Service and internment) to be magnificent and left £300 (£37,000 in today's value) for the purpose but in the event the Queen herself paid all the expenses. The Queen never attended any funeral, so Blanche's chief mourner, who by custom would be of the same rank and sex as the deceased, was her great-niece Frances, Lady Burgh. The 15 days between Blanche's death and funeral allowed family, friends and tenants to travel from Herefordshire, Wales and Yorkshire. Processions were a feature of Elizabethan funerals and Blanche's status ensured that hers would have included one. A contemporary letter, without mentioning Blanche by name (so perhaps unconnected), noted Robert Knollys' observation of the great sorrow at this time shown by the Queen and the ladies of the Privy Chamber.[2] The Queen was 56 years old and for the first time in her life she had no-one who closely remembered her childhood and young womanhood, or had known the mother whom she only ever mentioned in private. Blanche had been this precious link with Elizabeth's past. Perhaps, too, Blanche's example of living unmarried successfully had given the Queen the confidence to refuse marriage for herself. Whether or not Blanche had an influence on this aspect of the Queen's life and reign, she had certainly given her stability in her private life. Blanche's passing, so closely following that of the Earl of Leicester in 1588, must have been devastating for Elizabeth.

The funeral ceremonial was indeed impressive for this girl from the Welsh March who had grown up to become a Queen's confidante and longest-surviving friend. Blanche was buried near her beloved nephew John Vaughan, as she requested in her Final Will, and five years later her executor, Thomas Powell, who lived in the City of London, arranged for her tomb to be embellished with a beautiful monument. All involved carried out her wishes exactly, demonstrating the affection, regard and respect in which she was held. The angle of Blanche's face on her effigy and the phrasing of her epitaph indicate that she was buried in the chancel of Saint Margaret's Church, her monument being placed on the south wall. This was the church whose bells she had heard every time the Queen travelled through London, ringing when she left for her other palaces, such as from Greenwich to Otelands and on her return to Saint James'.[3] They rang with all the other church bells for the celebrations of the reign, such as the great Church Festivals, the Queen's birthday on 7 September and her Accession Day on 17 November. The church must have been not only Blanche's local parish church but a symbol of such celebration for her, and being buried there would maintain her link with the Queen.

In the 1570s Blanche had already written her own valediction for her monument in Bacton Church, setting out who she was and where she was trained, placing this within the context of the world's vanities. She says that Princes' Courts were filled with the gorgeously arrayed but the honours were all too fleeting. Although lodged within her tomb she has paid all the dues she owed. Her friends may speak of regretting her passing but this is the end of all her worldly state, drawing the moral that it is the same for all who gather acquisitions according to their rank. Blanche then returns to her life history. She was always the handmaid to a Queen and spent her time in the chief, or Privy, Chamber. She did not have to try to acquire possessions, even though time was passing, because she had no doubt that while her mistress lived she would always be looked after. (In fact, though, while Blanche had good reason to believe this as she had known of Lady Troy's pension, she had also taken steps in the past to furnish her possible retirement at Newcourt.) She had served her mistress from babyhood, right through to when she achieved her Crown and to the present day. She slides over the period of Elizabeth's dangerous childhood and young womanhood which may suggest how painful and uncertain this time really had been. Blanche then points out that she had spent her time listening to the cases and difficulties sent to her and raising them with the Queen. Her reward was in serving the Queen.

Blanche reiterates that she remained a maid, never married, was a sworn member of the Queen's Head / Privy Chamber and 'with maiden Queen a maid did end my life'. There can be little doubt from this that the Queen's and Blanche's unmarried status was supremely important to both of them. She calls the Queen 'Ellsbeth', which may be a diminutive or may be the way Elizabeth was pronounced at the time. All this was written over 12 years before her death and demonstrates that Blanche, even then an old lady by the standards of the time, was concerned with her own mortality and that of friends. She does not speak of a hope of salvation and indeed she mentions that death is the 'end of all'. In fact, her view of death is utterly pragmatic in that she has paid all her dues, which would include emotional as well as financial commitments, and she has been utterly faithful to the Queen, her mistress, serving her to the best of her ability. She implies that it would only be fair of God to take such service into account. All this complements her view of the Queen as a religious icon, as examined later.

In contrast to her Bacton epitaph, which she wrote herself, the inscription beneath Blanche's Saint Margaret's tomb monument (see overleaf) was written and placed there by Thomas Powell, her executor, who did not know that her father had never been known as Henry Parry. It is likely that he had received some instructions from Blanche, or he may have consulted her friends, especially Lady Burgh, Lord Burghley and Hugh Bethell, concerning the content but the result is a factual summary of Blanche's importance. Here her origins are stated, followed by her position as Chief Gentlewoman of the Privy Chamber and the Keeper of the Queen's Jewels. Her length of service is noted and her duties mentioned, showing that she was instrumental in helping those in difficulties. Her charitable bequests to the poor of Bacton and Newton are given in detail, indicating the hand of Thomas Powell who had been very involved with these as the 1590 Garnons Indenture shows. The bequests to Westminster are included but these were the concern of the Dean so were not given in detail. The fact that Blanche gave money 'to other places for good uses', may possibly allude to the expenses involved in the printing of the Welsh Bible for the juxtaposition with Westminster is interesting. The phrase also indicates that she was generous in other ways. It then reiterates that she was unmarried and closes with her age and date of death. The phrasing may suggest that Thomas Powell had seen a transcript of the Bacton epitaph.

HERE VNDER IS INTOMBED BLANCHE PARRYE, DAUGHTER OF HENRY PARRYE OF NEWCOURT WTHIN THE COVNTY
OF HEREF: ESQVIER, CHIEFE GENTLEWOMÃ OF QUEENE ELIZABETHES MOST HONORABLE PRIVIE CHAMBER AND KEPER
OF HER MA:TIES IVELLS, WHOME SHE FAITHFVLLIE SERVED FROM HER HIGHNES BIRTH, BENEFICIALL TO HER KINSFOLKE
AND COVTRYEMEN, CHARITABLE TO THE POORE, INSOMVCHE THAT SHE GAVE TO THE POORE OF BACTON,
AND NEWTON IN HEREFORDSHIERE SEAVEN SCORE BVSHELLS OF WHEATE & RYE YERELIE FOREVER WTH
DIVERS SOMES OF MONEY TO WESTMINSTEER AND OTHER PLACES FOR GOOD VSES, SHE DIED A MAIDE
IN THE EIGHTTE TWO YERES OF HER AGE THE TWELFE OF FEBRVARYE, 1589 [1590 in modern reckoning]

Blanche Parry's epitaph in Saint Margaret's Church, Westminster

Blanche's Tomb in Saint Margaret's, Westminster (Plate 14)
It was not until 1596 that the Churchwardens' accounts record 'Received of Mr. Powell [Thomas Powell] one of the Executors of Mrs. Blanche Parry for license and composition with the parish to erect and set up a monument for the said Mrs Blanche Parry in the parish church 20s.' An addition noted that 'Paid to the joiner for making the new pews under Mrs Blanche Parry's tomb 7s-6d', suggesting that pews had to be removed during the erection of the monument. However, the whole appearance of Blanche's statue suggests that this at least was sculpted from earlier drawings and perhaps studies of Blanche in the last months of her life.

Tudor period tombs and monuments were opportunities for theatrical expression, building on the theatrical experiences that were the descendants of the religious and political festivities of Blanche's youth, such as the Corpus Christi plays. All the evidence suggests that people at the time recognised their allotted role in life and usually played the parts expected of them. This could be seen in Queen Elizabeth's response to the varying pageants enacted before her. It could be seen in the elaborate ceremonial and masques performed at Court. It extended to the processions and ceremonial attached to local and civic affairs. It could even be seen in the drama of executions. Such illustrious victims as Queen Anne Boleyn, Queen Katherine Howard, Sir Thomas More and, in Elizabeth's reign, Mary, Queen of Scots and the Earl of Essex were not bound. They all walked to the scaffold, gave the expected speeches, forgave the executioner and knelt for the death blow. They followed a procedure, almost a play script, the choreography of execution, and witnesses noted every nuance of action and speech. This attention to the meaning of any publicly observed action was also extended to tombs and monuments. Indeed, tombs were seen as conveying a message, a final statement of the deceased's, or of their family's, summation of the life now ended.

Blanche initially made arrangements to be buried in the Parry family mausoleum at Bacton Church in Herefordshire but by 1589 she had decided to be buried near John Vaughan in Saint Margaret's Church, Westminster, a Royal Peculiar attached to the Collegiate Church of St. Peter, Westminster (Westminster Abbey). Thomas Powell made arrangements for her monument, which, from her statue's angle, has to have been originally positioned on the south wall of the church. Indeed, according to George Ballard in the 18th century,[4] it was 'on the fourth wall of the Chancel', placing it as near to the altar as the tomb of any contemporary aristocrat. In later years it was removed to the church tower. It now forms a pair, flanking the church's main doorway, with the plainer monument of Blanche's great friend Lady Dorothy Stafford. It is amazing that both monuments have survived restoration and war damage.

Between them, above the west door, in a 19th-century window commemorating Sir Walter Raleigh, the figure of Queen Elizabeth herself forms a neat juxtaposition.

Blanche's monument is exceptionally striking.[5] It is beautifully carved and richly decorated and we can meet her as she was when she was alive. Almost certainly the face of her kneeling statue is a good likeness, as it is not the bland countenance so often found on Elizabethan tombs. It is full of character and was evidently sculpted by someone who had known her. She has high cheekbones, pursed lips, slightly slanting eyebrows and piercing eyes. Her expression is studied, showing an intelligent depth of thought as she gazes fixedly towards the High Altar and into the next world, a concentration that may of course simply have originated in her need to focus, to compensate for blindness. If she was suffering from cataracts, it is possible she could still distinguish between light and dark. Her decorated, curved black, probably velvet, French hood allows her hair, which appears reasonably abundant, to frame her face, while the rear jewelled band is placed over the join with the veil. Her neck is hidden by a flattering white high closed goffered ruff, tied by tasselled band-strings, of the medium size fashionable from the 1570s when it was worn, as here, immediately below the chin. She has matching rufflets at her wrists, where the only damage is the loss of her (perhaps folded) hands. The pleats of a white cambric or lawn undergarment cover her décolletage, an exquisite fashion that hid the wrinkles attendant on ageing, over which she wears a double chain with what seems to be a pendant. Her black satin dress has full sleeves, no apparent waist, tabbed peckadils decorating the shoulders and a narrow mantle worn as a train. Blanche is clearly shown in the Queen's livery but her clothes are of the finest, showing impeccable style and a quiet good taste. As with the Bacton monument it seems likely that Blanche held something in her hands and, if the sculptors were given the same directions, it was probably similar to what is apparently a small pomander at Bacton.

She kneels on a dark red cushion with gold tassels and trim, again a mark of rank. The same colours are repeated on the trim of the black covering of the prayer desk in front of her. It holds a double book rest with two similar sized books in place perhaps to remind the onlooker that Blanche often received books for the Queen. It is also possible that they were intended to be the two companion editions of the Bible, in Welsh and English. The whole is placed in an arched recess, tastefully decorated with a guilloche pattern, the soffit having a strapwork setting of four Tudor roses alternating with five red inverted pyramids. The supporting pillars and the architrave are sumptuously decorated using marble, alabaster and gilding. The design below the two pedestals of the pillars includes coloured carvings of jewelled necklaces to signify Blanche's position as Keeper of her Majesty's Jewels. Two finials which surmounted the pillars are now missing but the central coat-of-arms is still in position.

The entry for Blanche in the Saint Margaret's burial register has a cross against her name to indicate that she was a member of the aristocracy. Her status was emphasised by the coat-of-arms surmounting her monument, which is a lozenge, the shape used for females, with eight quarterings.[6] It represents the arms of her father quartered with those of her mother and other armorial heiresses who had married into their families and were thus Blanche's direct ancestors. For instance, her grandmother, Joan Stradling, was not an heiress, so she is not represented, as she had a brother who was their father's heir. It is difficult to be certain of all the designations as it is possible the colours have been inadvertently changed over the intervening years and also that the design of the actual arms was slightly different in the 16th century but bearing these caveats in mind, the quarterings appear to be as follows:

1 and 8 – Definitely Parry of Newcourt, the arms of Blanche's father: *Argent a Fesse between 3 Lozenges Azure, a bordure of Azure*.

2 – Probably Gwilym / Gwillim from Mawd the heiress of Gwilym Llwyd of Tregunter who married Gruffudd ap Henry, bringing Trostrey to her marriage. She was celebrated by the bards and was Blanche's paternal great-great-grandmother. So this quartering was perhaps: *Argent a lion rampant Ermines collared Or*. The bardic poems certainly show that Mawd's memory was important to Blanche's family.

3 – Definitely Barr or de la Barre, for Mawd's mother, daughter of Gwillim / William de Barr (son of Gerald de Barr), suggesting she was an heiress: *Gules 3 bars gobonny Argent and Sable*. As all the evidence shows Blanche was meticulous in requiring accuracy it is evident that she believed Mawd's mother to have been an heiress. This Barr connection further linked Blanche with Sir James Croft, Comptroller of Queen Elizabeth's Household and also with the Sidney family (and through them with the Earl of Leicester).

4 – This should probably be the Furnival arms, from the mother of Elizabeth Eynesford (Simon Milborne's mother and Blanche's maternal great-great-grandmother). However, as both Elizabeth and her mother were heiresses, both should be represented.

5 – Definitely Milborne, as Blanche's mother, Alice Milborne, was a joint heiress: *Gules a Chevron Ermines between 3 Escallops Argent*.

6 – Probably Baskerville as Jane Baskerville was Alice Milborne's mother and so Blanche's maternal grandmother and as she was an heiress she brought her arms to her husband when she married Simon Milborne: *Argent a Chevron Gules between 3 roundels Azure*.

7 – Probably Blaket / Blackett as Jane Baskerville's mother was the heiress of John Blaket of Icomb, Gloucestershire, the manor Jane brought to her marriage and which was inherited by her daughter Blanche Milborne (later Lady Troy, sister of Alice Milborne): *Azure a bend cotised between 3 cross crosslets fitchy Or*.

These suggested designations show that the coat-of-arms used probable quarterings from five previous generations. As this was Blanche's personal coat-of-arms she would have used it with pride during her life, especially as it was proof of her gentle status.

The Saint Margaret's tomb is the work of a master. As Blanche arranged her Bacton monument herself, it is possible that she approved at least preliminary designs for this tomb as well. Magnificent and tasteful, it is a summation of Blanche's worldly status — a statement of her rank and of her exceptional closeness to the Queen. The only religious aspect is in her determined expression as she tries to overcome her blindness to gaze at the High Altar.

Paintings of Blanche

Apart from her possible inclusion in pictures alluded to earlier, there are two other paintings reputed to be of Blanche that must be mentioned. The first is a full-length portrait now in Tredegar House, Newport, Monmouthshire of a young woman wearing the fashionable court dress of the later 16th century, reputed to be by the Italian painter Frederigo Zuccaro, who was in England for only six months in 1575.[7] Both the style of clothes and the presumed date mean that the sitter cannot be Blanche, who was an old lady in the 1570s, but she is very probably a goddaughter. The second painting, a head-and-shoulders portrait, in the private hands of a Parry descendant, is noteworthy for the sitter's glorious eyes, a feature which has descended through subsequent generations. Her style of hat and ruff suggests a date after 1575, which again is wrong for the elderly Blanche, but both girls do show a family resemblance to Blanche.

However, there is another painting that is almost certainly a true likeness of Blanche. It is a head-and-shoulders portrait that is strikingly similar to that of the young girl described above. However, this portrait is of an elderly lady wearing a fairly large deeply indented ruff, a white cap edged with lace and a brimmed beaver hat that could be considered to be, but need not have been, in a Welsh style. Despite her age she has eyes that must once have been beautiful and while her face is lined, her angular features remain imposing. Her high cheekbones, straight nose and penetrating, intelligent eyes give her an enduring handsomeness. It would be fascinating to subject this picture to a modern examination, especially as the position of the sitter, the strongly modelled face, slightly pursed lips and eyes looking directly at the viewer, suggest that the artist was George Gower. Gower would become Sergeant Painter to the Queen in 1581 but he was already fashionable in the 1570s when Blanche was designing her Bacton tomb. According to Walter Pilley (writing in 1886): 'The portrait is painted in oils on an oak panel (glued up in two pieces) 17½ inches in height by 13⅞ inches wide ... The face is fairly but thinly painted ...'. 'A°1593' is written in the top left corner but without any apparent explanation. Nothing is known of the colours, as this arresting portrait is only known from a monochrome photograph that Walter Pilley,[8] a Hereford antiquarian, arranged to have taken in October 1886.

Blanche Parry (Pilley Collection, Hereford City Library)

At that time the picture belonged to Mrs. Laura Louisa Petherick Jenkins, the widow of Henry Jones Jenkins Esq., of 'Copelands', Holmer, immediately north of Hereford. Henry Jenkins had bought the picture in about 1860 at the Newcourt auction. When Mrs. Jenkins died in 1908 a sale was held, which was reported in the two local newspapers. On 27 June a notice placed in *The Hereford Journal* advertised the forthcoming sale of The Jenkins Collection which included 'two oil paintings "Queen Elizabeth" and "Blanch Parry" ... Two armchairs, Elizabethan age, once the property of Blanch Parry, Maid of Honour to Queen Elizabeth and used by that Queen ...'. A further post-auction report on 18 July notes:

> The Jenkins Collection: Art connoisseurs and dealers in antiques from many parts of England were attracted on Thursday [16 July] to Holmer where at the Copelands ... quite fancy prices were obtained ... Historic interest attaches to ... four chairs, once the property of Queen Elizabeth, who presented them to Blanche Parry, lady of the Bed Chamber and were purchased nearly half a century ago by the late Mr H.J. Jenkins at Newcourt Bacton, once the residence of Blanche Parry. These heirlooms were purchased for the Parry family, two of the chairs realising £25 ... For an oil painting of 'Queen Elizabeth in Court Dress' by Hondius, £30 was given and an insignificant-looking little picture in oils of Blanche Parry, to whom Good Queen Bess gave the furniture already referred to, was disposed of for 20 guineas.

The purchaser was a Mr. Parry of Harewood in Herefordshire, presumably a descendant of the family.[9] Nothing further is known and it is not certain if the picture still exists.

Nevertheless, the provenance appears to be secure. Blanche intended leaving 'all the household stuff at Newcourt' to William Vaughan in her First Will, which proves she owned household goods that were stored there, probably awaiting her possible retirement. Presumably the two / four chairs were included. Newcourt was still a viable house in 1801 when Mrs. Burton visited and it appears intact in the 1814 drawing. The above notice shows that the final stripping of the old house was in the 1860s when Mr. Jenkins evidently bought some of the items. Thanks to the foresight of Walter Pilley we know the appearance of the Blanche Parry portrait. These two paintings must have been sent to Bacton for a purpose and the most obvious one is that they were intended to provide likenesses for Blanche's tomb, a common practice.[10] As the finished result would have been inspected by family members who knew, or had seen, both ladies, the sculptor had to try to ensure accurate portrayals.

Blanche's Monument in Bacton Church (Plate 10)
Blanche's First Will, now dated to November 1578, means that Blanche herself dates her Bacton monument: 'I do authorise him [Lord Burghley] to give order by his discretion ... for the burial of my body at Bacton where I have prepared a tomb ...'. It pre-dates November 1578 and, although it is earlier than Blanche's tomb in Saint Margaret's, Blanche never saw it. She did not personally visit Bacton to arrange any details of this, her projected tomb at the time. She would have employed a designer and drawings would have been produced for her approval at Court. It is within this scenario that the painting of Blanche from the Jenkins Collection can be placed. In design the Bacton monument is in several ways a mirror image of the one in Saint Margaret's. In both Blanche turns towards the altar but here the sculptor was less skilled and turned the whole figure. Her clothes are the same, although here the sculptor was not sure where to place the mantle, turning it into a curious second sleeve. Blanche's loose dress seems to be a much tighter fitting garment, especially in the sleeves, which are depicted without folds. Comparison between the two monuments suggests that copies of similar drawings later adapted for the Saint Margaret's tomb were first used in Bacton. Unlike the Saint Margaret's effigy, the Bacton sculptor retained only one hand (holding what seems to be a small pomander) at Blanche's waist, allowing the other, holding a clasped book (a Bible or Prayer Book), to rest by her side. The one major difference between the portrayals is that at Bacton Blanche wears a pectoral cross hanging from her neck. This might mean that the pomander was meant to contain incense, suggesting that a ceremonial element was retained in Blanche's personal beliefs and perhaps, by inference, in those of the Queen. Certainly Elizabeth preferred churches to have ceremonial and tried to retain ecclesiastical ornaments in her private chapels. Blanche's monument complements these indications of the Queen's personal religious views.

Pevsner[11] calls the Bacton tomb 'a very curious monument' due to the relative heights of the two statues of Blanche and Queen Elizabeth and notes that it is not a skilled work. As the monument can now be dated to before 1578 it is likely that the sculptor was John Guldo / Gildon of Hereford,[12] one of the leading sculptors in the West Midlands during the 1570s. He was mentioned in Hereford documents of 1577-78 as a freemason, joiner and carver and he is known to have crafted and signed a 1573 tomb in Bosbury, a 1575 tomb in nearby Madley, a 1577 tomb in Astley in Worcestershire and a 1584 tomb in Abergavenny. Typical of his signature inscription is the one centrally placed on the long south side of the chest tomb in Saint Mary's Priory Church, Abergavenny: 'JOHN GILDON MADE THIS TOMB', in letters as large as the other letters of the epitaph. This tomb is of particular interest as it belongs to the Dr. David Lewis, who was known to Blanche and may have been related to her. (David Morgan was his servant.) Dr. Lewis' effigy lies with his head on a cushion surmounted by a Bible with two clasps and, above, a Prayer Book with one clasp. The decoration includes coats-of-arms, with figures and emblems symbolic of his career. The Madley tomb is also a chest tomb but the Bosbury one is placed under a coffered arch with Tudor roses and supported by pilasters, while tall Corinthian columns support a pediment. Pevsner describes it as elegant and dismisses the likelihood that another similar but unsigned Bosbury tomb is by Gildon as it is too rustic. However, it is worth noting that the Madley tomb has lost a part of Gildon's signature inscription and its erstwhile presence on smooth stone can only be deduced from the words that have survived. It seems very unlikely that John Gildon only produced the tombs where his name is still visible and it certainly seems that his style varied between the elegant and the less so.

Although unsigned it is possible that the Bacton monument was also the product of his workshop. Blanche would have employed the best craftsman available and the ornamentation is similar to the signed Bosbury tomb. The Bacton monument is a tomb-chest set in an arched recess, in white stone and alabaster, with two square Corinthian style pillars. There are four shields, one on a cornice above the shallow coffered arch, like that in Saint Margaret's, while three are set in strapwork below the figures. When the monument, originally placed on the north side of the chancel, was moved along the wall (nearer to the altar, when the organ was installed) it caused disturbance that could perhaps have resulted in the removal of a signature, which would have been on the lower front of the chest. The shield above the arch is of the Royal Arms, while the three on the chest have the quartered Parry coat-of-arms in the centre with lozenges of the same arms flanking it. The face of the arch appears to have a row of Tudor roses, while larger versions run in two rows on the soffit of the arch. Blanche's inscription is placed above the figures within the arch. In this inscription Blanche speaks of being within, but in the event no part of Blanche was buried at Bacton and stories about her heart or bowels being interned there are fictitious. The Queen is shown with royal regalia, heavily jewelled, wearing a collar of state, crowned, holding an orb, though her sceptre is missing, and facing forward. The whole monument must once have been dazzlingly painted. Although superficially similar in design to the Saint Margaret's tomb, the message to be discerned from the Bacton monument is different and is purely religious.

The Queen depicted as a Religious Icon on the Bacton Monument

Many have remarked on the curious positioning of the figures on this monument. Blanche is shown on the left, kneeling, and her size is such that if she stood she would be twice the size of the Queen. The most reasonable explanation of the Queen's short stature is that she is seated. In the monument's original position Blanche's gaze was directed towards the High Altar and indeed it is apparent that the two figures do not relate to one another at all. Hitherto, examination and description have gone no further in their analysis, but other points can be noted. The main coat-of-arms on the cornice above the monument was the Royal arms, the Parry arms being below the figures. So the Queen is the important figure here. The monument, then brightly painted, was originally one bay further west, which would have placed it just inside the site of the rood screen, within the chancel, on the north wall, that is to the left of the High Altar when viewed from the nave.

The relationship between these two figures marks an important change in the iconography used to depict Queen Elizabeth. Until about 1580 the relatively few portraits of the Queen were conventional likenesses used for diplomatic exchanges or for potential marriage suitors. Elizabeth had always had a deft and masterly touch in public relations but in the last two decades of her long reign many of her subjects came to believe that it was only the Queen who stood between them and chaos, a view denounced by both ardent Catholics and Puritans. The 1588 Spanish Armada only confirmed this general feeling of being beleaguered and the Armada portrait of the Queen is one of a series that is full of allegorical associations. The development of what became the glorification of the Queen began slowly and certain pointers can be discerned. The 1569 *Queen Elizabeth and the Three Goddesses*, attributed to Joris Hoefnagel, was painted showing Elizabeth (in place of Paris) awarding the golden apple, symbolising her role as the guardian of Protestant Europe and as a divinely-aided but human ruler. The transformation of Elizabeth into a focus for allegory only really began, however, in 1579.[13] By this date Elizabeth had embraced the quasi-divine function of 'touching' for the 'King's evil', the name given to scrofula, a condition with visible glandular swellings which was often the precursor of tuberculosis. This was the prerogative of the sovereign and through the years the custom had been ceremoniously followed by the more religiously minded. In the 1570s Elizabeth had the words of the ceremony translated into English, with overt Catholic prayers omitted, and thereafter she usually held the rite at Easter to stress the religious link between the monarch and Christ. On her summer progress in 1575 she 'touched' nine sufferers at Kenilworth.[14] This was a very visible way of refuting the Catholic propaganda (highlighted by the 1570 Papal Bull which had declared her deposed) as only God's Chosen would succeed in helping people to a cure.

Elizabeth's government was careful to control her image, especially as she grew older. In a series of later portraits her face is that of an unchanging younger virgin with elaborate, bejewelled clothes and symbolic attributes. These iconic depictions of her, utterly divorced from her actual appearance, helped to maintain stability in the country. The succession was in question, so the Queen had to appear ageless and it is in this context that the unique sculpture of Queen Elizabeth on Blanche's pre-1578 Bacton monument becomes important. It is not simply of passing interest but marks the beginning of the crucial change in the Queen's iconography.

The Bacton monument has a further layer of significance. The bards' poems show that Harri Ddu, Blanche's great-grandfather, had fought in France. The Parry family church at Bacton was dedicated to Saint Faith, whose feast day was 6 October (remembered as late as 1796) and the saint's image would have stood within the chancel on the left — precisely where Blanche later placed her monument. It is likely that this Saint Faith was originally Tyfoi or Foi, the disciple of the religious leader Dubricius or Dyfrig, the greatest of Herefordshire's saints who evangelised Archenfield / south Herefordshire in the 6th century.[15]

However, by the 15th century Tyfoi had become confused with the, by then, much more famous Faith / Foy of Agen in south-west France, thought to have been a beautiful 12-year-old virgin martyr of the 3rd century who died an excruciating death for her faith during the persecutions of the Roman Emperor Diocletian.[16] Apparently, between 877 and 883 AD, monks removed the saint's body from the monastery at Agen to Conques, where it became a focus of pilgrimage. This allowed the town of Conques, which stands in a spectacular location in the dense woods of the gorge of the River Dourdou, to prosper. The Benedictine Abbey of Sainte Foy in Conques still has a small 10th-century yew wood statue of the little saint covered in gold leaf, with added jewels and enamels (Plate 12). In mediaeval times it was known as the Majesté de Sainte Foy. (When examined in 1955 the 85cm-tall statue's head, which is larger than it should be for the body, was found to be hollow. It is thought to have been reused from an Imperial Roman statue and it does give a masculine appearance to this purported statue of a young girl.) The shrine enclosing the saint's remains is nearby in the same abbey. Conques was on one of the four routes through France to the Shrine of Saint James at Compostella in northern Spain. Huge numbers of pilgrims passed through Conques and spread the cult of Saint Faith to England, Spain and even the Americas, as shown by the many towns named Santa Fé in her honour.

Despite the probable original dedication of Bacton Church to Tyfoi, long before the 15th century the saint was equated with the famous Saint Foy of Conques. It is possible that Harri Ddu even visited the abbey there, as it was on one of the most famous pilgrimage routes in Europe. It seems reasonable to assume that the image of Saint Faith in Bacton Church, as in any medieval church, would have been a standardised copy of the statue at Conques, so although the Bacton statue has long been destroyed the Conques statue may show what it looked like.

The Conques statue and the statue of Queen Elizabeth on Blanche's monument are uncannily similar. Both are seated, the face looking straight ahead, the forearms held horizontally. The two faces are similarly framed by hair and crown. Indeed, the statue of the Queen is so similar to Saint Faith / Foy of Conques that it seems possible that Blanche was seeking to replicate a statue she had once known in Bacton Church. When young, she would have been a member of the Maidens' guild and thus would have helped raise funds for the candle, or light, which once stood in front of the saint.

A further point can be made. The powers credited to Saint Faith / Foy of Conques included an ability to cure blindness and by the 1570s Blanche may have already started to become blind. She may have suffered from cataracts and as this condition is progressive it would have felt natural for her to appeal to Saint Faith, whose image she had attended in her youth. However, Saint Faith's statue was no longer in Bacton Church, as all such images had long been removed and could not be reinstated. So Blanche, using the image of the Queen, replicated Saint Faith. Perhaps for her this had the dual purpose of glorifying the Queen she adored and supplicating Saint Faith. Anyone seeing the statue would have understood that Queen Elizabeth was being depicted as a religious icon. For more than two decades, from the 1570s to Elizabeth's death in 1603, the parishioners of Bacton would have taken part in ceremonies, such as on the Queen's Accession Day, in a church adorned with her statue. Many visitors from near and far must have come to Bacton Church especially to see the Queen's image and perhaps some of the older people noted the figure's resemblance to the old statue of Saint Faith.

As it can now be dated, the Bacton statue was apparently the very first known instance of the Queen being depicted as an icon and as such it paved the way for the allegorical portrayals of the succeeding decades. The drawings and discussions involved in the monument's commission were the precursor to the adoption of the concept behind the Queen's depiction as Gloriana. Blanche would have known about this development as she was with Elizabeth throughout her childhood and adolescence, and for the first 31¼ years of her reign, longer than any other lady and even longer than Lord Burghley.

Blanche's closeness to her was pivotal to Elizabeth's personal life and reign. She gave Elizabeth stability in the rapidly changing conflicts of the Court and politics of the time. This elegant, meticulous, fair and utterly trustworthy lady was not just a footnote. As the Queen's confidante she was firmly at the centre of the Court and the administration. Blanche Parry's place and influence were recognised by everyone at the time. She should be remembered now and accorded her rightful place in the history of the period.

Appendix 1
What happened to Newcourt

Blanche's brother, Milo ap Harry and his family lived at Newcourt after the death of Henry Myles. (Henry was a subsidy commissioner in 1515 and Milo in 1541.)[1] Rowland Vaughan and his wife Elizabeth were both the grandchildren of Milo ap Harry and it was Elizabeth who inherited Newcourt. Rowland Vaughan began the trench construction for his water-meadows while he and Elizabeth were still living at Newcourt and he mentioned and depicted the house in *His Booke*, published 1610. In this he described a system of water-meadows that capitalised on the lime-rich soil which had, for centuries, produced two cuttings of grass for the monks of Dore Abbey that had resulted in the superb quality of their wool-clips, taken from the progenitors of Ryeland sheep. Rowland Vaughan wanted to have a system less controlled by the vagaries of the weather which also gave him early grass to benefit from early spring market prices for his animals. However, by 1605, he had had to mortgage his manors of Bacton and Newton (the old manor of Jenkyn ap Ricard / Newcourt)[2] to his older brother Henry and by 1610 he had moved to the Whitehouse, extending his water-meadows into Turnastone parish. While at Newcourt he was recorded as sending gifts of a buck and doe 'out of his Park at Newcourt' to Watkin Vaughan of Moccas, a relation. However, little maintenance was spent on the site and by 1801 the gardens were described as having the remains of terraces with a summer house. Bradford quoted the description of Mrs Burton, the descendant of the Parrys, who visited the house in 1801. She said it retained some Gothic features, old stones in its outer wall and some 17th-century panelling. Fortunately a drawing of the house dated 1814 preserved its general appearance,[3] as it soon became a ruinous farmhouse.

The large park,[4] estimated to have been of several hundred acres, was shown on subsequent maps such as Speed's in 1610 and was still there on an

1822 Estate Map.[5] The area of the park can still be determined by the tracks, roads, field pattern and fieldnames such as 'park' and 'lawn'.[6] The emparked animals, including deer, were driven onto the lawn (a name still preserved in hunting with the first meet of the year being called the Lawn Meet). The present road at Newton is in the original park boundary ditch. Other traces of the bank and ditch can still be seen and can be compared to the 1586 survey.

In 2002 I was able to identify the site of the house on the ridge above Newcourt Farm, where two barns (a third barn was dismantled as unsafe in recent years) and the earliest parts of the farmhouse probably date from the same period. The farm would have supplied the main house. The area is shown on the tithe map and on an estate map. The site of Newcourt itself is now covered by scrub, trees and vegetation but the house platform can be found. On the east side of it is the ruin of Keeper's Cottage, parts of which are built of stone. It is likely that this was a service wing for the house and it may have been the documented bakehouse. The track from the house to the farm is clearly seen but the main approach was from the north, where a road links to a footpath through two 'Lodge Fields' and it would have run along the ridge. This carriage route would have been most impressive, providing wonderful vistas of the Golden Valley as it was then, with its orchards, meadows of cowslips, fields and many trees. This approach would have traversed the park and can now be followed first as a footpath and then by the field pattern to the site of the main entrance of Newcourt itself. As the track ran immediately to the west of the motte-and-bailey it is probable that the stone building on the motte was a service building for Newcourt. A second track may have given access across the park to Bacton Church where Blanche's family worshipped and where she had already prepared her monument in the mid-1570s.

Appendix 2
Blanche Parry's Wills

First (nuncupative) Will, November 1578

This Will is dated by internal evidence. Glasbury had been the property of John Vaughan, who had died on 25 June 1577 and is mentioned here as 'late deceased'. He had been granted a licence to transfer Glasbury to Blanche just 24 days before. Blanche had then sold the manor to Lord Burghley and John Morgan on 1 November and she would be granted a licence to alienate it on 27 November 1578. Corroborative evidence comes from Frances Vaughan being recorded as a Maid of Honour in 1579. Margaret Dane, who is mentioned as having charge of Blanche's money and plate, would die in 1579 (the last memorandum to her Will being dated 15 September 1579). As mention is made of the sale of 1 November with considerable detail concerning the intention involved but the licence of 27 November is not mentioned, it is likely that Blanche's illness was between 2 and 26 November 1578.

This Will was written by Lord Burghley from Blanche's dictation. In the transcript which follows, everything Lord Burghley wrote is shown in italics.[1] The additions and deletions provide a vivid picture of the discussions that ensued as Lord Burghley struggled to draw up the documents with clarity. The preamble said:

Left side of first sheet:

> I*n the name of God to whom I commend my soull by the*
> *merits of the passion of Jesus Christ my Redeemer*
> *last*
> *I do ~~in this manner~~ declare my* ↑ *Will ~~to be as followeth~~*
> *~~First~~ for all my goods chattels leases and all other*
> *worldly things to be disposed in manner and*
> *form following*
>
> *The gift of the lease*

Blanche does manage to list her leases but she is so ill that, uncharacteristically, she is prepared to leave details to Lord Burghley's good sense, giving him a free hand. Burghley's function was as supervisor and he found making lists very helpful. Indeed he was an inveterate list-maker, employing these methods in all his administrative work in running the kingdom and his own estates. He and his secretaries, used a + to mark the bequests that would have to be paid. The different handwriting seems to suggest that Burghley had the help of four secretaries, here denoted A, B, C and D, and ↑ is used to show interpolations from the line above.

Right side, same sheet, written by Secretary A:

Jesus
Daughters and heirs to Myle a Parry
having issue Elizabeth and Joan
£60 in money
+ Joan ↑ married to Watkin Vaghan
having issue Harry Vaughan *the children of*
this Joan to have every of them 20 marks. [a mark was 13s 4d, so £13 6s 8d each]
Elsabeth married to Rowland Vaughan
having issue, William, Kater and
Elsabeth.
My eldest sister Elsabeth a Parry
married to Thomas Vaghan of Tregunter
who had to son John Vaughan married
to the Lady Knevett who had to issue
Frauncis his son and Fraunces Vaughan his
daughter
My sister Sybble married to James
Whytney of Clifford who had to issue
Ewstawnce Whytney *to have £5 in money*
My sister Margett married to Howell
Watkyn of Pen Pidle who had issue
Tho. Powell to have 20 marks by year
out of the leases Water Powell and *Thomas Powell* ~~*20 marks per annum out of the leases*~~
in the north ~~*whilst he go*~~ *to school*
to have the lease of the woods jointly with his wife *during the lease*
John Morgan my kinsman John Parry *to*
have annuity of 20 marks of out of Ryse and the leases
Clerk of the Queens household my
kinsman
£5 per annum out of the leases
Rodger Vaughan my servant 53s-4d
Robart Duppa my servant Robart Rampton
my servant

Dorse, left side:

out of the leases *To have a lease of parcel of Wheldrake*
to have £5 by year↑*so as* *as is promised to Francis Vaughan and Bedell*
he will
avoid from Harry and Richard brethren to John Vaughan
a fine of *he hath a lease*
William My friend, Hugh Bethell *to remit £20 of his fine*
Vaughan Elnor Bull + *£5 in money*
~~Margeret Wilton 20~~
My Lady Haward *£10 in money*
My godson Blanch Parry *son to James Parry*
Thomas Powell *20 marks as is specified before*
~~Elsabethe Acton-- *20 s*~~ [shillings] ~~*in money*~~
Jane Vaughan *£20 in money*
John Morgans wife ~~*the*~~ *joined with her*
husband the lease of
of plate *the wood*
a piece ↑ *to James ap Parry of Poston*

a piece of plate to John ap Harry of Morehampton
Cath. Vaughan to have £300
Elis. her sister £100
plate and other goods to be divided betwixt Wm Vaughan
Francis Vaughan
and his sister Frances
and to

Debts

£80 to the Queen by Bethell out of the fines
of Wheldrake
The leases of Ryss and Wheldrake to be granted to Francis Vaughan
and to with condition that they shall pay
the annuities above mentioned and to save harmless John Morgan
for his bonds in the Exchequer concerning the said leases or
for any other bond wherein he standeth bond for her or is otherwise charged
for her.

On a separate second sheet Lord Burghley dealt with the crucial details of Blanche's property, penning notes as Blanche talked. Probably because the property closely involved Burghley personally, he wrote all the points himself. One small point is that Burghley invariable writes 'Elizabeth' whereas his secretaries tend to write 'Elsabeth' which was perhaps how the name was pronounced (and is nearer to the spelling of her name on Blanche's Bacton epitaph).

Be it remembered ~~that the Intention of Mistress Blanch a Parry is that~~ where ~~she doth~~ Mistress Blanch a Parry hath bargained and sold the manor of Glasebury in the county of Radnor by deed Indented bearing date the of November to the Right Honourable William Lord Burghley, Lord Treasurer of England and to John Morgan of Westminster esquire.
The meaning and intentions of the said Blanch ~~is and the con~~ on the one part and of the said Lord Burghley and John Morgan on the other part is that if God shall call the said Blanch out of this life before any redemption shall be thereof from the said Lord Burghley and John Morgan as, by a clause in the said indenture she hath authority to do, then the said Lord Burghley and John Morgan shall make an estate of the said manor to the use of her cousin William ~~Morg~~ Vaughan now within age son ~~to the m~~ and ~~isu of the~~ heirs of Elizabeth that was one of the daughters and heirs of Milo ap Harry brother to the said Blanch ap Harry and of the heirs of his body.
The remainder for lack of such issue to ~~the 2 sisters of~~ the ~~said William Morg Vaughan and the heirs of their bodies~~ her cousin Francis Vaughan son and heir of John Vaughan late deceased and the heirs of his body
and for lack of such issue to the ~~heirs~~ Frances Vaughan sister to the ~~said~~ foresaid Francis and daughter of the said John Vaughan.
The ~~execution thereof~~ manner of the execution whereof the said Blanch commits to the ~~disc~~ wisdom of the said Lord Burghley and John Morgan

At this point Blanche rouses herself as she remembers that her favourite nephew would need money and Burghley continues in the first person. Blanche is still meticulous as, for example, she asks that only proved debts be paid:

and I will that the said William Vaughan shall ~~after the foresaid legacies be paid~~ have £300 to be in safe custody by the order of the Lord Treasurer towards the repairing of the house of New Court when he shall come to full age.
Item because there are many things requisite to be devised by me that can not for lack of time at this present be put into writing I do require my good Lord and friend my Lord Treasurer and I do authorise him to give order by his discretion ~~to that this my that my goods not be~~ for the

burial of my body at Bacton where I have prepared a tomb with such costs as he shall think meet and there --- to bestow upon the steeple and church that shall by him be thought meet for the performance of my intent
and also I do require him to be a mean to the Queen's Majesty, my dear sovereign lady and mistress, that a favourable account may be made of all jewels and other things belonging to her majesty within my charge that my heirs may thereof have a discharge
and ~~wherein he sta~~ what so ever my said Lord Treasurer shall think further meet than is above expressed to be disposed towards the relief of my kinfolks and servants.
I ~~le~~ will the same to be performed by ~~the fors~~ my foresaid kinsfolks to whom I have devised my goods ~~so as in~~ whom I will and charge to be ordered by ~~him~~ the said Lord Treasurer for the distribution thereof amongst them
And himself shall take order that out of the same goods my debts that shall be proved due may be paid and that the several legacies mentioned within this Will may be also ~~perfor~~ delivered paid and performed.

The manor of Ketherogh and Usk and 1 tenement falley [Fawley] *brontllish* [Bronllys] *to Wm Vaughan and the heirs of his body*
remainder to Catherine and Elizabeth their heirs
remainder to Francis Vaughan and his sister.

Co. Brecknock vel Radnor
The manor of Glasberry sold to Blanche ap Harry by John Vaughan for 1000 in respect that she should pay his debts which was by estimation above £700 the rent is £20.
John Vaughan gave it to his mother being sister to Blanche ap Parry for term of her life ~~and~~ without rent saving that she should pay £6-13-4 to Miles Whytney now dead
and £5-16-8 to Roger Vaughan 2nd son to brother to John Vaughan,
to David Watkyn his servant £4.
Blanche ap Harry hath made a lease to Robert Vaughan younger brother to John Vaughan of the manor of Glasbury for term of his life, yielding £20 per annum.

Co. Hereford
She had the manor of Fawley of £26 which she gave to John Vaughan and his heirs after her life and reserved power to make a lease thereof for 21 years which is esteemed worth 1000 marks.

Leases

Co. York
Of the manor of Ryss [Rise] *yield to the Queen's Majesty £60 per annum etc.*
Whereof she made by granting of leases £700 and she hath £50 de claro of the demesnes
nota she had a lease for £21 years
and she hath a lease of Ryss in reversion to bring after her decease pro 21 annis [years]
Of the manor of Wheldrake near Sutton that is Fr [Frances] *Vaughan during her life without reversion and after her life pro 21 annis rent £67.*
She hath now but £67 because she made leases for term of 10 years.
She hath a lease of the woods of Ryss Wheldrak and of yielding the rent of £10 the profit ~~hath~~ riseth by wood sales made by Bethell.

Nota that John Morgan ~~standeth bond~~ and his brother Walter Morgan stand bound for answering of the rents.

Money lying with Mrs Dane
Chests of plate at Mrs Danes
2 beds and 4 pieces of hangings at John Morgan's house
The advowson of the vicarage at Glasbury for 3 turns.

The necessary sworn witnesses were recorded on the dorse, right side, as: *William Vaughan*, *Francis Vaughan*, *Frances Vaughan*, *Catherine* and *Elisabeth*. It is likely that these five had been called to Blanche's bedside for Blanche says 'I have by my speech to Wm Vaughan … and he did thereto agree' to provide a house for the vicar of Bacton. The most poignant moments are written in the first person as Blanche remembers those dear to her like William Vaughan and the need that 'a favourable account may be made of all jewels and other things belonging to her majesty within my charge that my heirs may thereof have a discharge', a discharge certificate to protect her relatives, a very important consideration when the value in Blanche's charge is appreciated.

Following his usual practice Lord Burghley's secretaries listed the legacies to be paid on a third sheet, with secretary B noting that these were 'To be added to Mrs Blanch a Paryes Will':[2]

	Francis Vaughan and Frances his sister	The leases of Rise and Wheldrake charged with certain annuities hereafter expressed	
Leases }			
	John Morgan and Susan his wife	The lease of the woods there	
	John a Pary	£6-13-4	
	Thomas Powell	£13-6-8	
	Henry Vaughan	£5	
Annuities }	Roger Vaughan	£5	} £38-13-4
	Robert Duppa	£5	
	Robert Rampton	53s-4d	
	Morrice hir servant	20s	
	Joan Vaughan	£60	
	Her 5 children	£66-13-4	[£13-6-8 each]
	Katherin Vaughan	£300	
	Elizabeth Vaughan	£100	
	Estanes Whitney	£5	
	Blanch a Pary	£10	
	Hugh Bethell	£20	
Legacies in }	Elioner Bull	£5	} ~~£943-6-8~~
Ready Money }	Jane Vaughan	£20	} £948 6 8
	James a Powell	£5	
	Nicholas Pigeon	£10	
	William Vaughan	£300	
	John Vaughans mother	£20	
	Anthony Martin	£10	
	Katherin Whitney	£5	
	John A Pary	£6-13-4	
	James Whitney	£5	
	The Lady Haward	£8	
Debts pardoned }	Francisce Vaughan	£20	
	Robert Vaughan	£15	} £93
	John Morgan	£50	
Household stuff	William Vaughan	The beddings and hangings at Westminster and all the household stuff at Newcourt	
Poor in Bacton	The poor of Bacton	Twenty kine	
Plate jewels etc }	All plate, jewels and other goods whatsoever to William Vaughan and his two sisters, Francis Vaughan and Frances his sister		

Lord Burghley then wrote on the dorse, right:

+ 20 kine to be bought to be bestowed
amongst the poor people and
they to give ~~20s~~ 2s a piece
as long
+ the vicarage to be bought to be appointed to the vicar
to dwell ----- [too faint to read]

Debts } *Lady Howd* *£8*
Frasc Vaughan *£20*
Morgan *£50*
Rob Vaughan *£15*
4
To his ↑ children 20 nobles a piece [a noble was 6s-8d, so £6-13-4 each]
To Jho Vaughans mother £20
To Wm Vaughan the hangings and bedding in the house
at Westminster

Secretary B continued on a fourth sheet, heading it as a 'Brief of Mrs Blanch A Paries Will'.[3] The reference to Frances Vaughan confirms the date as 1578/79. Secretary A wrote, again endorsed by Lord Burghley:

Anthony Martin	£10
Katherin Vaughan	£5
Jo. a Pary	£6-13-4
Morice her servant	20s *by year out of the lease of Ryse*

To every } Gentleman of the chamber present }
Grooms and maids } rings of 20s a piece
To ye Queen a pair of sables with 8 claws of gold

Lord Burghley, having noted these bequests to the Queen and members of her Household, continued:

Where as the vicar of Bacton lacketh a house to inhabit in
and that my nephew Roland Vaughan and his wife did
grant away the house wherein the vicar was accustomed
to dwell; I will and require my Lord Treasurer [Lord Burghley] *to take*
order that Wm Vaughan at his full age shall
make a grant of that house or some other house meet for
the purpose to be assured to the vicar and his successors
whereof I have by my speech to Wm Vaughan in presence
to inhabit ↑ in ~~and in the respect of the vicar~~
~~I will that~~ of my said Lord Treasurer give him charge and
he did thereto agree.
And for further relief of the vicar, I will that there be
poor
bought 20 kine [cows], *to be distributed to the ↑ parishioners of*
Bacton and they to give to the vicar 2s by year for the
use of every cow, as long as may be by some
composition agreed ~~with the~~ betwixt the vicar and them
that shall have the said kine

At this point Blanche becomes more confused. She starts to say 'John Vaughan's mother' but interpolates 'my sister' and the patient Lord Burghley writes exactly what she said. Then she remembers Lady Howard's debt and here she corrects herself in time. Frances Vaughan she calls her 'cousin' meaning kinsman / kinswoman:

> *Item I do give to Jno Vaughan my sister Jno Vaughans mother £20*
> *Item I do forgive to the lady Haward £8 which ~~I owe her~~ she oweth me*
> *and the like to my cousin Fra Vaughan the Queens maid for £20*
> *and to Robert Vaughan for £15 and to Thomas Morgan for £50*
> *so as he do give to every of his 4 children £6-13-4*
> *Item I will that Wm Vaughan shall have the bedding and hangings at my*
> *house at Westminster and all the household stuff at New Court.*

On the third side:

Item I give to Anthony Mertyn [Martin] *£10*
To Kathuryn Whytney *£5*
To Jho ap harry *£6-13-4*
To James Whitney £5 [line added by Secretary C]
To Moryce my servant I will 20s yearly to be paid to him
out of the profits of the leases of Ryse as long as
the term may endure
Item I will that to every of the ladies and gentlewomen of
the privy chamber and the Grooms of the same and
every of the maids of honour, that shall be at the
Court when God shall call me out of this
Life, rings made like hoops with deaths head of
the value of 20 s a piece
Item I will that there be delivered to her Majesty a pair of sables
garnished with 8 claws of Gold

When Blanche recovered, Lord Burghley, with a lawyer's care, filed his notes for the future. He may even have kept them up-to-date as it is likely that Katherine Vaughan and Katherine Whitney, with a £5 bequest, was the same person, suggesting she had married.

Final Will 1589

By 1589 a number of relatives and friends had pre-deceased Blanche, including and most importantly her great-nephew William Vaughan who had died, without direct heirs, in 1584.[4] William reciprocated Blanche's regard and appointed her his executrix, bequeathing her his estate, probably in a nuncupative Will on his own death-bed, and asking her to pay his debts.[5] Blanche also realised that she would die before the Queen and so provision for her own retirement was no longer necessary.

Lord Burghley estimated the value of the annuities in Blanche's First 1578 Will as £38 13s 4d, the legacies as £948 6s 8d and the debts pardoned as £93, though no jewels were specifically mentioned. In contrast the sums from her Final 1589 Will were £2,708 6s 8d besides the annuities, jewels, plate and the 100 marks (£66 13s 4d, a mark being 13s 4d) for the farm for William Berrowe. An idea of the value suggests that Blanche's total estate may have been between a half and a million pounds in modern terms. Her bequests were carefully allotted as she operated a sliding scale according to the individual's relationship to her and the frequency of contact with her. By 1589 Burghley also required a rudimentary Family Tree[6] to help him determine the beneficiaries. He was becoming deaf and Blanche must have thought she needed to provide a safeguard against the onset of forgetfulness so she made a bequest to

Burghley's son, Sir Robert Cecil, to ask him to remind his father to carry out her instructions. In the event this was unnecessary.

Blanche's Final Will and Testament is dated 21 June 1589 with codicils dated 23 June, 27 October and 2 December 1589. The probate copy has survived.[7] Written largely by Lord Burghley to Blanche's dictation, she was presumably able to sign it, albeit shakily. It is a more considered document, for Blanche says she *makes* her Will and she is putting her affairs in order:

> **In the name of God Amen** the one and twentieth day of June a thousand five hundred and eighty and nine and in the one and thirtieth year of the reign of our sovereign lady Elizabeth by the grace of God of England, France and Ireland, defender of the faith etc.
> I Blaunche Parrye one of the Gentlewomen of the Queen's Majesty's Privy Chamber, whole in body and mind thanks be to Almighty God, do make this my Testament and last Will in the name of the eternal living God the father, the son and the holy ghost in whose name I was baptised, in whom only I hope and believe to be saved. Amen.
> First I bequeath my soul into the hands of God, father, son and holy ghost and my body to be buried in the parish Church of St Margarets within the City of Westminster, near unto my nephew John Vahan, if it please God to call me near London.
> Item I give to the Queen's most excellent Majesty, my sovereign lady and mistress, my best diamond.
> Item I give to the Right honourable my very good lord Sir Christopher Hatton, Knight, Lord Chancellor of England, one table diamond.
> Item I give to the right honourable, my very good Lord, the Lord Burleigh, Lord High Treasurer of England, my second diamond.
> Item I give to the right honourable my very good lady, the Lady Cobham, one ring with a pointed diamond and a chain of knobs enamelled work.
> Item I give to my very good lady, the Lady Dorothy Stafford, one diamond set in gold with a broad hoop.
> Item I give to the right honourable, my very good lord, the Lord Lumley, one ring with a pointed diamond, eight pieces of hanging being in my house, two short carpets and one carpet of four yards long.
> Item I give to the right honourable Sir John Perrott, knight, one piece of plate weighing forty ounces.
> Item I give to the right honourable, the Lady Frances Burghe, my niece, One hundred pounds.
> Item I give to my cousin, Katherine Knowles, one girdle of fryers knots of gold with a jewel of masory work set with stones, two pair of holland sheets, two pair of pillowberes, a table cloth of damask imagery, a towel and a dozen of napkins of the same and two hundred pounds in money.
> Item I give to my cousin Anne Vaghan, wife of Frances Vaghan, esquire, one chain of gold and a girdle which the Queen's majesty gave me.
> Item I give to Mr. Thomas Knevett one piece of plate weighing three score [60] ounces.
> Item I give to the Lady Blanche Somerset twenty pounds.
> Item I give to Blanche Parry, son of James Parrye, ten pounds.
> Item I give to William Powell, James Powell and Henry Powell, my sister's sons to every one of them one hundred pounds.
> Item I give to Blanche Whitney, my god-daughter, twenty pounds.
> Item I give to   my sister Margaret's daughter, being unmarried, one hundred pounds.
> Item I give either of her other two daughters fifty pounds.
> Item I give towards the amending and repairing of the highway between Newcourt and More Hampton and Newcourt and Doure, in the county of Hereford, twenty pounds.
> [added in the margin] Item I give to Mistress Frances Burghe, my god-daughter, twenty pounds.
> Item I give to Mistress Elizabeth Burghe twenty pounds.

Item I will that my Executors shall bestow the sum of five hundred pounds in purchasing of lands which shall be worth ten pounds by year and to build a convenient almshouse for four poor people to be chosen from time to time within the parish of Backton in the county of Hereford of the oldest and poorest within the said parish, whether they be men or women there to be relieved of the profits of the said lands for ever.

And the said alms house to be builded as near the parish church of Backton aforesaid as the land may be provided for that purpose, which said almshouse I will shall be founded as law will allow at the charge of my Executors.

Item I give to Mistress Lettice Knowles twenty pounds.

Item I give to Mistress Frances Knowles twenty pounds.

Item I give to my niece, Mistress Joane Vaghan, if she be living at my decease forty pounds.

Item I give to John Parry of Dulas gent. twenty pounds.

Item I give to John Vaghan of Sutton gent. five pounds.

Item I give to Master Martin, the Sewer, five pounds.

Item I give to Mistress Preston twenty pounds.

Item I give to William Berrowe, my servant, if he continue in my service until my decease one hundred pounds.

Item I give to Mawde Berrowe, his mother, forty pounds.

Item I give to my cousin Anne Whitney one hundred pounds, which one Newton and one Birde do owe me.

Item I give to my cousin Elinor Bull one hundred pounds, which Mr. Mounteagewe oweth me.

Item I give to Mr. Morgan the apothecary one ring worth three pounds.

[added in the margin] Item I give unto Mr. Mounteagewe a ring worth three pounds.

Item I give to every woman servant, whom I shall have in my service at the time of my decease, four pounds.

And to every yeoman who shall then serve me five pounds.

Item I give to Mistress [added in the margin Elizabeth] Broke a table with two rock rubies in it.

Item I give to my gentlewoman, who shall serve me at the time of my decease, six pounds thirteen shillings and four pence.

Item I give to Mr. Standen and to his wife, either of them, one ring worth three pounds.

Item I give to Mr. Hewes, the Queens Majestys linen draper, one ring of gold worth five pounds.

Item I give to the poor people of the parish of Backton, in the county of Hereford, ten pounds.

Item I give to the poor people of Newton near the park pale of Newcourte, in the said county, ten pounds.

Item I give to Ewstones Whitney of Clifford, esquire, twenty pounds.

Item I give to Lewes Parrye five pounds.

Item I give to the poor of the City of Westminster twenty pounds to be distributed by the discretion of Mr. Deane of Westminster.

Item I give to Francis Vaghan esquire, my nephew and to Hugh Bethell gent. all those my Letters Patents which I have from the Queens Majesty of the Manor of Risse in the county of Yorke and of the woods there and of certain lands and tenements in Wheldrake and the woods there in the said county as well in possession as reversion with all my right, title, interest and term of years possession and reversion of, in and to the said Manor of Rysse and woods there, the said lands and tenements in Wheldrake aforesaid and the woods there, by virtue of the said Letters Patents for and during the several term and terms in the said premises yet to come and not expired together with the said Letters Patents and every of the same with all my right and title in and to the same and every of them they, the said Francis and Hugh, yielding and paying, performing and doing such rents and other things as by the said several Letters Patent or any of them shall be done to our said sovereign Lady the Queens Majesty her heirs and successors and also yielding and paying such yearly rents or annuities as by this my last Will and Testament hereafter shall be limited and appointed given or set down to any person or persons of the profits of the said leases or either of them at such days and Feasts as the said rents or annuities shall be by this my said last Will assigned and appointed.

Item I also give to the said Francis Vaghan one silver gilt basin and ewer.

Item I give to the said Hugh Bethell one basin and ewer of silver.

Item I give to John Parrye, gentleman, one of the Clerks of the Queens Majesty's Household, the yearly rent or sum of thirteen pounds six shillings and eight pence of lawful money of England to be paid yearly to him at the Feasts of the Annunciation of the blessed virgin Mary and Saint Michael the Archangel or within one month next after either of the said Feasts at the Chapel in the Rolls London if it be there lawfully demanded of the profits of the leases aforesaid during the term in the said Manor of Rysse by even portions if he the said John Parrye so long shall live.

Item I give to James Morgan gent. [James is probably an error for John] the yearly rent or sum of thirteen pounds, six shillings and eight pence of lawful money of the profits of the said leases to be paid to him at the said Feast days and place aforesaid by even portions during the term in the said Manor of Rysse if he, the said John Morgan, shall so long live.

Item I give to James Thomas gent. the yearly rent or sum of six pounds thirteen shillings four pence of lawful money of England to be paid to him of the profits aforesaid at the Feasts and days and place above said by even portions during the term in the said Manor of Rysse if he so long shall live.

Item I give to Mother Harrys the yearly rent or sum of six pounds thirteen shillings four pence of the profits of the said Leases to be paid to her at the days and place above said during the said term if she live so long and do demand the same.

Item I give to William my Chamber Keeper the yearly rent or sum of four pounds of lawful money of the profits of the said leases to be paid at the said days and place if he so long live and demand the same.

Item I give to Richard Vaghan gent. the yearly rent or sum of eleven pounds of lawful money of the profits of the said leases to be paid at the days aforesaid during the term in the said lease of the Manor of Rysse if he so long live and do demand the same at the said Manor all the said annuities to be paid by even portions.

Item I give to Francis Vaghan, son of the said Richard Vaghan, twenty pounds.

Item I give to my said cousin Anne Whitney one pair of white holland sheets of three leaves.

Item I will there shall be bestowed upon my funerals at the time of my burial the sum of three hundred pounds at the discretion of my Executors.

Item I give to Mark Staneborne, my Boy, fifty pounds.

Item I give to Roger Harrys five pounds.

Item I give to the Lady Katheryne Gate a cup of plate weighing forty ounces
and to either of her two daughters ten pounds a piece.

Item my meaning is that if any of my said Sister's children shall happen to die before he or she shall have the benefit of this my will then the portions of him, her or them so dying shall be divided amongst the rest of the said children.

And likewise if either of the daughters of Mr. Knowles shall happen to die the other to have her portion.

And also if either of my Lord Burghe, his daughters, shall happen to die then the other to have her Legacy or portion.

Item the rest of all my goods moveable and unmoveable not bequeathed I give and bequeath to Thomas Powell and Hughe Bethell gent. whom I make Executors of this my said last will and testament.

And I do humbly desire my said good Lord, the Lord Burleighe, Lord High Treasurer of England, to be Supravisor of this my said last will.

And that it will please his Lordship to see the same performed according to the meaning of me set down in this my said will for charities' sake and towards his Lordship's charges herein I give his Lordship fifty pounds.

And to Mr. Robert Cicell [this spelling of Cecil is nearer to the Welsh] fifty pounds to remember [remind] my said Lord.
Item I give to Mr. Coppe, my Lord Treasurer's man, one ring worth five pounds.
In witness whereof I have to this my said last Will and Testament put my hand and Seal the day and year above written in the presence of Robert Freake, William Billesbye, Bartholomewe Dodington.

Blanche Parrye

I do affirm that my cousin Mrs. Blanche Apparrye did confess this to be her last Will and required me to seal it up which I did. And now the seventeenth of February I have opened it.

William Burleighe

A Codicil, annexed to the Will of me Blanche Parrye the 23 day of June 1589.
Item I give Rowland Vaghan, my cousin, one hundred pounds.
Item I give to the six pages of the Queen's Majesty's Privy Chamber, every one of them twenty shillings [six pounds in total].
Item my will further is that if any person or persons to whom I have by my last Will given or bequeathed any sum or sums of money, or other things, do at any time after my decease make any trouble or suit or do withstand or go about to overthrow, deny or annihilate my said Will which beareth date the one and twentieth of this instant June, or shall not hold him or her self contented and pleased with the said Legacies to them, him or her given by the said Will as aforesaid. That then they, he or she who shall so trouble, molest or incumber my Executors or shall stand to deny or withstand the probation of the said Will shall lose and forgo the benefit of all such legacies, gifts and bequests to him, her or them so given or bequeathed.
And also I will that all the legacies given or bequeathed by my said Will shall be delivered, paid and performed within one and a half next after my decease.

The 27 of October 1589 a **Codicil** to be annexed to the Will of me Mistress Blanche Parrye.
Item I give to my cousin, Katherine Knowles, one basin and ewer gilt, a gown of velvet, a round kirtle of velvet and a petticoat of crimson satin and a great nest of bowls which my Lord Chancellor gave me.
Item I give to Anne Whitney, my waiting gentlewoman, one hundred pounds.
Item I give to Mistress Alice Dacre six pounds, thirteen shillings, four pence.

6th of December 1589

Second of December 1589 A **Codicil** made by me Mrs. Blanche Parry to be annexed to my Will. Whereas by my Will I have appointed five hundred pounds or thereabouts to be bestowed for the building of an Alms House in Backton in the county of Hereford and for the providing of ten pounds land yearly or thereabouts for the same.
I do now in lieu thereof, for that I cannot provide land in Backton aforesaid for building of the said house, assign and appoint and will that my Executors shall purchase so much lands as shall yield above all charges yearly for ever the number of seven score [140] bushels of corn, viz. wheat and rye, to be bestowed and distributed yearly amongst the poor people of Backton aforesaid and Newton in the said county for ever.
And that the Dean and Chapter of Hereford shall from time to time have the oversight of the bestowing and distributing of the said corn, which said corn I will my Executors shall provide in form aforesaid with as much speed as conveniently may be.
Item I give to William Berrowe my servant, the fine or sum of money which shall be made or given for the farm in Wheldrake in the county of York, now in the tenure of Thomas Haxby or his assigns for the years which shall be to come in the said farm at the time of my decease.
Item to Mrs. Payne one ring and to Mr. Williams, my Lord Cobham's man, one ring.

Probate was granted on 5 March 1590 on the oath of 'Anthony Law notary public as procurator for Thomas Powell and Hugh Bethell the executors'. However, by then Blanche's death had been noted, with a list of bequests, by Lord Burghley in 'A Breviat of Mres Blanche apparyes wyll':[8]

Who died Febr Was buryed 27 Feb 1589 [1590 in modern reckoning]
Feb 1589 The breff of Blanch ap Parrys legacyes

These 17 bequests were repeated in 'Legacies given by Mistress Blanche Parryes Will' written by secretary D in February 1590, which then continued with the full list. They were a working summary of the bequests to be paid and as such were largely similar to Blanche's Final Will. One exception was the bequest for Blanch Parry, son of James Parry, who had been given £10 in Blanche's Final Will but here was given £20. Here too the table for Mistress Elizabeth Brooke was described as having two rock rubies, while in the Final Will there were three. These were negligible slips, though Blanch Parry must have been delighted if he did receive double his intended bequest. The second page had a section headed 'Annuities out of the said leases' which concluded with:

Sum of this will besides annuities	£2708-6-8
Jewels plate with the codicil	besides 100 marks to Wylliam Berow for the Farm

The list of 'Legacies by codicil' followed and there is no mention here of the third codicil dated 2 December 1589 which concerned the alternative to the building of the Bacton almshouses and the bequests of rings to Mr. Payne and Mr. Williams. Provision was also made for the fine of the farm to be given to William Berrowe though it is clear that this fine had already been included and mention in the codicil only served to clarify the bequest. Therefore, this codicil shows that the legacy lists were written between 27 October and 2 December 1589. It was the working list of payments prepared by the careful Lord Burghley.

The Aftermath

Blanche tried to smooth the way for her executors and to ensure that her provisions were carried out as she wished. She must have realised that some family members would be unhappy with the bequests because she stated that if any beneficiary made any 'trouble or suit' or in any way tried to overturn the provisions of her Final Will then he / she would lose any bequest. Blanche appointed Lord Burghley as her Will's supervisor, with £50 for expenses, asking him to carry out her wishes 'for Charities sake'. Charmingly she also left £50 to his son to remind the busy Lord Burghley (who was, after all, also fully occupied with running the country!) to do the work. That he did so as conscientiously as he could is shown by his lists of payments that needed to be made.

Blanche Parry died on Thursday 12 February 1590 and her Final Will was opened by Lord Burghley on the 17th. Lord Burghley then made his list of the legacies that had to be paid. Blanche was buried on the 27th, for which she had left £300 though in the event the Queen paid for her funeral. Probate was granted on 5 March 1590 on the oath of a notary public which suggests that Thomas Powell and Hugh Bethell, Blanche's named executors, were not then available perhaps because they had already left for Yorkshire. Between them they had to see that the payments were made to the poor of Bacton, Newton and Westminster and to ensure the roads around Newcourt were repaired. Blanche had made it clear that she bequeathed Francis Vaughan and Hugh Bethell all the Letters Patent which she had had from the Queen for the manor and woods of Rise and for the lands, tenements and woods in Wheldrake, all in Yorkshire. The Letters Patent showed the number of years left and the rents that had to be collected and dues paid. From this income Francis Vaughan and Hugh Bethell were required to pay the annuities, based on an individual yearly rent of £13 6s 8d, given in Blanche's Final Will. These were to:

John Pary, of the Household	£13 6s 8d	
James Morgan (a mistake or John's son?)	£13 6s 8d	
James Thomas	£ 6 13s 4d	} Total = £45
Mother Harrys	£ 6 13s 4d	all from the
William, chamberer,	£ 4	manor of Rise
Richard Vaughan	£11	

William Berrowe had a farm in Wheldrake.

The payments were to be made within a month of the Feast of the Annunciation of the Blessed Virgin Mary, called Lady Day, 25 March, and the same for the Feast of Saint Michael the Archangel, Michaelmas, 29 September (two of the four quarter days used for hiring servants and paying rents). Evidently the annuities were to be paid in two instalments for the length of time remaining on the manor's leases. However, in 1591, Francis Vaughan agreed to sell his share of the Letters Patent to Hugh Bethell,[9] so presumably Hugh continued to pay the annuities from the manor of Rise until the leases expired or the beneficiaries themselves died.

In addition, Hugh Bethell and Thomas Powell, as Blanche's executors, had to arrange for the implementation of the codicil made in lieu of the building of an almshouse at Bacton in Herefordshire. By this she had stipulated that land should be bought which would annually provide seven score bushels of wheat and rye to be distributed among the poor of Bacton and Newton. A bushel, equivalent to 8 imperial gallons, was a measure of dry capacity and the total here amounted to 140 bushels, which were 140 large sacks of corn. Once the arrangements had been made the Dean and Chapter of Hereford Cathedral were required to oversee the annual distribution.

The Garnons Indenture, dated 2 July 1590 (32 Elizabeth)[10] was made 'between John Garnons of Garnons in the county of Hereford esquire and Robert Garnons son and heir apparent of the said John Garnons on the one part and Heughe Bethel of Ellerton in the county of York esquire and Thomas Powell of the City of London, gent., executors of the last will and testament of Blaynche Parry late principal Gentlewoman of the Queen's Majesties Privy chamber deceased on the other part …'. The inclusion of Robert Garnons was a precaution to ensure the arrangements would be maintained into the future. There was a family connection with Blanche as John Garnons' mother was the daughter and heir of Watkin ap Henry, the bastard son of Blanche's brother Milo ap Harry. John and Robert Garnons received '£340 of the goods and chattels of the said Blaynche Parry …' In return Hugh and Thomas were to receive 'six score bushels [120 sacks] of good sweet and merchantable rye and of twenty bushels of good sweet and merchantable wheat to be clean' and made ready 'according to the usual measure commonly used' in Hereford market place. This was to be issued every year, the corn coming from the manor and farms of Garnons and Barrs Court in Herefordshire and from the other lands, messuages and tenements belonging to John and Robert Garnons in Hereford and the parishes of Mansell Gamage, Byford, Shutton and Peterchurch. This spread the area from which the corn would come and allowed for localised poor harvests. Interestingly, it supports Hugh's family connection being with Garnons and the Mansell Gamage area, which perhaps was the reason the corn was to be obtained here.

The dates for the delivery of the corn had not been set out by Blanche so they were agreed to be arranged in seven equal portions. These would be on the feasts of: All Saints

- 1 November; St. Thomas the Apostle - 21 December; the Purification of the Virgin Mary - Candlemas 2 February; Easter; Pentecost; St. Bartholomew - 24 August; St. Michael the Archangel - Michaelmas 29 September.

Of these Easter, whose date changed each year being moveable between 22 March to 25 April and Pentecost - Whitsunday, which was 50 days (six weeks) after Easter, were spring feasts. In 1590 Easter Sunday was on 19 April.[11] So the delivery intervals were not always exactly the same. The place for delivery was 'the house called the Common Bakehouse' in or near Hereford. Twelve days were allowed after each feast day for delivery. However, provision was also made if any of the corn was not delivered to Hugh Bethell, Thomas Powell, their heirs or assigns, who would be the Dean and Chapter of Hereford Cathedral. In this event those assigned to collect could lawfully enter the designated area and could carry away the said amount of corn. Failing this, for every twelve days of non-delivery a sum of £3 6s 8d would have to be paid by John and Robert Garnons or their heirs and goods could be impounded until full payment was made. John and Robert Garnons reiterated that they owned the property and various legal injunctions were added to ensure the smooth delivery of the corn for the future. The arrangements all seemed to be very efficient and Blanche's executors appear to have acted conscientiously. However, as Hugh Bethell lived in Yorkshire and Thomas Powell in London, neither was in a position to monitor the situation.

It is strange that there seems to be no record of the Dean and Chapter being informed of their purported role, a curious omission in view of the care taken to implement the other provisions in Blanche's Will. In addition, confusion arose over the £500 for the purchase of land for an almshouse, indicating that the Will was not read in its entirety. However, the poor do seem to have received their dole, though it is difficult to determine how it was managed. At some point the Garnons estate ceased, or diverted, the payments and land was bought. Quite how the position changed from corn obtained as determined by the Garnons Indenture, to corn from purchased land is not clear. One hopes the poor continued to receive their due.

On 19 January 1757 a letter was written from a J. Scudamore to the then Dean of Hereford, Francis Webber.[12] The letter said:

> .... About a year and a half ago I put into your hands the copy of Blanche Parry's Will, wherein it appears she left an Estate to pay the poor of Bacton and Newton two score bushels of wheat and rye and the Dean and Chapter for the time being Trustees of this Charity. The poor are miserably used by the Tenant and in short for sometime past have received such corn that it has been impossible to make bread and it would be out of great goodness in you to inquire into this matter and recommend it to the Chapter to extent their authority and oblige the tenant to pay in eatable corn, or to turn him out; and I will engage to find such a tenant that the poor shall have no reason to complain of ...

The poor were certainly not getting the 'sweet corn' envisaged in the Garnons Indenture. Indeed, the picture here of the poor being short-changed is appalling, though typical of the poverty in rural Herefordshire at that time. The influential Mr. Scudamore, related to the Scudamores of Kentchurch and Holme Lacy, was able to initiate an enquiry, though the Dean and Chapter took 3½ years to write a six page letter in mitigation to Lord Healey, Lord High Chancellor of Great Britain. This letter dated 5 June 1761 said that a William Newton was administering the Charity, though without apparent authorisation. They thought that the executors had spent the £500 on buying a farm called Upper Moor in the Parish of Bodenham which was let for an annual rent of more than £20. This money had been paid to William

Newton for several years and he had then used a small part of it to provide the corn for the poor of Bacton and Newton, retaining the rest for himself. The Dean and Chapter said that they would now require a full accounting from William Newton, although John Pritchard, the Overseer of the Poor of Bacton, had refused to join with them in this demand. The Dean and Chapter humbly desired to be acquitted of the charge of not fulfilling their duty and asked that a local gentleman of fortune and character should be asked to overseer the management of the Charity.

The situation was formalised by an entry in the Bacton Parish Book[13] for 29 August 1762:

> Agreement for the securing of yearly payments hath settled and charged an estate, Upper Moor Farm in Bodenham, in possession of William Newton and it not appearing that the said William Newton has made any nomination or appointed days for the delivery and payment of the said corn, only that the year begins the 24th August and ends 24th August the year following. But for the more certain payments of the said corn it is hereby agreed upon between William Newton and the parish of Bacton and St. Margarets [which now includes Newton] in the manner following, viz:
>
> the first 20 bushels to be delivered in Hereford the 1st Saturday after All Saints Day;
> the second 20 bushels after St. Thomas' Day;
> the 3rd 20 bushels the 1st Saturday after Candlemas;
> the 4th 20 bushels the 1st Saturday after Good Friday [Easter];
> the 5th 20 bushels the Saturday before Whitsunday [Pentecost];
> the 6th 20 bushels after the 1st Saturday after Midsummer Day / 24th June;
> the 7th 20 bushels the 1st Saturday after Lamas Day [1st August];
>
> and in a like manner from year to year; in Witness thereof we have set our hands in Witness the day and year first written above:
> William Newton, Morgan Pritchard, James Pritchard, John Waters, Will. Prosser
>
> Overseers of the Poor.

The only dates that differed from the Garnons Indenture was that 24 August became 24 June and the 29 September delivery was brought forward to 1 August; Lamas was traditionally celebrated by making a loaf from the first sheaf of harvested corn. This meant that deliveries were at fairly regular intervals.

The Bacton Parish Book shows that corn was fetched from Hereford and when corn was not available money was received instead, presumably to buy local corn. On 6 June 1893 Blanche Parry's Charity, by then the £14 half of the £28 rentcharge from The Upper Moore Estate, became a part of the Bacton Parochial Charities. A similar arrangement pertained for her Newton (now Newton Saint Margaret's) bequest which also had eventually become money (£14) and was then subsumed into a similar grouping of smaller charities. At Bacton, Blanche Parry's Charity was included on a Board erected by the Church door. Today, the £28 is still paid annually, being divided between the two parishes, and is a part of the sum used for the benefit of the respective parishioners. Although its value has considerably diminished (from the £3,500 value in 1590) it remains a regular and annual payment. Blanche Parry continues to be remembered in the Church where her family lie buried and by those now living beyond what was once Newcourt's park pale.

Abbreviations and Further Reading

Bradford (1935) — Charles Angell Bradford F.S.A. *Blanche Parry, Queen Elizabeth's Gentlewoman* (London c.1935)

BL — British Library

CSP Dom. — Calendar of State Papers Domestic

Faraday (2005) — M.A. Faraday, ed. *Herefordshire Taxes in the Reign of Henry VIII* (Woolhope Naturalists' Field Club, Herefordshire 2005)

HFNS — *The Herefordshire Field-Name Survey*, Ruth E. Richardson ed., copies in HRO and on the Herefordshire On-line website which has additional information. For discussion on meanings of field-names see Transactions of the Woolhope Naturalists' Field Club (1996) vol. XLVIII part III

HRO — Herefordshire Record Office

IPM — Inquisition Post Mortem

LP — *Letters and Papers, Foreign and Domestic, of the Reign of Henry VIII 1509-47*, ed. J.S. Brewer *et al.*, 21 vols. and addenda (London 1862-1932)

Merton — Charlotte Isabelle Merton, *The Women who served Queen Mary and Queen Elizabeth: Ladies, Gentlewomen and Maids of the Privy Chamber 1553-1603*, PhD thesis, Trinity College, Cambridge

Nichols — John Nichols, *The Progresses and Public Processions of Queen Elizabeth*, in 3 vols. (London 1823)

Richardson (2000) — Ruth E. Richardson, *Herefordshire Field-Names*, in *A Herefordshire Miscellany*, editors David Whitehead and John Eisel (Woolhope Naturalists' Field Club, Lapridge Publications 2000)

Richardson & Musson (2004) — Ruth E. Richardson & Chris Musson, *Herefordshire Past & Present* (Logaston Press 2004): the history and archaeology of the area

Shoesmith & Richardson (1997) — Ron Shoesmith & Ruth E. Richardson, editors *A Definitive History of Dore Abbey* (Logaston Press 1997)

TNA — The National Archives (formerly Public Record Office)

Vaughan (1610) *His Booke* — Rowland Vaughan (1610) *His Booke: Most Approved and Long experienced Water-Workes Containing The manner of Winter and Summer drowning of Meadow and Pasture ... As also a demonstration of a Project for the great benefit of the Commonwealth generally, but of Herefordshire especially*, republished and prefaced by Ellen Beatrice Wood (publisher John Hodges, London 1897)

Wedgwood & Holt (1936) — Col. The Rt. Hon. J.C. Wedgwood and A.D. Holt, *History of Parliament 1439-1509* (HMSO 1936)

Sources and References

Websites
www.blancheparry.com or www.blancheparry.co.uk
www.doreabbey.com or www.doreabbey.co.uk or www.doreabbey.org

Sources for the 9 Bardic Poems

Guto'r Glyn: The 5 poems are published in Welsh in John Llywelyn Williams, editor Sir Ifor Williams (1939, republished 1961), *Gwaith Guto'r Glyn (Guto'r Glyn's Work)*, Caerdydd Gwasg Prifysgol Cymru (Cardiff: University of Wales Press). I am grateful for the permission to use these Welsh texts. Three of these, *To Harri the Black of Ewyas, Gwladus Hael (the Generous),* and *The Death of Harri Ddu of Ewyas* have been translated into English and published in *Medieval Welsh Poems: An Anthology*, translated by Richard Loomis and Dafydd Johnston (Binghamton, NY, 1992), pp. 179-184. Copyright Pegasus Press, Asheville, North Carolina. The series is *Medieval and Renaissance Texts and Studies*, New York series. I am most grateful for the permission to use these English translations.
Eurig Salisbury, with comments by Professor Gruffydd Aled Williams, translated the remaining two poems, *To Harri ap Gruffudd* and *A Semi-Satire to Harri Gruffudd of Euas,* and transcribed and translated the following from the original manuscripts:

Gwilym Tew: *An Awdl asking for a stallion on behalf of Harri Stradling*, also in Anne Elizabeth Jones (1980) *Gwilym Tew: astudiaeth destunol a chymharol o'i lawysgrif, Peniarth 51, ynghyd ag ymdriniaeth a'i farddoniaeth* (Gwilym Tew: a comparative study of the text of his manuscript, Peniarth 51, dealing with his poetry therein), PhD thesis, University of Wales. This poem is Gw 452.

Howel Dafi: *A Poem to Harri Mil* (Henry Myles, Blanche's father) Peniarth MS 67. 66.

Huw Cae Llwyd: *To Troy in praise of Sir William Herbert*. Peniarth MS 189, 91. According to Leslie Harries (editor *Gweith Huw Cae Llwyd ac Eraill*, University of Wales Press, Caerdydd 1953) the poem was composed *c*.1463-1469. However, between 1469 and 1490 is a more concise rendering, which was given by William Gwyn Lewis (*Astudiaeth o ganu'r beirdd i'r Herbertiaid hyd ddechrau'r unfed ganrif ar bymtheg*, PhD thesis 1982). The copyright for the above five translations remains with Eurig Salisbury, 2006.

Lewys Morgannwg: *Elegy to the Lady Blanche* Llansteffan MS 164, 118 (*c*.1624) published in A. Cynfael Lake, editor, *Gwaith Lewys Morgannwg*, vol. 1, Aberystwyth, 2005. I am most grateful to Dr. Lake and Professor Geraint Jenkins for permission to use the modern Welsh and the English translation.

Abbreviations and Further Reading

Bradford (1935)	Charles Angell Bradford F.S.A. *Blanche Parry, Queen Elizabeth's Gentlewoman* (London *c*.1935).
BL	British Library.
CSP Dom.	Calendar of State Papers Domestic.
Faraday (2005)	M.A. Faraday, ed. *Herefordshire Taxes in the Reign of Henry VIII* (Woolhope Naturalists' Field Club, Herefordshire 2005).
HFNS	*The Herefordshire Field-Name Survey*, Ruth E. Richardson ed., copies in HRO and on the Herefordshire On-line website which has additional information. For discussion on meanings of field-names see Transactions of the Woolhope Naturalists' Field Club (1996) vol. XLVIII part III.
HRO	Herefordshire Record Office.
IPM	Inquisition Post Mortem.
LP	*Letters and Papers, Foreign and Domestic, of the Reign of Henry VIII 1509-47*, ed. J.S. Brewer *et al*, 21 vols. and addenda (London 1862-1932).
Merton	Charlotte Isabelle Merton, *The Women who served Queen Mary and Queen Elisabeth: Ladies, Gentlewomen and Maids of the Privy Chamber, 1553-1603*, PhD thesis, Trinity College, Cambridge.
Nichols	John Nichols, *The Progresses and Public Processions of Queen Elizabeth*, in 3 vols. (London 1823).
Richardson (2000)	Ruth E. Richardson, *Herefordshire Field-Names*, in *A Herefordshire Miscellany*, editors David Whitehead and John Eisel, (Woolhope Naturalists' Field Club, Lapridge Publications 2000).
Richardson & Musson (2004)	Ruth E. Richardson & Chris Musson, *Herefordshire Past & Present* (Logaston Press 2004), the history and archaeology of the area.
Shoesmith & Richardson (1997)	Ron Shoesmith & Ruth E. Richardson, editors *A Definitive History of Dore Abbey* (Logaston Press 1997).
TNA	The National Archives (formerly Public Record Office).
Vaughan (1610) *His Booke...*	Rowland Vaughan (1610), *His Booke - Most Approved and Long experienced Water-Works containing The manner of Winter and Summer drowning of Meadow and Pasture ... As also a demonstration of a Proiect for the great benefit of the Common-wealth generally, but of Herefordshire especially*, republished and prefaced by Ellen Beatrice Wood (published John Hodges, London 1897).
Wedgewood & Holt (1936)	Col. The Rt. Hon. J.C. Wedgewood, and A.D. Holt, *History of Parliament 1439-1509* (HMSO 1936).

References

Preface

1. SP Dom Elizabeth I, 1566.
2. Until 1752 the legal year in England changed date on 25 March, the feast of the Annunciation of the Blessed Virgin Mary, called Lady Day. In this book the modern dates will henceforth be given.
3. Additional information can be found on the website: www.blancheparry.co.uk.
4. Merton. This is invaluable for any study of these women, though it is wrong concerning Blanche's relationship to Sir Thomas Parry.
5. Edited Christopher Haigh (1984), *The Reign of Elizabeth I*, Macmillan Education.

Chapter 1

1. Sir Joseph A. Bradney (republished 1993), *A History of Monmouthshire*, vol. 3 part 1, Academy Books. HRO F37/10 grant of the manor from Vaughan to Hoskins. Also research by Barbara Griffiths on the Parry Family Tree and by Dewi Williams on Ewyas Lacy.
2. TNA IPMs C142/42 no.95 of Henry Myle, Blanche's father; C142/69 no.130 and C142/73 no.94 of Mylo ap Harry, Blanche's elder brother; C142/71 no.131 of Henry Myle, Mylo's son. These show the name change of this core land to *Mererickeston*, anglicised by a 1630 grant to *Tremorythige al. Moreithickeston*.
3. See Sources for the nine Bardic Poems, p.167.
4. 'To Harri ap Gruffudd' by Guto'r Glyn.
5. The other versions of his name included Gruffudd ap Harri, Gruffydd ap Harry, Griffithe ap Henry, Griffin ap Harry and Griffithe Aphenry which was an attempt to anglicise the name.
6. Nichols. Vol. III page 242, concerning the Cecil Pedigree at Theobalds.
7. David Powel (1584 reprinted for John Harding 1811), *The Historie of Cambria by H. Lhoyd, Gentleman augmented by David Powel*.
8. HRO AL2/4 Letters Patent, Henry IV, 1401-5, 13 September 1403 Pardon for Gruff ap Henri of Ewyas Laci and 14 September 1403 grant to William Beauchamp.
9. TNA SC 8/213/10624, Abbot Jordan Bykeleswade's 1398 Petition to the King.
10. See note 8 above.
11. See A.J. Winnington-Ingram (1967), *Hereford and the English Bible*, (Hereford Cathedral). Also the *Dictionary of National Biography* on Sir John Oldcastle and Derek J. Plumb (1987), *John Foxe and the Later Lollards of the Thames Valley*, PhD thesis (Corpus College, Cambridge) for the latest research.
12. HRO AL2/15 Calendar of Close Rolls 23 January 1417 John ap Harry required to refrain from doing hurt or adhering to Sir John Oldcastle.
13. The other versions of his name included Henry Griffith, Henry ap Griffith, Harry Ddu ap Gruffydd and Harri Ddu o Euas.
14. Robert Cooke, *The Visitation of Herefordshire 1569* (Exeter, privately published by William Pollard 1886).
15. TNA E 315/405 f.20.
16. HRO AL2/5 Patent Rolls 14 March and 16 May 1450 commitment by Henry Griffiths, esquire and Thomas Fitz Harry.
17. HRO AL2/15 Close Rolls 8 September 1452 recognisance of Henry Gryffyth of Neweplace within the lordship of Ewyas in the march of Wales. All conversions are from the TNA currency converter 2006.
18. HRO AL2/5 Patent Rolls 22 March 1460 grant for life to Henry ap Griffith of the office of Steward.
19. In *Cerdd i Harri Mil*, A Poem to Harri Mil (Henry Myles, Blanche's father).
20. HRO AL2/5 Patent Rolls 28 July 1460 commission to Walter Devereux, James Baskerville, Eustace Witteney, Henry Griffith, Simon Mylburn, Richard Crofte and Thomas Monyngton, esquires.

21. H.T. Evans (1915/1995), *Wales and the Wars of the Roses*, Alan Sutton Publishing Ltd, quoting CPR 360 and 367, CPR 554, 22 March 1460 and ibid 51, 1453, CPR 608, 28 July, CPR 1461, 451.
22. HRO AL2/5 Patent Rolls 1 July 1463 and 28 March 1465 commissions.
23. See note 14.
24. See Williams (1939, 1961), under Guto'r Glyn in the Sources for Bardic Poems, p.167.
25. See Loomis and Johnston (1992), under Guto'r Glyn in the Sources for Bardic Poems, p.167.
26. The other versions of his name included Miles Aparry, Myle ap Harry, Mylo ap Harry and Myles Parrye.
27. See summary in Anthony Fletcher & Diarmaid MacCulloch (4th edition 1997), *Tudor Rebellions*, Longman.
28. Calendar of Patent Rolls, Henry VI, 7 June 1557, general pardon.
29. W.E. Griffiths (1974), 'The Herefordshire Escheators of the 15th century'. *Transactions of the Woolhope Naturalists' Field Club,* Vol. XLI part II (1974), pp.198-212; Wedgewood & Holt (1936).
30. HRO AL2/5 Patent Rolls 6 June 1473; Evans (1915/1995) see note 21.
31. Patent Rolls 1 May 1484 and 8 December 1484, commissions of array naming William Earl of Huntyngdon and Simon Milborn / Milburn among the nine knights. Miles ap Herry was among the seven others. The list ended with the Sheriff of Herefordshire.
32. TNA PROB 11/8 Will of Milo Aparry esquire 10 February 1488, proved 21 November.
33. Charles Angell Bradford (1935), *Blanche Parry, Queen Elizabeth's Gentlewoman*, describes the circumstances of Mrs. Burton's removal of the windows, with references. Mrs. Mary Burton was a descendant of the Parry family and her husband was incumbent at Atcham. It was said that at a time when there was no rector at Bacton, the windows were in danger of being damaged by boys throwing stones, and Mrs. Burton decided that they must be moved to a safer place. In 1811 she secured the churchwardens' permission by making them 'merry'. The parishioners were furious and sued for the windows' return but to no avail. Rev. J.G. Munro (Rector of Bacton 1891-1903) negotiated for their return by offering replacement cathedral glass but to no avail. In 1894 at Atcham the wind was said to have damaged another window commemorating Blanche herself, occasioning replacement.
34. See note 19.
35. The other versions of her name were Aeles and Alis.
36. Caroline A.J. Skeel (1904), *The Council in the Marches of Wales, a study in local government during the sixteenth and seventeenth centuries*, Hugh Rees Ltd., London.
37. TNA C49/69/9 order for Henry Miles to appear before the King, 1514.
38. HRO AL2/15 Close Rolls Henry VII 9 May 1505 recognisance to keep the peace by Sir Walter Herbert, William Herbert of Troye and Henry Mile of Newecourt esquires.
39. TNA E314/100 memorandum of debts claimed by Abbot John Longdon from Henry Mile; E111/24 answers of Henry Myle esquire to the complaints of the Abbot of Dore.
40. TNA E315/405 memorandum concerning Henry Mile esquire 1516.
41. TNA C142/42 no.95 IPM of Henry Myle.

Chapter 2

1. TNA C139/52/72 m.1, 4 IPMs of Henry VI.
2. See, for example, Cardinal Gasquet (1909 fourth edition), *Parish Life in Mediaeval England*, Methuen & Co. Ltd. London.
3. It is Robert from whom the Whitneys in the USA descend. See also Henry Melville (1896) *The Ancestry of John Whitney*, New York, The De Vinne Press.
4. There is debate about the paternity of Catherine and Henry Carey, whose mother was Mary Boleyn, sister of Queen Anne and former mistress of Henry VIII. If one or both were the king's this could not be acknowledged as it would have been considered incest, calling into question Elizabeth's legitimacy. Nevertheless, Elizabeth favoured both.

5. Michael Powell Siddons, transcribed and edited (1996), *Visitations by the Heralds in Wales (and Herefordshire) 1531*, also (2002) *The Visitation of Herefordshire 1634,* both published by The Harleian Society, London.
6. Huw Cae Llwyd, whose circuit included the Herbert family, composed *To Troy, in praise of Sir William Herbert*, which begins: 'May the Lord our Father keep the flowers [i.e. descendants] of Dafydd Gam ...' (translator Eurig Salisbury).
7. W.A.Shaw (1906), *The Knights of England*, London. William Herbert was created a Knight Bachelor between Easter and Michaelmas 1516.
8. TNA PROB11/21 Will of Sir William Herbert, Knight, 15 March 1523.
9. Clifford Brewer (2000), *The Death of Kings*, Abson Books, London.
10. Christopher Dyer (1989), *Standards of living in the later Middle Ages*, Cambridge, and similar books.
11. Iona & Peter Opie (1959), *The Lore & Language of Schoolchildren*, Oxford Paperbacks, and similar books.
12. Mulcaster's two books were (1581) *The Positions* and (1582) *The Elementaries.*
13. See the Parry IPMs for extent of lands. Ditton, known as Dotton in 1292, is confirmed as being in Dorstone by the Delabere IPMs, owners in the 15th century.
14. Brian Smith (2004), *Herefordshire Maps 1577-1800*, Logaston Press.
15. BL Lansdowne 102 no 94 property conveyance of the manor of Glasbury in Lord Burghley's handwriting and notes for Blanche Parry's Will.
16. BL Lansdowne MS 62 f 119 an earlier Will of Blanche Parry.
17. Gwent Record Office, Cwmbran, MAN/A/151/0022 grant 28 Elizabeth with a later addition by Sir John Hoskins. Also MAN/A/151/0024 survey of 1624.
18. A superb Welsh-type late medieval rood loft and screen has survived in nearby Saint Margaret's Church.
19. Eamon Duffy (1992), *The Stripping of the Altars, Traditional Religion in England c.1400-c.1580*, Yale University Press, New Haven and London. Also (2001), *The Voices of Morebath, Reformation & Rebellion in an English Village*, Yale University Press, New Haven and London. Also Diarmaid MacCulloch (2003), *Reformation, Europe's House Divided 1490-1700*, Allen Lane an imprint of Penguin Books.
20. In 1348 Bishop John Trillek listed 16 altars in Vowchurch Church: the High Altar, Virgin Mary, Saints John the Baptist, Apostle Bartholomew, Laurence, King Ethelbert, Blaise, Martin, Gregory, Thomas of Hereford, Mary Magdalene, Agnes, Cecilia, Katherine, Margaret and Milburga.
21. BL Lansdowne 62 f 119 Brief of Mrs Blanch A Paries Will.
22. Clergyman were usually designated 'Sir'.
23. CSP Dom & Foreign of Henry VIII, vol.XI, no.1370 (1536). HRO copy *The Story of Aconbury* by Rev. D.E. Jones and in D. Whitehead in *Archaeological News* no.51.
24. HRO AL2 Letters Patent 10 June 33 Henry VIII, Hugh ap Harry of Aconbury and Elinor his wife granted licence to alienate.
25. Roger, the eldest son, is mentioned in Queen Elizabeth's pardon roll of 1559 as of Porthaml and Newcourt. He was a commissioner re the Stradling icon. His son Rowland was the MP who married Elizabeth. Her sister Joan married Roger's brother.
26. HRO 8 February 1528 marriage banns recorded in the Register of Bishop Charles Booth of Hereford.
27. Charles Nicholl (1992), *The Reckoning, the Murder of Christopher Marlowe*, Picador.
28. Eric Ives (1986), *Anne Boleyn*, Basil Blackwell.

Chapter 3

1. Calendar of the Manuscripts of the Most Hon. the Marquis of Salisbury part XI Dublin 1960, a report on the subversive activities of the Earl of Essex and Mr. Roger Vaughan in 1601 which John Garnons forwarded to Sir Robert Cecil. The unnamed writer was married to John Garnons' goddaughter.

2. Edward Hall (1809), *Chronicle, collated editions of 1548 and 1550*, London, contemporary account. David Starkey (2000) *Elizabeth: Apprenticeship* and (2003) *Six Wives, The Queens of Henry VIII*, both Chatto & Windus London.
3. LP 1536 no 203 Lady Bryan's letter to Cromwell.
4. LP 1537 no 911 the Christening of Prince Edward.
5. A. Cynfael Lake (2005) transcriber and translator, see Sources for Bardic Poems, p.167. Additional comments Professor G.A.Williams. Copyright Dr. Lake.
6. Nichols from BL Cotton MS Vespasian C xiv.
7. LP 1536 no 1187 Household lists.
8. LP 1536 no 639 Kateryn Champernon to Thomas Cromwell.
9. Roger Ascham (1570), *The Scholemaster*, Book II includes two paragraphs and a poem detailing his grief at the untimely death of *Myne owne John Whitney*.
10. Translated by Maurice Hatch and Alvin Vos, edited Alvin Vos, *Letters of Roger Ascham* (Peter Lang 1989).
11. Calendar of State Papers, Edward VI, 1549, letter concerning the Seymour affair.
12. *Household Account of the Princess Elizabeth 1551-1552*, reprinted in The Camden Miscellany LV, Camden Old Series, vol II, 1853.
13. TNA PROB 11/40 Will of Sir Charles Harbert of Mitchel Troy, Monmouthshire.
14. See note 10.
15. BL Lansdowne 1236 f 35.
16. A. Jefferies Collins (1955), *Jewels and Plate of Queen Elizabeth I, the Inventory of 1574, edited from Harley MS. 1650 and Stowe MS. 555*, Trustees of the British Museum, London.
17. Merton, thesis.
18. Bradford (1935); TNA LC2/4/3 f 53 lists cloth issued for Queen Elizabeth I's Coronation 1559.
19. BL Lansdowne MS 59 f 43.
20. See note 17.
21. Lady Stafford's monument is to the left of the door as one enters Saint Margaret's, Westminster and like Blanche's, which is on the right, has been moved. Originally she faced the altar.
22. See note 16.
23. See note 10.

Chapter 4

1. One of many sources for these restrictions is Roger Ascham.
2. Rowland Vaughan (1610, reprinted 1897).
3. Merton offers persuasive arguments to demonstrate the falsity of Vaughan's point of view.
4. TNA LC2/4/3 f 53; Bradford (1935).
5. (1995), *The Journals of Two Travellers in Elizabethan and Early Stuart England - Thomas Platter and Horatio Busino*, Caliban Books.
6. John Nichols (1823), *The Progresses and Public Processions of Queen Elizabeth*, in three volumes, London.
7. John Steane (1993), *The Archaeology of the Medieval English Monarchy*, Routledge.
8. See note 6.
9. See note 6.
10. See note 6.
11. See note 6.
12. TNA LC5/33, fol.50.
13. TNA LC5/33 fols.15, 50, 51, 71, 91, 118. Warrants dated 20 October 1562, 4 May and 2 November 1563 and 31 May and 27 September 1564; Merton.
14. Dr. John Johnston (1578), *A Description of the Nature of Four-Footed Beasts, written in Latin, translated into English*, London. Copy belonging to the University of Wisconsin,

U.S.A. (Edward Topsell 1607). *The Historie of Foure-footed Beastes* has an illustration of a moschatte.

15. Painting in the collection of the Duke of Buccleuch and Queensberry. For Bacton embroidery see Lionel Cust 1913 in *Burlington Magazine*.
16. Janet Arnold (1980), *'Lost from Her Majesties Back' Items of clothing and jewels lost or given away by Queen Elizabeth I between 1561 and 1585*... edited from The Duchess of Norfolk deeds MS C/115/L2/6698 in the NA. The Costume Society.
17. Nichols vol II.
18. Thomas Knyvett as Keeper of Whitehall Palace led the 1604 search of the vaults that apprehended Guy Fawkes. Thomas was ennobled as Baron Escrick and 10 Downing Street now stands on the site of his London house.
19. Dr. Parry would become Bishop of Gloucester in 1607, being translated to Worcester in 1610 where he served until his death in 1616.
20. Bradford (1935).
21. TNA PROB 11/65 Will of Lady Latimer.
22. See note 6.
23. The painting belongs to the Trustees of Lady Beauchamp's Will Trust.
24. George Gascoigne (1585, reprinted 1903 and 1910), *The Queen's Majesty's Entertainment at Woodstock 1575*, with an Introduction by A.W. Pollard.
25. See note 6.
26. H.D.W. Sitwell (June 1962), *The Jewel House and the Royal Goldsmiths. The Archaeological Journal*,Vol.CXVII, pp.131-155. This names royal goldsmiths as Robert Brandon, Hugh Keall / Kayle and Richard Martin.
27. SP Dom. 12/8 No.24 f 51-2, 1559.
28. State Papers Domestic of Elizabeth.
29. See note 12.
30. BL Egerton MS 3052.
31. A. Jefferies Collins (1955), *Jewels and Plate of Queen Elizabeth I, the Inventory of 1574*, British Museum.
32. Bradford (1939), *Hugh Morgan, Queen Elizabeth's Apothecary*, Heron & Co. London. J.O.Swahn (1991), *The Lore of Spices*, Senate Publishing Ltd., London. Hugh Morgan was one of four known apothecaries at the Elizabethan Court. In 1602 he first used vanilla as a sweetener in candies to the delight of the sweet-toothed Queen.
33. Edited by Simon Adams (1995), *Household Accounts and Disbursement Books of Robert Dudley, Earl of Leicester, 1558-1561, 1584-1586*, Cambridge University Press.
34. TNA PROB 11/61 Will of Margaret Dane.
35. TNA LC5/33 f 91.
36. Margaret's various benefactions, now a trust fund, still operate as do the links she established with Bishop Stortford in Hertfordshire, her husband's home town, where she followed his example in providing for a school.
37. BL RM Appendix 68 f 7.
38. See note 13.
39. Janet Arnold (1980), *'Lost from Her Majesties Back' Items of clothing and jewels lost or given away by Queen Elizabeth I between 1561 and 1585*....... edited from The Duchess of Norfolk deeds MS C/115/L2/6698 in the PRO. The Costume Society. Gives details of clothes and sables. The specific references to Blanche taking delivery of jewels for French hoods are:
    October 1579 of 29 gold buttons set with rubies.
    Twice in October 1580, 19 gold buttons, each set with a diamond.
    23 November 1580, 19 gold buttons set with five turquoises 'sent up by Mrs. Twist', the entry repeated with the added note 'to set upon a billement'.
    17 April 1581 14 pieces of roses of diamonds, 23 pieces of 'another sort' of diamonds and 13 spinel rubies in a delicate rose red variety, 'being all of her own charge before'.

1581, 'delivered to Mrs. Blaunch Pary at whitehall' 37 gold buttons, each set with a rich diamond, entry repeated 18 April 1581 'at whitehall'.
23 April 1581, 2 gold buttons each set with a single table ruby, a name which applied to the top facet of a brilliant cut stone.
The repetition of 19 and 37 suggests a standardisation in the patterns for the decorative features of French hoods.

40. A. Jefferies Collins (1955), *Jewels and Plate of Queen Elizabeth I, the Inventory of 1574*, British Museum.
41. These two chains were probably the ones described as being ornamented by two great enamelled roses, which were recycled between 1588 and 1589 to be made into buttons for the Queen.
42. BL Royal MSS Appendix 68.
43. Elizabeth's jewellery can be seen in her portraits. See also, editor Susan Doran, guest curator David Starkey, (2003), *Elizabeth, the Exhibition at the National Maritime Museum* (Chatto & Windus).
44. The Radcliffe Inventory included: 59 jewelled flowers or ouches (clasps or buckles), 5 crosses, a crucifix and a gold ship, 3 brooches, 27 tablets and pendants including one of 'unicorn horn', 38 bracelets and 68 gold chains, one 'enamelled black with pearls in gold links' measuring 6¾ yards. 12 'carkanetts' and laces, with 13 buttons and aglets (the metal tag of a lace), 8 beads of 'gold, agate and pearls', 31 loose stones and pearls, 3 collars, 2 colletts and 16 girdles. The 11 furs were mostly sable and all were jewelled or had gold attachments. The 68 bodkins, mostly for confining the hair, nearly all of gold, included a gold bodkin 'garnished with two diamonds and two small rubies noted as remaining in the bed chamber', as presumably it was a current favourite with the Queen. There were 12 'habillaments' and 17 'attiers' (jewelled nets or caps) for decorating the hair, 2 looking glasses, 2 knives and 7 gorgeous fans of ostrich feathers or swansdown all heavily jewelled with gold handles. The 83 'sundry' items included a gold toothpick set with emeralds, diamonds, rubies and pearls and a small gold eyebath, 24 clocks and watches (including the 'cunningly wrought ones' that Thomas Platter would see at Whitehall). 9 books with covers of gold, silver or gilt. 104 rings included the two seal rings mentioned in the text. The pictorial items included the items mentioned. The list for Mary Radcliffe was signed by William Jenison junior with the observation, in Latin, that 'it agrees with the original'.
45. SP Dom. Elizabeth 1568/69.
46. Manuscripts of the Most Hon. the Marquis of Salisbury, preserved at Hatfield House, Hertfordshire, CP 12/59.
47. SP Irish Elizabeth; Bradford (1935).
48. SP Dom. 1584.
49. Statutes of the Realm 27 Eliz c2; 4&5 Philip and Mary c3; 31 Eliz c4.
50. Susan Doran (2003) (see note 43).
51. Dr. Christiane Lukatis 17 March 2004.
52. Jennifer Loach (1999), *Edward VI*, Yale English Monarchs.
53. SP For 1569.
54. See note 5.
55. Merton referring to Princess Elizabeth's interview with the Count of Feria, 10 November 1558.

Chapter 5

1. Nichols, vol III, p 543.
2. HRO BG11/17/11 f 176.
3. HRO BG11/23/1 Hereford City Records.
4. Rev. John Montgomery Traherne (1840), *Stradling Correspondence*, Longman, Orme, Green and Longmans; and William Bird, Cardiff.
5. Gareth Jones (1977), *A New History of Wales, The Gentry and the Elizabethan State*, Christopher Davies. SP Dom. Elizabeth I.

6. Christopher Haigh (1998 and 2001), *Elizabeth I*, Longman.
7. Eric Ives (1986), *Anne Boleyn*, Basil Blackwell, especially pages 161 and 314.
8. Merton from Rodriguez-Salgado and Adams, *The Count of Feria's dispatch to Philip II, 1554*, Camden Miscellany XXVIII 1984.
9. One of Wycliffe's translators was Nicholas Hereford who after recanting was appointed to the staff of Hereford Cathedral. The Cathedral Library has a 1420 manuscript copy of the Lollard Bible.
10. Derek J. Plumb, *John Foxe and the Later Lollards of the Thames Valley*, PhD thesis (Corpus Christi College, Cambridge, 1987).
11. Caroline A.J. Skeel (1904), *The Council in the Marches of Wales*, Hugh Rees Ltd., London, quoting Bagot manuscript.
12. The tradition of dissent may have contributed to Almeley being the site of an early Friends / Quaker Meeting House in the 17th century.
13. TNA C43/2/22 19 Henry VIII (*c*.1528) feoffees of Simon Milborne, and C1/658/36 (1529-1532). Wedgewood & Holt (1936), *History of Parliament 1439-1509*, HMSO. HRO Lists of Herefordshire MPs.
14. Compare this with her coupling of the Dean of Hereford Cathedral with the Chapter — see page 128.
15. His boyhood home was Ty Mawr, Wybrnant, Betws-y-Coed, Conwy. The stone-built upland farmhouse has been beautifully restored to its probable 16th/17th century appearance. There is an exhibition of Bibles.
16. William Morgan became the Bishop of Llandaff and then of Saint Asaph where he is buried.
17. Anthony Fletcher & Diarmaid MacCulloch (4th edition 1997), *Tudor Rebellions*, Longman, gives a lucid account of the order of events concerning the Northern Rebellion.
18. All letters in this section are from the Calendar of State Papers, Domestic Series, Edward VI, Mary, Elizabeth, 1547-1580. (1871), HMSO.
19. Merton from Historical Monuments Commission *Salisbury*, letter to Cecil 1568.
20. General editor Earl Jowitt (1959), *The Dictionary of English Law*, London.
21. The exact date is given in *The History of Parliament 1558-1603*.
22. Cumbria Record Office DSTAN/2/3.
23. East Riding Archives DDRI/26/9.
24. HRO list of the Mayors of Hereford written into the (20 Henry VII), 'Rental of Dynmore and Garway taken before Thomas Leyland in the time of Mr. Lancelot Docwra Kt. Preceptor.'
25. HRO BG11/17/6 Miscellaneous papers 1378-1687, Hereford City Documents No.78 page 181.
26. SP Dom Elizabeth I, 1568.
27. TNA SP Dom 1564.
28. Edited James Orchard Halliwell (MDCCCXLII), *The Private Diary of Dr. John Dee*, London printed for The Camden Society.
29. Edited The Rev. John Montgomery Traherne (1840), *Stradling Correspondence*, London. Blanche's letter is CLXXXIV.
30. BL Addit. MSS. 23212 fol.187. Charles Angel Bradford (1939) *Hugh Morgan, Queen Elizabeth's Apothecary*, Heron & Co. Ltd. London.
31. Lambeth Palace Library MS 3198 ff.189 and ff.59. Talbot Papers.
32. The Earl of Shrewsbury owned Coldharbour, which was near Cannon Street Station, Sheffield Castle and only a mile distant, Sheffield Manor.
33. The story of William and Jane Shelley is given in detail, with references, in *Notes and Queries*, 10th Ser. Vols. III and IV.
34. Alan Haynes (2004), *The Elizabethan Secret Services*, Sutton Publishing.
35. HRO A63/11/316 relating to law-suits of Thomas Coningsby.
36. TNA CP24/11.
37. Much of the story is set out in *Notes and Queries*.

38. BL Lansdowne 54, 46.
39. TNA SP46/34.
40. TNA SP46/18.

Chapter 6

1. Katherine S.H. Wyndham (1979-1980), *Crown Land and Royal Patronage in Mid-Sixteenth Century England*, The Journal of British Studies, Vol.19, part 2.
2. Cal Patent Rolls 1559.
3. Calendar of the Manuscripts of the Most Hon. the Marquis of Salisbury preserved at Hatfield House, Hertfordshire, 1883.
4. There had been a similar arrangement for the daughters of Blanche's brother Milo ap Harry.
5. William Rees (1947), *A History of the Order of St. John of Jerusalem in Wales and on the Welsh Border, including an Account of the Templars*, Cardiff.
6. HRO K11/3253.
7. TNA C66/1011.
8. HRO original tithe maps, reduced sized copies published by *HFNS*. For Fawley see 1843 Fownhope.
9. HRO AS58/2/16, 1588 copy of Indenture between Blanche Parry, Francis Vaughan and Richard Cox. Original withdrawn from TNA 1899.
10. TNA C/115 f 1.2587. See Elizabeth Taylor (1986), 'The Seventeenth Century Iron Forge at Carey Mill', *Transactions of the Woolhope Naturalists' Field Club*, Vol.XLV part II.
11. See note 9.
12. HRO 1843 Sutton Saint Michael tithe.
13. Close Rolls vol 15, 8 Elizabeth, part 5,
14. Pilley Collection in Hereford City Library.
15. TNA REQ2/167/32 Blanche v John Jones re lease of tithes of Wisteston Chapel formerly belonging to St. John of Jerusalem.
16. HRO A63/111/23/1 the Hospitallers' Rental 1505.
17. TNA REQ2/170/42 although granted to Blanche by Letters Patent, John Haworth maintained this land in Wellington was copyhold of the manors of Upleadon and Garway, both formerly owned by Dinmore Commandery.
18. TNA REQ2/127/6 first document: Blanche's petition, and third: Richard Cox's answer 22 June 1566. TNA REQ2/111/37 second: Blanche's complaint 6 June 1566.
19. See note 9.
20. TNA STAC 5/P15/4.
21. TNA Cal Patent Rolls 3279 m.25.
22. TNA SP/46/36/10 and E178/3323. Also *Brycheiniog* vol XXII (1986-1987). And see Plate 9.
23. TNA STAC 5/P8/8, 5/P13/3, 5/P17/13, 5/P18/26, 5/P19/22, 5/P49/8, 5/P59/25, 5/P61/34.
24. TNA PROB 6 PCC Administration Act Books 1585 f 134 Canterbury, Sir Roger Vaughan 31 March 1585.
25. BL Lansdowne MS 47 number 47.
26. See note 23.
27. TNA C66/1154; Cal Patent Rolls 2010.
28. BL Lansdowne MS 106 no 33.
29. Robert's execution was obliquely remembered in his brother Christopher's epitaph in Aughton Church; written in Old French it translates as 'Christopher, the second son of Robert Aske, chevalier, ought not to forget the year of our Lord 1536'. See Victoria County History of Yorkshire East Riding (1976) vol III.
30. *South wood* is *Southscogh* in the 13th Cartulary of Fountains Abbey (ed. W.T. Lancaster). At OS SE 6844.
31. Phil Thomas (2003), *The Priory Church of St. Mary the Virgin and St. Lawrence at Ellerton in the East Riding of Yorkshire. A Little Guidebook*, Ellerton Church Preservation

Trust. Nearly 300 acres of ings in Wheldrake with 100 acres in Thorganby were designated a nature reserve 1971-1972.
32. Hull University Library DDJ/14/395 Thorganby Enclosure Award.
33. TNA Patent Rolls 402 m.16, m.17, m.18. 14 June 1567. TNA C66/1109.
34. Richardson (2000).
35. Ruth E. Richardson (February 2001), 'The Early History of Drama', *The English Review*, Vol.11, Num.3.
36. These lists will be given in full on www.blancheparry.co.uk.
37. TNA Patent Rolls 348 m.4, 13 December 1572.
38. TNA Patent Rolls 1111 m1, m2, m3 7 July 1574. TNA Patent Rolls 1387 m16, 16 July 1582.
39. Calendar of the Manuscripts of the Duke of Rutland vol 4, 15 December 1583 Belvoir Castle.
40. BL Lansdowne 102 no 94 property conveyance of the manor of Glasbury, in Lord Burghley's handwriting and notes for Blanche Parry's Will.
41. BL Lansdowne 109 no 90.
42. Eric St. John Brooks (1946), *Sir Christopher Hatton*, Jonathan Cape, London.
43. Bradford and Jones' *Brecknock* vol.i p. 119.
44. See note 25.
45. Frederick Clifton Pierce (1895), *The Descendants of John Whitney*, Chicago. Transcribed by the Whitney Research Group, 1999, extracts on Internet: whitneygen.org. Also Henry Melville esq. John Whitney, Puritan Emigrant.

Chapter 7

1. Lambeth Palace Library MS 3198 f 552 Talbot Papers. Markham had been a standard-bearer for the Queen's Gentlemen Pensioners in 1567.
2. Hatfield CP37/105. The letter is probably from Dr. Stanhope, who had walked with Knollys at the Earl of Leicester's funeral on 10 October 1588.
3. Nichols demonstrates the regularity of these peals.
4. Pilley Collection 906 Hereford City Library.
5. Blanche's tomb is fully described by The National Association of Decorative and Fine Arts Societies (NADFAS).
6. Described by NADFAS. The suggested quarterings: 1 & 8 Parry, 2 Owen, 3 Barr, 4 Fane, 5 Milborne, 6 Dobyns?, 7 Furneau? The alternatives in the text are tentatively suggested by the author.
7. Roy Strong (1995), *The Tudor and Stuart Monarchy, Pageantry, Painting, Iconography. II Elizabethan*, The Boydell Press.
8. Walter Pilley (1848-1913), a baker and confectioner, was Mayor of Hereford in 1910 and 1911. He bequeathed to the city a huge, and invaluable, collection that included books, manuscripts, letters, pictures, wax seals and coins.
9. Hereford City Library, Pilley Collection 906. Includes a newspaper cutting saying the portrait 'is now in the possession of Mr. Parry of Harewood' and a photograph of the portrait of Queen Elizabeth I.
10. Alan Haynes (2004), *The Elizabethan Secret Services*, Sutton Publishing, describes how those searching for two Catholic priests, Robert Persons and Edmund Campion, were provided with woodcut portraits to aid identification.
11. Nikolaus Pevsner (1963), *The Buildings of England, Herefordshire*, Penguin Books.
12. J.W. Tonkin (1977), *Herefordshire*, Batsford.
13. See note 7.
14. Christopher Haigh (2001), *Elizabeth I*, Longman.
15. D.M. Annett (1999), *Saints in Herefordshire, a Study of Dedications,* Logaston Press.
16. http://www.conques.com.

Appendix 1

1. Faraday (2005). The original rotulets, or documents, are TNA E179/117/106 lay subsidies. Rotulet 1 shows eight entries for Bacton and four for Bacton and Newcourt together, while rotulet 7 shows eight for Bacton alone and four for Newcourt.
2. HRO F37/10 feoffment of 11 February 5 Charles (1630) in the records of the Whitehouse Estate, Vowchurch; HRO F37/4 rent book.
3. Preserved by Walter Pilley in the Pilley Collection in Hereford Library.
4. David Whitehead (2001), *A Survey of Historic Parks & Gardens of Herefordshire*, Hereford and Worcester Gardens Trust.
5. HRO F33/1 for maps.
6. HRO *HFNS* booklets and the original tithe maps and apportionments.

Appendix 2

1. BL Lansdowne 102 no 94 property conveyance of the manor of Glasbury in Lord Burghley's handwriting and notes for Blanche Parry's Will. All transcriptions Sue Hubbard.
2. BL Lansdowne 62 no 119.
3. See note 2.
4. BL Lansdowne 47 no 47 William's death is given as 26 Elizabeth.
5. TNA STAC 5/P15/4.
6. BL Lansdowne 109 no 90.
7. TNA PROB 11/75. Will published privately by Sir Thomas Phillipps in 1845.
8. BL Lansdowne 62 no 51.
9. East Riding Archives DDRI/26/9.
10. TNA C147/88.
11. Edited C.R. Cheney, revised Michael Jones (1945-2000), *A Handbook of Dates for students of British History*, Cambridge University Press.
12. Notes held at Bacton Church from Hereford City Library Pilley Collection 906.
13. HRO property of Bacton Parish.

Index

Aconbury nunnery 32-34
Almeley, Herefordshire 10, 87-89
Ascham, Roger 44, 46, 56
Ashley, John 44, 53, 56
Ashley, Kate 42, 43-44, 46-69, 51, 53, 55-56, 63, 66, 109
Atcham Church 19

Bacton Church 15, 19, 25, 31-32, 62, 84-85, 147, 150, 165
Bacton parish 31-32, 127-128, 162-165
Ballard, George 4, 137
bards and bardic verses 7-8, 11, 13-17, 20, 39-41
Baskerville, Jane (Blanche Parry's grandmother) 21, 139-140
de Barr, William 9, 139
Beard, Benjamin 106
Beauchamp, Joan 9
Berington, Thomas 115
Berrowe, Maud 130
Berrowe, William 98, 128, 130, 132, 162
Bertie, Richard 55
Bethell, Hugh 34, 97-98, 124, 127, 132, 162-164
Bingham, Sir Richard 78
Blythe, Bishop George 88
Boleyn, Anne 28, 35, 37, 38-39, 57, 62, 83-84, 87
Boughton, Louis 100
Bourne, Anthony 103
Bourne, Elizabeth 103-104
Bradbelt, Dorothy 4
Bradford, Charles Angell 4-5
Brecknock Mere 116-119
Brereton, William 35
Breynton, John 115
Buckingham, Thomas 110
Buckingham, Stephen 110
Bull, Elinor 72, 132
Burgh, Lady *see* Vaughan, Frances
Burgh, Thomas 124
Burghley, Lord *see* Cecil, Sir William
Byddel, Robert 104
Bykelswade, Abbot Jordan 9

Camden, William 128
Carey, Catherine, Lady Knollys 50, 71
Catherine of Aragon 28, 38, 42, 62, 83
Catholicism 44, 84-86
Cecil, Sir Robert 106, 127, 129, 158
Cecil, Sir William, Lord Burghley 4, 9, 30, 52, 60, 67, 73-74, 77-78, 80, 81, 86, 91, 93, 96, 100, 104, 107-108, 116, 118-120, 124, 125-127, 130, 151-158, 162
Champernon, Kate *see* Ashley, Kate
Cleubury, Abbot Thomas 87
Cobham, Lady Frances 53-54, 72, 129
Conques, France 146-147
Coppe, Mr. 130
Council of the North, the 92-94
Cox Indenture 7, 115
Cox, Richard 112-115
Croft, Sir James 6, 9, 49, 88, 139
Croft, John 88
Cromwell, Thomas 43

Dafi, Howel 8, 13, 17, 20
Dale, Sir Valentine 102-103
Dane, Mrs. Margaret 69-70, 110, 151
Dane, William 69-70
Ddu, Harri ap Gruffudd (Blanche Parry's great-grandfather) 8, 11-17, 146-147
Dee, Arthur 100-101
Dee, Dr. John 52, 100-101
Desmond, Earl of 2-3, 77
Denny, Sir Anthony 56
Dinmore, Herefordshire 110, 112-113
Dissolution of the Monasteries, the 32-33, 84, 109, 113
Dore Abbey 5, 8, 9, 11, 13, 15, 19, 23, 85, 87, 149

Dormer, Jane, Duchess of Feria 52, 85
Dudley, John 1-4, 69
Dudley, Robert, Earl of Leicester 1-4, 9, 53, 63, 66, 69, 80-81, 91, 104, 128, 134, 139
Dynas, Breconshire 116-118

Edward IV, King 14-15, 18
Edward VI, King 39, 40, 79, 84
Elizabeth I, Queen
  birth, christening and early life 37-40, 42-43
  coronation 52-53
  daily routine 59, 61-62, 63
  education 42, 44, 46-47
  household
    as Princess 43-45, 48-49, 50-51
    as Queen 52-55, 61-64
  imprisonment in Tower of London 50
  loyalty to servants 48, 53-54
  New Year gifts 55, 66-70
  pets 61-62
  portraits 145-146
  as icon 145-147
  relationship with Blanche Parry, *see* Parry, Blanche
  religious influences and views 44, 50-51, 84 *et seq.*, 143, 145-146
  royal progresses 59-60
  unmarried status 135
Elizabeth I Receiving Dutch Emissaries see *Painting of the Presence Chamber, the*
escheators 18
Eynesford, Elizabeth 139

Faith, Saint 146-147
Fawley, Herefordshire 110-115
Fiennes de Clinton, Edward 80-81
Foy, Sainte 146-147

Gam, Dafydd 17, 41
Games, Thomas 107
Gardiner, Dame Isabella 33-34
Gardiner, Bishop Stephen 79
Gargrave, Sir Thomas 93, 96
Garnons, John 98, 163-164
Garnons Indenture, the 98, 163-164
Garnons, Robert 98, 163-164
Garnons, William 98
Gascoigne, George 66
Gate, Sir Henry 92-96, 97
Gildon, John 101, 143-144
Glasbury, Radnorshire 117, 120
Glyn, Guto'r 8, 11, 13, 14, 15-17, 28
Glyndwr, Owain 9, 21
Goodman, Dean Gabriel 90, 128
Gower, George 141
Great Seal of England, the 74
Grey, Lady Jane 50
Grey, Lady Katherine 65
Grey, Lady Mary 65
Grindal, William 47
Gunter, Mawd (Blanche Parry's great-great-grandmother) 8-9, 139

Hardwick, Bess of 83
ap Harry, Blanche *see* Parry, Blanche
ap Harry, Hugh 113
ap Harry, Sir John 25
ap Harry, John of Dulas 114, 132
ap Harry, Miles (Blanche Parry's grandfather) 8, 17-19
ap Harry, Milo/Myles (Blance Parry's brother) 34, 149
ap Harry, Symond (Blanche Parry's brother) 34, 114, 130, 132
Hatton, Sir Christopher 55, 60, 81-82, 105, 129
Haxby, Robert 132
Haxbye, John 123
Henry VII, King 21-22
Henry VIII, King 39, 40, 54, 57, 83-84
ap Henry, Gruffudd (Blanche Parry's great-great-grandfather) 8-11, 87, 139
heraldry 17
Herbert, Sir Charles 41, 45
Herbert, Joan 45

Herbert, Sir Walter 22
Herbert, Sir William, 1st Earl of Pembroke 14-15, 18, 21
Herbert, Sir William of Troy Parva 26-27, 40
Hereford Cathedral 85, 164-165
Hereford, Mayor of 98-100
Hesse-Kassel, Landgrave 79-80
Hoby, Sir Thomas 64
Howard, Katherine 57
Hunsdon, Lord 4, 95-96
Huntingdon, Henry, 5th Earl of 66-67

Jenkins Collection, the 30, 142
Jenkins, Henry Jones 142
Jenkins, Mrs. Laura Louisa Petherick 142
Jerningham, Sir Henry 103
Jones, David 117
Jones, William 73

Kassel, Staatliche Museen 79
Ketherogh 120
Killegrew, Henry 79-80
Knollys, Frances 132
Knollys, Sir Francis 50
Knollys, Lady *53*
Lettice (Robert Knollys' daughter) 132
Knollys, Lettice (Robert Knollys' sister) 3, 132
Knollys, Robert 69, 118-120, 131, 133
Knowles, Katherine 67
Knyvett, Lady Anne 64, 92, 120, 124
Knyvett, Francis 92
Knyvett, Sir Henry 92
Knyvett, Katherine 64, 92
Knyvett, Thomas 55, 64

Lanthony Secunda 110, 112-113
Lee, Rowland 32-33
Leicester, the Earl of *see* Dudley, Robert
Lewis, Dr. David 101-103, 144
Llangorse Lake *see* Brecknock Mere
Lollardy 10-11, 19, 87-89
Lumley, Lord 130

Margaret, Lady Bryan 38-39
Margaret, Countess of Salisbury 38, 54
Markham, Thomas 133
Mary I, Queen
- childhood 39, 40, 42
- death 52
- household 43
- marriage 51
- reign 49-52
- religion 84, 109

Mary, Queen of Scots 3, 79, 81-82, 92-93
Mayew, Bishop Richard 25, 87
Milborne, Alice (Blanche Parry's mother) 20-21, 139
Milborne, Blanche, Lady Troy (Blanche Parry's aunt)
- career at court 5, 37-44
- elegy 40-41
- godmother to Blanche Parry 21
- inheritance 140
- marriages 26-27
- retirement 44-46

Milborne, Elizabeth 89
Milborne, Sir John 89
Milborne, Simon 14, 20, 21, 89, 139
monuments, general significance of Tudor 137
Morgan, David 101-103
Morgan, Hugh 69, 126
Morgan, John 116, 120, 132
Morgan, Susan 132
Morgan, William 90
Morgannwg, Lewys 8, 26, 27, 39-42
Mulcaster, Richard 29
Myles, Henry (Blanche Parry's father) 7, 8, 19, 20-24, 31, 34, 149
Myn, Francis 117
Mystery Plays, Hereford 84-85

Newcourt (Blanche Parry's family home) 8, 11, 15, 23, 28-31, 131, 142, 149-150

Norwich, Mrs. Elizabeth, Lady Carew 53

Oldcastle, Henry 89
Oldcastle, Sir John 9-11, 87
Oldcastle, Sir Thomas 11
Ormond, Earl of 2-3, 77

Painting of the Presence Chamber, the 78-82
Parr, Katherine 27, 44, 57
Parry, Blanch 106, 130, 162
Parry, Blanche
appointment as gentlewoman 47
Cecil, Sir William, relationship with 4, 9, 119-120, 125, 130
childhood 27-29
christening 25-26
coat-of-arms 139-140
death and funeral 133-134
depictions of Blanche 65-66, 78-82, 138-139, 140-143
education 29, 32-34
epitaphs
Bacton 5, 32, 46, 83, 134-135
Saint Margaret's, Westminster 58, 75, 83, 135-136
Elizabeth I, and
bequests to the Queen 128-129
during Elizabeth's childhood 46-47
at Elizabeth's coronation 53
Elizabeth's care for Blanche 56, 65, 109, 123
Elizabeth's grief at Blanche's death 133-134
Elizabeth's 'personal assistant' 6, 76-78, 82
intercession with Elizabeth on behalf of others 91-108
during Queen Mary's reign 50-51
New Year's gifts 68-70
religious influence upon 83-84
in the Tower of London 50
family 7-24, 34
family tree 8, 12, 126
friends at Court
Sir Christopher Hatton 55
Lady Dorothy Stafford 54
Herbert family, links with 13-15, 21-22, 47
lands
Herefordshire 110-115
Wales 115-121
Yorkshire 97, 121-124
lawsuits 113-115, 117-120
Milborne, Blanche, Lady Troy, relationship with 26, 35-36
monuments
Bacton 85, 143-147
Saint Margaret's, Westminster 82, 134, 137-140
religious background and views 31-33, 84-91, 135, 140, 143
responsibilities
attendance on Elizabeth 61-62
keeper of the Queen's books 68
keeper of the Queen's jewels 70-71, 73-75
responsibility for the Queen's linen 71-73
responsibility for money and papers 75-76
channel for parliamentary business 78
siblings 27, 34
status at Court 1-6, 44-49, 55-61, 64-66, 72, 73, 77-82, 124-125
unmarried status 31-32, 34-35
wardships 110
Welsh Bible, publication of 89-91
wills
first will 30, 32, 54, 65, 72, 106, 116, 120, 124, 125-127, 143, 151-157
last will 30, 54, 55, 67, 69, 82, 90, 102, 106, 118, 124, 127-132, 157-162

Parry, Dr. Henry 64
Parry, James 105-108, 130
Parry, John 64, 106-107, 130
Parry, Sir Thomas 9, 51
Pendred, Mr. 76
Pendred, Mrs. 37
Perrot, Sir John 102, 129
Perrot, Thomas 102
Philip of Spain, King 51, 83, 84
Pickering, Sir Christopher 92
Pilley, Walter 141-142
Platter, Thomas 78, 82
Powel, David 86, 91
Powell, Hugh 117-119
Powell, Thomas 127, 130-131, 134, 135, 162-164
Privy Chamber, the 5-6, 56, 59, 73, 79

Qwrtnaye, Blaunche 50

Radcliffe, Mary 64, 74-75
Radcliffe, Sir Thomas, 3rd Earl of Sussex 93-95
Raglan Castle 7, 22
Richard, Duke of York 13-14
Rise, Yorkshire 123

Saint Margaret's Church, Westminster 90, 126, 132, 137
Salesbury, William 90
Sandes, Elizabeth, Lady Berkeley 50
Scory, Bishop John 128
Scudamore, Eleanor (Blanche Parry's sister-in-law) 34
Scudamore, J. 164
Scudamore, Mary 71-73, 100-101
Seymour, Jane 27, 39
Shelley, Jane 105-106
Shelley, William 105-106
Somerset, Lady Blanche 129-130
Somerset, Elizabeth, Countess of Worcester 35
Somerset, Lucy, Lady Latimer 65
Stafford, Lady Dorothy 54-55, 83, 129, 137
Stradling, Damascyn 85-86
Stradling, Sir Edward 86, 101-103
Stradling, Sir Harri 17
Stradling Icon, the 85-86
Stradling, Joan (Blanche Parry's grandmother) 7, 13, 19, 21, 85, 139
Stradling, Sir Thomas 85-86
sumptuary laws 49, 72, 81

Teerlinc, Levina 65
Tew, Gwilym 8, 11
Thorganby Church, Yorkshire 121-122
Throckmorton, Francis 105
Trostrey, Usk 9, 120
Troy, Lady *see* Milborne, Blanche
Twist, Anne 73
Tyndale, Sir William 87
Tyrwhitt, Sir Robert 44, 48

Usk 120

Vaughan, Anne 67
Vaughan, Catherine 131
Vaughan, Elizabeth (Blanche Parry's great-niece) 31, 149
Vaughan, Elizabeth (Blanche Parry's sister) 34
Vaughan, Frances, Lady Burgh 62, 64, 92, 124, 131, 134, 151, 158
Vaughan, Francis 92, 98, 115, 127, 129, 131
Vaughan, John (Blanche Parry's nephew) 35, 64, 91-97, 115-116, 120, 121, 126, 134, 151
Vaughan, Katherine, Lady Knollys 52, 67, 69, 118-119, 131-132
Vaughan, Robert 117, 120
Vaughan, Sir Roger 86, 116-117
Vaughan, Rowland (Blanche Parry's great-nephew by marriage) 31, 57-59, 129, 131, 132, 149
Vaughan, Rowland of Porthaml 65
Vaughan, Thomas (Blanche Parry's brother-in-law) 23, 34

Vaughan, Watkyn (Blanche Parry's nephew by marriage) 78, 90, 149
Vaughan, William (Blanche Parry's great-nephew) 30, 115-117, 120-121, 125, 129, 131, 157

Walsingham, Francis 80-81, 82, 91, 131
wardships 18, 110
Warren, Lawrence 110
Warren, William 110
Wars of the Roses, the 5, 14-15, 17, 18
Watkins, Dean John 128
Webber, Dean Francis 164
Weldrake, Yorkshire 121, 123-124, 128
Welsh Bible, the 89-91, 135, 138
Welsh surnames, development of 7, 8
Weobley Castle, Herefordshire 15
Weston, Francis 35, 92
White, Sir Nicholas 77-78, 91
Whitney, Anne 132
Whitney, James 26, 132
Whitney, John 44
Whitney, Sybil 132
Williams, Thomas 91
Wistason, Herefordshire 112-113
women, influence in Elizabethan Court 57-59, 83
Wriothesley, Thomas 43
Wyatt, Sir Thomas 49-50
Wycliffe, John 10, 87

Zuccaro, Frederigo 140